12·99

‖‖‖‖‖‖‖‖‖‖‖‖‖‖‖‖‖‖‖‖
D1557495

THE CROSS AND THE FASCES

RICHARD A. WEBSTER

THE CROSS AND
THE FASCES

Christian Democracy and
Fascism in Italy

STANFORD UNIVERSITY PRESS
STANFORD, CALIFORNIA
1960

STANFORD UNIVERSITY PRESS
STANFORD, CALIFORNIA

Library of Congress Catalog Card Number: 60-13868

PRINTED IN THE UNITED STATES OF AMERICA

Published with the assistance of the Ford Foundation

PREFACE

Since the fall of the Fascist dictatorship there has been a sifting and re-evaluation of the whole history of united Italy by the post-war generation of Italian historians. The problems of Italian socialism, of Giolitti's democracy, of Italian foreign policy, have been taken up in a free critical spirit, without chauvinism and superficiality. The impulse given by Croce and Salvemini, men of an antithetical cast of mind, but both of them historians and teachers of a rare order, has borne fruit in every province of Italian history-writing, leading to achievements of truly European importance.

One of the notable new directions taken by younger Italian historians has been in the history of the Catholic movements in the peninsula. Although given a few passing glances in Croce's classical history of united Italy, and discussed only in external sociological terms by Salvemini, the Italian Catholic movements were always important during the whole period of liberal and democratic governments in the Kingdom of Italy. When, after World War II, the Catholic party emerged unexpectedly as the ruler of the Italian Republic, an investigation of its past and of the inner life of Italian Catholicism became a prime task of the new historiography. This study has been inspired and stimulated by the achievements of postwar writers such as Spadolini, Fonzi, Scoppola, and De Rosa, who have produced richly documented studies of the Catholic movement from 1870 to 1926; above all, this new current in Italy owes much to the jurist-historian A. C. Jemolo, whose work began under Fascism.

Part I of this study is based largely upon the work of contemporary historians, though I have often gone to primary sources to illustrate specific points that they have not always emphasized, as, for example, in dealing with the links between Italian Nationalism and the Catholic conservatives, in discussing Italian Catholic attitudes in 1914–15, and in describing the travail of the Popular Party in 1924. Part II, on the other hand, is drawn from primary sources almost entirely.

In discussing the Catholic movements of 1870–1926, I have tried to keep two problems in mind. First, the relation between the Italian Catholic movements and the Holy See, with its worldwide concerns, and second, the position of these movements within the politics of the Italian State. Neither of these perspectives may be slighted in any account that strives for comprehension of historical reality.

In this study I have not attacked directly the problem of relations between Church and State, but it comes up unavoidably in any history of Catholic movements. Like most great problems that torment Western European civilization, it is never finally solved, but takes on new forms in each century. In the Old Regime, concordats and alliances of Altar and Throne provided settlements that often lasted for a long time, though the claims of monarchs and Popes could never be truly harmonized. But in the modern State, which has such far-reaching controls over the lives of its citizens, the Church becomes to a great extent dependent upon the influence and authority it can exert among the masses. Old diplomatic channels often remain open, but become less important than a direct appeal to the believers of the nation by the Pope or his representatives. Even in a dictatorship, the Church's direct communication with the masses is a powerful weapon.

Yet a Catholic social or political movement can endanger Church-State agreements, in which case the movement is often ignored or deserted by the Church in order to gain a concordat settlement. Thus the Church mourned neither the Italian Popular Party in 1926 nor the German Center Party in 1933, but came to agreements with the victorious Fascist and National Socialist regimes through conventional diplomatic channels. However, in both cases the Church's position in negotiating with the dictators was greatly strengthened by her mass organization and following.

On the other hand, when the political climate is right, Catholic movements can shape Church-State relations to the advantage of the Church. The most recent example of this is the Christian Democratic Party of Italy, which since the proclamation of the Republic in 1946 has dominated each successive government and assured to the Church a real prestige and influence in Italian affairs far exceeding what the 1929 pacts provided for.

Catholic movements within an indifferent or unbelieving society are an innovation of our own time, but seen in a long perspective they constitute a new element in an ancient problem, another chapter in a history of spiritual travail that began with the very introduction of Christianity into Europe.

Naturally a work of this sort has problems of research and exposition. The Vatican is a closed world, in general, and there is no *Vatican Confidential,* if one excepts the scandalous novels of M. Peyrefitte, to initiate the researcher into its mysteries. However, in the course of time facts *do* come out, and indications of Vatican sentiments are never lacking in the form of notes in *Osservatore Romano* and *Civiltà Cattolica*; but these notes are the barest public guide to a complicated world of thought and action. Most of the iceberg lies below the level of visibility. Nevertheless, it is possible by putting together testimonies of one sort or another to form some idea of the Vatican in the 1930's—see especially Part II of this work. (There are other gaps. The Fascist ministry archives, which would have yielded interesting information on the enemies of the Regime, are closed, and the important Biblioteca Nazionale Centrale collection of parochial and episcopal bulletins was in process of being reorganized during my year of research in Florence.)

One word of advice to the reader: if he should encounter difficulties in picking his way through the maze of tendencies and currents in the Catholic world of Italy, let him use the biographical method. By following Miglioli, Martire, Cavazzoni, Gemelli, De Gasperi, Gronchi, and others through the various stages of their careers as picked up in successive chapters, the reader will be able to keep the main narrative thread in hand and be aware of the currents and states of mind that these men represented within Italian Catholicism.

It would be impossible to list all the Italians who have helped me at one time or another, but explicit mention must be made of the Biblioteca Nazionale Centrale of Florence, the Biblioteca del Senato and the Biblioteca della Camera dei Deputati of Rome, the Istituto per la Storia del Movimento di Liberazione in Italia of Milan, and the Biblioteca Civica of Trent, institutions without which this research could never have been undertaken and carried on. I am especially grateful to certain private citizens: Avvocato Francesco Berti, Professor Fausto Fonzi, Professor Carlo Francovich, Dottor Sergio Bertelli, Dottor Dino Fiorot, Dottor Enzo Enriquez Agnoletti, who at one point or another gave me useful documentation or references. An especial word of thanks to the Honorable Piero Malvestiti.

This work was presented as a doctoral thesis at Columbia University, and thanks are due to the patient readers and committee: Professors René Albrecht-Carrié, S. B. Clough, who sponsored it, Peter Gay, Enrico de' Negri, and Michael T. Florinsky. I profited much from their suggested revisions and amplifications. Of course they are not responsible for eventual flaws and errors.

Some parts of the concluding chapters have appeared in Italian in the periodical *Il Mulino* (Bologna) in the issues of January 1958 and August 1959.

RICHARD A. WEBSTER

Berkeley, California
  October 1960

CONTENTS

Preface   v

Prologue   ITALY IN PASSAGE FROM LIBERALISM TO
                DEMOCRACY, 1860–1913   xi

PART I   THE FIRST ITALIAN CHRISTIAN DEMOCRATIC
                MOVEMENTS AND THEIR FAILURE, 1870–
                1929

Chapter One   ORIGIN AND DEVELOPMENT OF THE
                   CATHOLIC MOVEMENT IN ITALY, 1871–1913   3

Chapter Two   ITALIAN CATHOLICISM AND THE LIBYAN
                   WAR: FIRST CONTACTS WITH THE ITALIAN
                   NATIONALIST PARTY   26

Chapter Three   THE CATHOLIC ALLIANCE WITH SALANDRA,
                   1914–15   38

Chapter Four   WORLD WAR I AND THE FOUNDATION OF
                   THE ITALIAN POPULAR PARTY, 1915–19   50

Chapter Five   THE ITALIAN POPULAR PARTY, "SHORT
                   FRUIT OF LONG LABOR," 1919–22   57

Chapter Six   THE DEATH OF THE POPULAR PARTY, 1922–
                   27   78

PART II   THE REVIVAL OF CHRISTIAN DEMOCRACY IN
                ITALY: 1929–45

Chapter Seven   THE CATHOLIC CHURCH AND THE FASCIST
                   REGIME   109

Chapter Eight   THE CLERICO-FASCISTS AND THEIR
                   MEDIATION BETWEEN THE CHURCH AND
                   THE FASCIST REGIME   119

Chapter Nine   DE GASPERI, THE EXILE OF THE VATICAN   129

x   *Contents*

Chapter Ten   THE ITALIAN CATHOLIC UNIVERSITY
                    FEDERATION   137

Chapter Eleven   SCATTERED CHRISTIAN DEMOCRATIC
                    MOVEMENTS   144

Chapter Twelve   FATHER GEMELLI AND THE CATHOLIC
                    UNIVERSITY OF MILAN   153

Chapter Thirteen CATHOLIC PARTICIPATION IN THE
                    RESISTANCE   162

Epilogue   THE TRIUMPH OF CHRISTIAN DEMOCRACY
                    IN ITALY AFTER 1945   178

Appendix One   CONCLUDING NOTE ON CHRISTIAN
                    DEMOCRATIC PROGRAMS, 1899–1948   187

Appendix Two   THE ELECTORAL SITUATION OF ITALIAN
                    CATHOLIC PARTIES, 1919–48   189

Notes   191

Bibliography   215

Index   225

Prologue

ITALY IN PASSAGE FROM LIBERALISM
TO DEMOCRACY, 1860–1913

The Italian Risorgimento began as a national revolutionary movement, and the romantic exile Mazzini gave it a democratic stamp. But after the failure of revolutionary efforts to achieve unity and independence in 1848–49, the constitutional Kingdom of Sardinia united most of the peninsula by diplomacy and war, adroitly using the parties and the red-shirted militia of Italian democracy without letting them exert any real control. The aristocratic Liberal Cavour succeeded where Mazzini had failed.

The resultant Kingdom of Italy was not a democracy, but a constitutional oligarchy. The State was in the hands of a Liberal elite, governing through a parliament chosen by a narrow propertied electorate. The rule of this Liberal Right, which lasted from 1860 to 1876, created many conditions favorable to commercial and industrial progress: railroads, stable government finances, the end of ecclesiastical tenure and mortmain in the countryside. But this achievement was largely paid for by consumer taxes, the largest single item in the revenues of the State. Government monopolies of salt and tobacco, stamp taxes, internal customs, and the infamous 1868 tax on grain milling, which struck directly at the working classes, proved to be of great help in balancing the budget, but estranged masses of nonvoting taxpayers. In much of Italy the State appeared as a foreign invader.[1]

The lower classes, thus alienated from the national State, were still for the most part preindustrial. They provided a fertile ground for Bakunin's anarchism, in those areas where papal misrule was still remembered and the Church had lost credit. Yet the Catholic country masses were equally hostile to the State, since it had "imprisoned" Pius IX and fostered a regime of capitalism and high taxes in the countryside. Had opposition to the State been organized and directed, Italy might well have undergone a revolution in the 1870's.

Instead there was a "parliamentary revolution" in 1876, which brought to power those old democratic followers of Mazzini who had passed over to the Monarchy in 1859–60. The most important single result of their triumph was the partial broadening of the suffrage in 1882, which brought several million lower middle-class and urban working-class citizens into the electorate. The great liability of the new half-democratic half-liberal Italy was the South, where the illiterate masses still could not vote and most constituencies were in the hands of local cliques. The holders of these rotten boroughs assumed an importance in Parliament far out of proportion to their real weight in the life of the nation. On the other hand, the Italian working class, far from satisfied, became attracted to new forms of Socialist doctrine imported from Germany.

The central problem of Italian politics between 1882 and 1912 was one of finding an electoral system and a parliamentary tactic capable of producing a stable government, while holding off a proletarian revolution. The new Right, under Crispi, Di Rudinì, and Pelloux, tried repression and foreign adventure from 1893 to 1898, outraging not only the nascent Socialist Party but also a large part of the constitutionally and democratically minded bourgeois political leadership of Italy. In the crisis of 1898–1900 the Right failed in Parliament and in the country; after 1900 the new constitutional Left took over.

The greatest leader of the constitutional Left, Giovanni Giolitti, improvised a solution. Good administration replaced ideology and adventure. The industrial North was appeased by high protective tariffs and social reforms, while the South, still dominated by local land magnates and notables, provided, with some help from Giolitti's prefects, a reservoir of tame deputies ready to join any governmental majority. The Radicals were weaned away from the Socialists and Republicans, with whom they had been allied during the crisis of the 1890's, and were transformed into a "ministerial" group in the Chamber, balancing the Government's conservative supporters from the Southern political fiefs. By this sort of "transformism" Giolitti prevented any regular alternation of parties in power; instead, he broke them down into small parliamentary factions, fodder for shifting government majorities.

Giolitti's system worked and assured Italy ten years of peace and industrial progress. However, it contained the seeds of its own destruction. It engendered a powerful opposition among political outsiders, Liberals, Democrats, and Socialists, who saw that the system perpetuated one small circle of "Giolittians" in the high offices of the State, leading to dangerous political stagnation; the methods by which some of Giolitti's officials "made" elections in the backward regions of Italy aroused disgust and cynicism, discrediting parliamentary government.

But the system of 1903–13 was also endangered from within, for Giolitti actually met the nation's demands for greater political democracy. He envisaged universal suffrage as one of the goals of his administration, and finally put it through the Chamber in 1912, though with a few salutary restrictions on illiterates. But then Giolitti could no longer control elections and parliaments by his old methods, and in the parliamentary elections of 1913 the newly enlarged organized Catholic vote, especially important in North Italian rural constituencies, had to be reckoned with. If the urban and rural proletariat were to enter Italian politics under the leadership of the Socialists, the Catholic masses could not be excluded without upsetting the parliamentary balance essential for forming governments. The "Giolittians" themselves called for the organized Catholic vote.

All politically alert Italians therefore had to turn their attention to a mass movement that had for decades gone practically unnoticed in the developing life of the nation.

PART I

THE FIRST ITALIAN
CHRISTIAN DEMOCRATIC MOVEMENTS
AND THEIR FAILURE

1870–1929

. . . I believe that there is in this democratic phenomenon some leaven taken from Christianity. . . . I tell you, gentlemen, that no monarchy, no republic will ever solve the social problems of the future, without the cooperation of the religious feeling, which in Italy can only be given by the Catholic Church . . . It is necessary to admit this principle, affirmed by Count Cavour in a memorable speech on the abolition of the ecclesiastical tribunal, that religion and freedom are jointly necessary for the progress of modern society.

A. Fogazzaro, *Deniele Cortis* (1885), Ch. VIII.

One righteous man who professes and practises Catholicism is more profitable to the glory of the Father, of Christ and of the Church, than many congresses, than many circles, than many Catholic electoral victories. . . . Social action, my friends, is certainly good as a work of justice and brotherhood, but, like the Socialists, certain Catholics mark it with the stamp of their religious and political opinions, refuse to share it with men of good will unless they accept that stamp; they reject the good Samaritan, and this is abominable in God's eyes. They preach the just distribution of wealth, and that is good, but too often they forget to preach at the same time the poverty of the heart; and if they deliberately leave it out, for reasons of opportunism, this is abominable in God's eyes. Cleanse your action of these abominations.

A. Fogazzaro, *Il Santo* (1906), Ch. VII.

Chapter One

ORIGIN AND DEVELOPMENT OF THE CATHOLIC
MOVEMENT IN ITALY, 1871–1913

THE "INTRANSIGENT" ORIGINS OF THE CATHOLIC
MOVEMENT IN ITALY

The pontificate of Pius IX (1846–78), after a brief illusory era of good feeling, turned into a last-ditch defense of the Pope's traditional positions against the attacks of European Liberalism. The Pope reaffirmed the status of the Church as a sovereign society superior in certain ways to any state, and clung to the Temporal Power exactly as he had received it from his predecessors, abating not a jot or a tittle of the Holy See's territorial rights. In 1870 he secured recognition by an ecumenical council of the old papal claim to absolute jurisdiction and infallible defining power within the Church. But in that very year Pius lost the last of the Papal States to the Kingdom of Italy; as his spiritual dominion flourished, his political fortunes waned. Rome became the capital of Italy in spite of the Pope.

Spurning offers of pensions and indemnities that the Italian Liberal government was quick to make, Pius retired to the precincts of the Vatican as a protesting "prisoner," and carried on the war against Liberalism of all shades. In his last years the pontiff sponsored the formation of a militant auxiliary of Italian Catholic laymen faithful to the Papacy. Like so many European states, Italy had a "Clerical" movement, as its opponents called it.

Before the French Revolution such a thing would have seemed strange in a Catholic country. There had been Franciscan and Jansenist movements, but almost never a Catholic movement as such. The State itself defended religion, often with a heavy hand. Only in the nineteenth century, and particularly after 1848, did such a movement become necessary, as the Church found itself forced to resort to modern "mass" means of self-defense. In the cities her position, already weakened by the widespread unbelief of the middle classes, was attacked at the base by Socialist agitation among the masses; Socialism almost always portrayed the Church as a prop of the most antiquated part of the existing social structure. The Church's basic strength was to be found in the small towns and in the country, but there she was faced with growing migration to the cities. There was only one defense against the agnosticism of the middle classes and the aggressive irreligiousness of the mass movements, whether democratic (in the European, "Jacobin" sense) or Socialist: a Catholic mass movement aimed first at safeguarding Catholic interests, many of which were often no longer protected by the State, and ultimately at a Catholic "reconquest" of national life.

In Italy the Catholic movement developed slowly and hesitantly, compared with its counterparts in Germany, Austria, and Belgium. The reasons for this delay must be sought partly in the general lag in Italian development, but chiefly in the peculiarities of Italian politics, especially the "Roman Question."

Not only had the Kingdom of Italy put an end to the Papal States, but also, like the revolutionary regimes of France, it had confiscated and sold Church properties throughout the whole peninsula, a measure by which both the State's finances and the rising forces of agricultural enterprise benefited. The finishing touch was the abolition of theological faculties in the Italian university system. In all practical matters the divorce between the Italian State and the Church was an accomplished fact, though in many areas, such as the nomination of bishops, occasional contacts continued.

Hence the Catholic movement in Italy was in a special sense the child of adversity. It arose as an "intransigent" protest against the despoiling "subalpine usurpers," in the words of Pius IX, and aimed at restoring the old political and economic power of the Church in Italy, a chimerical notion that died hard. The first militant Catholic movement in Italy, the Catholic Congresses that began in 1874, was an auxiliary of the Holy See, seconding the aspirations of Pius IX and Leo XIII toward a more or less integral restoration of the rights of the Church.[1]

Yet the very fact that the Catholic movement since 1874 was all-Italian in scope, though organized in diocesan and parochial committees, marked an implicit acceptance of unification. Catholic militancy had nothing to do with legitimism, for the rights of the Pope were on a different plane from those of the dispossessed Italian princes.

In another way the militant Catholic movement of the nineteenth century faced reality. From their beginning the Italian Catholic Congresses had shown concern for the hard-pressed lower classes, though they often spoke a paternalistic language unsuited for the age of democracy and socialism. Slighted and despoiled by the *bourgeoisie,* the Church turned to the masses.

In the 1870's and 1880's the intransigent Catholic press battled unceasingly against the State and the Liberal ruling class. Italy's economic and social troubles furnished excellent issues: the increasing tax burdens and cost of living, rising unemployment, speculation in Church properties seized by the State and sold to the *bourgeoisie,* were all laid to the account of Italian Liberalism, guilty not only of heresy but also of social exploitation. Intransigent Catholic agitation took on a democratic and even demagogic tone with the passage of time.

The Milanese journalist-priest Don Davide Albertario is the most typical representative of Catholic intransigency as it became a mass movement in the late nineteenth century. "Let us approach the working man, who is escaping us," he said at the Catholic Congress of Bergamo (1877), "let us go into the workshops and factories, . . . let us sanctify democracy, for which the future is reserved." Albertario's politics had a certain one-track simplicity: "the Christian transformation of society would be brought about with the support of the people, under the Church's guidance, against all forms of Liberalism." Therefore, said Albertario, Catholics must shun the "bourgeois Liberals who call upon the priest's help in order to hold back the passion of the masses," for the priest, like the masses to whom he ministers, is a victim of Liberal tyranny.[2]

Little wonder that in the early decades of the Kingdom of Italy the government often lumped "Clericals" together with Republicans and the partisans of the Socialist International as "subversives," and that in the repressions of 1898 Don Davide Albertario was imprisoned in a military fortress.

Yet the intransigent Catholic Congresses laid the foundation for a Catholic mass party in Italy, not only by agitation and demagogic journalism but also by concrete organizational work, by setting up rural banks and cooperatives to assist the Catholic peasant and landowner. Catholic political life in Italy has borne ever since the imprint of nineteenth-century intransigency; Catholic leaders have been quick to see the power of democratic appeals and organizing methods, but have only rarely been willing to see anything positive and worth saving in the freedoms and guarantees of Liberalism.

However, the Catholic movement in Italy did not continue along the "subversive" lines of the 1870's and 1880's. Indeed, for one moment, in the repressions of 1898, it seemed as if the "Clericals" might become an agrarian auxiliary to the working-class revolution in Italy, but this alarming possibility soon faded. The intransigents had begun organizing the Catholic laity of Italy, but after 1898 lost control of the movement they had founded.

The intransigents, with their everlasting jeremiads against the new Italy, by no means represented the Italian Catholic laity as such. Many Catholics had worked and fought for Italian unity, not even drawing back at the seizure of Rome in 1870; the most distinguished of them, Count Alessandro Manzoni, was a senator of the kingdom and had voted to make Rome its capital. Officials of the Catholic Congresses were widely resented for their arrogance; these "bishops in tall hats" were especially disliked by some of the Italian prelates.[3]

Italian bishops were often less intransigent than their parish priests. Bishops had to be acceptable to the royal government before they could take possession of their sees. Therefore the Pope tended to nominate clerics of a moderate cast of mind, compromisers with the new order. Though the theoretical divorce between Church and State in Italy was complete, there was at least in this matter an unspoken practical understanding.

There was thus in Italian Catholicism a "conciliatorist" tendency which found a strong point among the bishops. The most outspoken of the conciliatorists was the patriotic bishop Monsignor Bonomelli of Cremona, aided by his more discreet neighbor Monsignor Scalabrini, who held the see of Piacenza. The conciliatorist laity included the popular novelist Antonio Fogazzaro.

The conciliatorists never formed a mass movement. Most of them were men of substance, with a "stake in the country." To

Catholic landowners it became clear that the central State was a bulwark of social order that had to be defended in spite of its past plundering of Church lands—which was now an accomplished fact, like the State railroads and protective tariffs. Leaders of the old "black" aristocracy of Rome, though still performing their ceremonial role in the papal court, took an active part in the economic and political life of the new Italy.

Between 1882, when the suffrage was broadened, and 1888 many Catholic landowners and nobles called for the formation of a "national" Catholic conservative party. But in 1888 relations between the Holy See and the Italian State, still embittered by the Roman Question, suddenly took a turn for the worse. Far from allowing the formation of a Catholic conservative party, which would strengthen the Italian State, the Vatican favored intransigent opposition to Italian Liberalism and the organization of the Italian Catholic masses, socially and economically, *outside* of the Italian political system.[4]

The crisis of the 1890's made both intransigent and conciliatorist positions seem irrelevant to the new situation of Italian Catholics. Leo XIII's *Rerum Novarum* (1891) marks in many ways the beginning of a new course in the Vatican's policy and a new direction to be imparted to the various Catholic movements of Europe. In his declining years the great pontiff turned away from some of the diplomatic maneuvers that had profited the Holy See so little; the Roman Question gave way to the Social Question. The Church's true strength was seen as lying in the Catholic masses, not in the making of concordats and exchanging of envoys. The new Italian State was by now anchored in the European system, and all hopes of intervention by some Catholic power or powers were futile.

By 1898 the Clericals' intransigent opposition to the State had in fact put them in seeming alliance with the Extreme Left, and the repressions of May struck at both forms of "subversion." This was an absurd and dangerous situation for Italian Catholics. The fiery intransigent Don Albertario, who had fought a running journalistic battle with the conciliatorist bishops of Lombardy, now found himself in jail and grateful for the intercession of his old foe, the patriotic bishop of Piacenza.[5] Intransigent opposition to the Italian State no longer fitted the purposes of the Holy See;

a settlement of the Roman Question could wait, if necessary, but the menace of the anti-Clerical Left was immediate.

Therefore, after 1898 the Italian militant Catholic movement took a new turn. It had begun on an intransigent base, emphasizing political separateness, but it now developed along more conciliatory lines, attaching greater importance to the social and economic organization of the Catholic masses within the existing state system. The polemic between intransigents and conciliatorists faded away in the early twentieth century, as other issues came to the fore.

Catholics had to face an immediate problem: whether or not to vote. The Holy See had forbidden them to vote in national elections; originally a counsel *(non expedit)*, under Leo XIII it hardened into a prohibition. As long as suffrage was restricted to men of means, as in the first years of the new State, this electoral boycott was not important, for the constitutional Liberals had the situation in hand. But the broadening of the franchise, with the rise of revolutionary and irreligious mass parties, made Catholic abstention seem outdated and dangerous. Catholic abstention was part of the nineteenth-century conflict between the Church and the Italian Liberal State: Now that the worst of the conflict was over, why go on abstaining? In municipal elections conservative, "moderate" Catholics freely joined with the Liberals to shut out the Left; why not on a national scale? If, on the other hand, militant Catholicism were regarded as a force of reform rather than as a mere conservative auxiliary, why not use the vote to further Catholic social aims?

While militant Catholics of different tendencies often agreed that it was necessary to take an active part in the political life of the nation, there was no agreement on how this was to be done. All during the stormy period 1898–1900, and until Pius X imposed a temporary solution in 1904, the problem of political participation was an apple of discord; in the varying answers put forth, all the tendencies that have been at work ever since within the Italian Catholic movement may be distinguished, at least embryonically. In the more advanced nations of Western Europe *Rerum Novarum* was the summation of a long debate, but in Italy it marked a beginning, the first great step beyond the dead point of the Roman

Question and the struggle against Liberalism. Albertario's intransigence died with him, but his social campaign was taken up by a new generation of Italian Catholic leaders, the first Christian Democrats.

THE BEGINNINGS OF CHRISTIAN DEMOCRACY WITHIN THE ITALIAN CATHOLIC MOVEMENT

The fundamental division within the Catholic Congresses movement was between those who believed in a Catholic mass party, with a program of its own, and those who envisaged Catholic organization only as a papal auxiliary; in other words, between the Christian Democrats, who had been inspired by *Rerum Novarum* to aspire toward a Catholic reconquest of society, and the remaining intransigents of the nineteenth-century Catholic Congresses, who stayed within the limits of the old anti-Liberal campaign.

The upholders of a Catholic party were themselves divided. All were publicly agreed that Italian Catholics would not violate the Holy See's prohibition on voting, that they would obediently wait for it to be rescinded. However, the more eager elements of the Christian Democratic group, headed by a young priest from the Marches, Don Romulo Murri, treated the prohibition as a political weapon, active rather than passive in its nature. Murri held that it worked against the centralized Liberal State, as it kept Catholic conservatives from supporting the State. The prohibition, he thought, would keep Catholics away from parliamentary politics until they could have a mass party of their own, based on the ever-spreading network of Catholic rural credit organizations, cooperatives, and trade unions, and advancing a program of local autonomy and corporative "class representation" in the State. Murri hoped to revive the supposed medieval alliance between the Papacy and the guild-dominated Italian communes, the true expression of the Italian people. Abstention from parliamentary representation was thus a logical and necessary stage in the development of a Catholic party, in Murri's conception.[6]

After 1898 the "moderate" group of Milan, led by a young lawyer, Filippo Meda, successor to Don Davide Albertario, and by the journalist Marquis Filippo Crispolti, took the cautious line of "preparation in abstention." This element did not share Murri's anti-Liberal views; it would, with conditions, accept the Italian parliamentary state and defend it.*

Both sides looked to Professor Giuseppe Toniolo as their inspirer, and even today he is often regarded as the greatest Italian Catholic social thinker.[7] A professor of economics and law at Pisa, Toniolo was one of the few devout Catholics holding a chair in an Italian university at that time. Like so many Catholic leaders of the period, he was born in the Veneto. His idea of Christian Democracy was largely drawn from his studies of Tuscan economic history, in which he concluded that the greatness of Florence was due to its corporative social system; this system, he held, was founded upon scholastic principles of justice. San Bernardino of Siena and Fra Girolamo Savonarola, with their attacks on usury and their furthering of the *monti di pietà*, with their ideal of government by the representatives of various crafts and social categories, were the true heroes of this glorious period of Italian history. Machiavelli's power-state was really a foreign importation.

The ideal society conceived by Toniolo is essentially static, organized in corporations that "vertically" include both masters and workmen; the State, far from being the heretical monster of Machiavelli and his successors, is simply the supreme organ of the corporations, an agency that apportions the goods of life in accordance with social justice and charity. Ultimate authority of

---

* Though Meda (born in 1869 in Milan) was himself intransigent and "Clerical" in background, he clearly rejected some of the exaggerations of the Catholic protest. He began in 1889 by writing an article distinguishing between the dynastic and traditional rights of the deposed princes of the Italian states, now clearly beyond recovery, and the imprescriptible rights of the Head of the Church. By 1898 Meda had gone farther: he accepted the accomplished fact of Italian unity as good in itself, although he rejected the "Liberal revolution" by which it had been won. Meda held that the only reason for Catholics to boycott parliamentary elections lay in the Pope's specific order, which could be rescinded or modified either by an agreement between the Holy See and the Italian State, or by a radical change in Italian politics, which might require Catholics to vote. Meda quite orthodoxly held that the Pope was final judge when his own rights were in question, and could hence order Catholics to uphold papal rights by abstaining from national elections; but Meda did not believe that Catholic opposition to a parliamentary Italian state had any deeper doctrinal roots. Indeed, he thought that the participation of Catholics in parliamentary elections, unavoidable sooner or later, would be hastened if the Pope could be sure of a mature, prepared Catholic voting public. See De Rosa, *Filippo Meda*, pp. 1–35.

course resides in the Church. Toniolo's corporativism has no place for the *stato forte* of Fascism, just as it has no place for the "abstractly" representative Liberal or Socialist state, which is an instrument of revolution; it has, in fact, little relation of any kind to the realities of modern politics and social change.

Faced with the tremendous changes brought about by industry, Toniolo and his school thought that the new proletariat could be eliminated by the fostering of small landholdings and by granting the workers a share in the profits of industrial enterprise.

This kind of Christian Democratic political thought had anti-Liberal implications, as unfolded in Murri's movement; but it could also be understood in a "moderate" reformist sense by practical-minded Catholic leaders like Meda and Don Sturzo. In fact Murri's hostility toward the Liberal State was the one element he had in common with the old intransigents; it reflected some of the deepest feelings of the Catholic countryside.

Toniolo himself was peaceful and moderate in his attitudes. In 1903 he broke with Murri, regretfully accusing him of "open indiscipline" and warning that he might become a second Lamennais.[8]

While Toniolo's social thought was essentially "theocratic" and preindustrial, his importance as a personality was considerable. He enjoyed the confidence of Leo XIII and had a moderating influence on the impulsive young Christian Democrats of Murri's camp. His devoutness enhanced his role of peacemaker and mediator among the various "social" Catholics of Italy. Throughout his life he observed a filial obedience toward the Papacy. When the Vatican seemed mistrustful or cold toward the aspirations of publicly minded Italian Catholics, his advice was always to submit and wait. It was—and is—often the only way, as many found out during the Fascist period.

In the last years of Leo XIII both extreme and moderate Christian Democrats were opposed by the old leaders of the Catholic Congresses, the intransigents of the Veneto, headed by the president of the Congresses, Giambattista Paganuzzi. The intransigents stood for the restoration of the old order, pure and simple. Their idea of the Catholic "reconquest" was political rather than social, and they distrusted both the ardent preachings of Murri and the more cautious preparations of Meda and Crispolti. It was not, be it noted, that the intransigents altogether neglected the sphere of social organization, for they had been the first to organize Catholic cooperatives and credit institutions in the Veneto; but they regarded social organizations as a papal auxiliary in the struggle against the Liberal State. It was logical that these veterans should have their chief strongholds in the Veneto, which was late among the regions of North Italy in developing agrarian capitalism and had, like Lombardy, inherited some of the solid traditions of Austrian Catholicism.

The Papacy tried to keep a balance between these two sides, whose rivalry came at times to resemble a war between two generations. Leo belonged to the generation of the intransigents, but his sympathies tended toward the young Christian Democrats.[9] Up to the year of his death (1903) an open break was avoided. In the encyclical *Graves de communi* (1901) Leo authorized the term "Christian Democracy," but gave it a purely social meaning: namely, the participation of all elements in the governing of society, to the benefit of all, but especially of the lower classes.[10] Such a formula was more apt, by its vagueness, to accommodate the two points of view than to resolve the difference between them, which was in fact left as a problem for the next pontiff, Pius X (1903–14).

THE ORGANIZATION OF THE CATHOLIC MOVEMENT UNDER PIUS X: THE NEW ELECTORAL POLICY

The new Pope, who as Giuseppe Sarto had occupied the sees of Mantua and Venice, was not a humanist and diplomat, like his predecessor, but a plain man with little taste for social innovations. Every bit as uncompromising as Leo in maintaining the sovereign claims of the Holy See, he showed a practical understanding of Italian politics quite new in the recent annals of the Papacy, and had the great advantage of seeming intransigent to many of his fellow churchmen but moderate to the outer world. His pontificate coincided with the years in which Giovanni Giolitti succeeded in dominating the parliamentary system and in making it work; in its conservative fashion, the Vatican supported the new and fragile stability which Giolitti brought into Italian political life.

Pius's first moves were to impose a solution from above upon the disunited Catholics of Italy. He dissolved the *Opera dei Con-*

gressi, which after much dissension had been wrenched away from the intransigents (1904), and replaced it with a new loose federation of "unions," each controlled by the Holy See. Local organizations were put under the bishops. It was made clear that for the moment there would be no Catholic party in Italy, to the deep disappointment of both the Murri extremists and the Meda-Crispolti moderates. At the same time, there was no return to intransigence; social and economic organization of the masses, generally rural, would be continued on a constitutional plane. Thus all three jarring sects were discomfited.[11]

As in 1848, the Church could not allow itself to be drawn directly into a political struggle; it could not itself become a center, a rallying point for the masses rising to political awareness, nor could it commit itself directly for or against the Liberal State. This was the political meaning of the 1904 decisions. Murri's great mistake was to see the Church as a *direct* agent and organizer of social action. The Church could not let itself serve as an instrument in any one country, without at the same time endangering its freedom of action and damaging its international and spiritual character. Nevertheless, under Pius X the Church could and did take a barely disguised *indirect* part in Italian affairs.

Pius X's decisions of 1904–5 were influenced by at least two considerations outside of Italian politics: the tangle in France, where political indiscretions on the part of independently minded Catholics had caused the victory of an anti-Clerical bloc and the separation of Church and State, and also the Modernist crisis, which affected the whole Catholic world. By preventing the rise of a Catholic party, Pius X averted two probable misfortunes: a new wave of anti-clericalism among the Italians, and an attempt to "modernize" the Church by some of the bolder Demochristians. Of these latter, some (Modernists, like Murri) eventually left the Church, while others (orthodox, like Don Sturzo) submitted and turned to the concrete tasks of social organization.

But Pius X could not stop at such a negative position. As the Socialists and other groups of the Left gained ground in the nation, a Catholic electoral intervention in the interests of "order" became urgent. During the repressions of 1898 Socialists and Catholics had been momentarily joined by a common enmity toward the Liberal State; but in the succeeding years they were soon separated by militant anticlericalism on one side and by a cautious conservatism on the other.

After the failure of the Socialists' 1904 general strike, Giolitti cleverly arranged a general election. Again the question of Catholic abstention came up, for the elections of 1904 "immediately took on the character of a test of strength of the Government and of the party of order against subversives of every shade"; not only was order at stake but also religion, for the "blocs" of the Left, made up of Socialists, Republicans, and Radicals, were united by anti-Clerical feelings rather than by any positive social program, and hence tended to give the problems of Church and State an exaggerated importance in their election propaganda.[12]

Tittoni, then Foreign Minister, known for his moderate attitudes toward the Catholics, urged that the Catholics participate in the defense of order. He worked through an intermediary, the conservative deputy Count Suardi of Bergamo.

The appeal reached Pius X through a visit of Catholic activists from Bergamo. In conversing with one of them, Paolo Bonomi, the pontiff tacitly allowed Catholics to use the ballot in emergency conditions. "Do as your conscience dictates," he is reported as saying, "the Pope will keep silent." In this typically indirect way the Holy See's prohibition was relaxed but not abolished—Catholics would vote only in critical areas. In a few cases they were permitted to run for seats in the Chamber, though they would sit as *cattolici deputati* rather than as *deputati cattolici*.

In the elections of 1909 this permission was broadened. Thirty-eight moderate Catholics entered the Chamber pledged to support the existing order; their failure to assert Catholic interests vigorously led to some polemical remarks in the *Osservatore Romano* and answers in the Milanese Catholic press. In the general elections of 1913, held under universal suffrage, Giolitti's constitutional Center forces needed Catholic votes, and a price for them was exacted. Giolitti's candidates negotiated a "pact" with Count Gentiloni, the indiscreet, arrogant head of the Catholic Electoral Union, whereby Catholic votes were delivered to those Government candidates who in return gave *privately* certain promises of respect for Catholic views. In this way the Catholic vote, enlarged by universal suffrage, became a pawn, moved by the Vatican through an intermediary, in the Italian political game. It had no normal means of self-expression; the Catholic masses began voting as a minor under papal guardianship.*

The contradictions were plain. The Vatican had escaped the danger of an Italian Catholic party, which under Murri would have cut loose from any hierarchical control and might have dragged the Church into dangerous adventures. Murri's party would have been Catholic without being papal, and its leader would have been a political primate imperiling the unity of command within the Church.† But the Vatican had been thereby compelled to compromise itself in the Italian political struggle, and to create an unnatural situation that only the unripe Italian democracy of 1913 could have tolerated. The Vatican's almost open descent into the political market place was unwelcome not only to austere anti-Giolitti Liberals like Senator Luigi Albertini, editor of the great *Corriere della Sera,* but also to many Catholics themselves, who after all had political interests and aims of their own to which the Vatican, pursuing larger ends, often failed to give due weight.[18]

In fact, Italian Catholicism was beginning to come of age; the paternalistic formulas of Pius X were never applied in another Italian election. And it was in the reign of Pius X that Italian Catholics acquired a real political life of their own, that a Catholic Left, Center, and Right could be made out against the official background of uniformity. The Catholic bank, cooperative, and labor union rose to real importance in the national life, and became a possible underpinning for a future Catholic party.

Yet the age of Pius X and Giolitti was only in part one of peaceful progress; many, including Giolitti himself, were not wholly aware of how the cracks were widening beneath the smooth

---

* Originally Pius X allowed the bishops to relax the ban on Catholic voting, but this led to such confusion that the matter was put in the hands of the *Unione Elettorale,* at the head of which he appointed Count Gentiloni. However, the "Gentiloni Pact" was in fact transmitted to the Count as an order after it was first cleared with the Cardinal Secretary of State. The whole transaction was carried on in strict secrecy; indeed, one Liberal candidate had been taken to see Count Gentiloni and had accepted his conditions, but after the election, which he won thanks to Catholic support, he solemnly denied any knowledge of the matter! See the account by one of the Vatican's trusted intermediaries, Marquis Filippo Crispolti, *Pio IX, Leone XIII, Benedetto XV, Pio XI, ricordi personali* (Milan, 1939), pp. 109–12.

† By 1909 the thwarted Murri was outside the Church, and stayed so until shortly before his death in 1944.

surface. This truth is exemplified even in the relatively calm area of State and Church, where the measures taken by Pius X really settled none of the fundamental difficulties and had a temporary and stopgap effect. The Roman Question remained unresolved, and the Holy See accepted the existence of Italy only at a practical level. Instead of a genuine reconciliation, merely a tacit truce had been reached, and that solely because of the Socialist menace. The essentially political problem—in what way would Italian Catholics take part in the nation's political life?—was still unsolved, and had grown more urgent since the introduction of universal suffrage. In some part its solution hinged on the Roman Question, but much depended upon the various elements of Italian militant Catholicism, of which some account must now be given.

LEFT AND RIGHT WITHIN THE ITALIAN CATHOLIC MOVEMENT

The Catholic Left was of several sorts. There was one little group, the Demochristians, made up of some of the survivors of Murri's *Lega democratica nazionale* who had not followed the leader into heresy. In the course of a debate with Murri at the Congress of Imola (1910) E. Cacciaguerra declared, in an emotional moment, that he was afraid of coming to the same end as Lamennais. Although the Demochristians avoided this fate, they were very much on the edge of the Catholic world. After the death of Leo XIII and the change of views in the Vatican, the *Lega* had come around to a rigidly separatist position, the exact opposite of Murri's earlier hopes, and the Demochristians maintained it. Democracy, they held, would simply assure a perfect religious liberty and would relegate religion to the realm of private choice. The Church would profit thereby, for it would have an unlimited field of religious action, free from the political interference that had so often compromised it in the past.

The most talented Demochristian was Giuseppe Donati, whose separatism and faith in democracy were later to lead him into working with Don Sturzo in the Popular Party. Like so many other young intellectuals in the age of Giolitti, Donati passed under the influence first of Prezzolini's *La Voce,* to which he was a contributor, and then of Salvemini. He took an active part in Salvemini's campaign against Giolitti's system, distinguishing himself in the attack on economic protectionism, the device by which

Giolitti had secured for himself the support of the North Italian industrial "aristocracy" at the cost—so it was alleged—of impoverishing other elements of the nation. From Murri to Salvemini was a hard journey, and few Catholics made it. Donati's association with Salvemini was never entirely broken, and Donati's political faith owed as much to the Apulian reformer's concrete political thought as to any orthodox Catholic sources. This unusual political education was to set Donati apart, even during the period of his greatest influence among Italian Catholics in the 1920's. While most Demochristians were still locked in the moral and religious struggles of the pontificate of Pius X, Donati had come out of them. He had arrived at a clear idea of the separation of the religious and political spheres, and his political program, while inspired by Christian ethics, shut the Hierarchy out of national politics.

From their beginnings in 1910 until their absorption into the Popular Party after World War I, the Demochristians remained a provincial movement centered in the country towns of the Romagna, with all the intensity and narrowness of such groups.[14] However, they had sympathizers in many parts of Italy, among whom were a parliamentary deputy from the Friuli, elected in 1913, and a young schoolteacher from Pontedera, near the Tuscan coast, Giovanni Gronchi.

The part that the Demochristians played in Italian political debate during the closing years of Giolitti's political ascendancy (1910–15) was greater than their small numbers would lead one to believe, and their journal *L'Azione* of Cesena was a meeting place for young nonconformists such as Dino Grandi and Ferruccio Parri.* Up to a point, nationalists and reformers alike were drawn together by the common struggle against Giolitti's political machine and the "skeptical and materialistic" state of mind in which it acted. Only war and crisis were to show how narrow was their common base of discussion.

Another element of the Italian Catholic Left was headed by Guido Miglioli, who had organized the sharecropper peasants of the Cremona region into a solid and militant phalanx. Miglioli first made his voice heard on a national level at the Catholic Con-

---

* Grandi was later a leading member of the Fascist Grand Council, while Parri headed the Resistance forces of North Italy in 1944–45.

gress of Genoa (1908), when the defense of catechism instruction in the schools was being discussed; he pointed out that the catechism was no platform for a political campaign, and that the masses would vote for the Catholics rather than the Socialists only if they were convinced that their economic interests were thereby being protected. "It is necessary that we organize them, that we give them bread; then, once their faith is gained, we will get them to vote for religious instruction too."

Miglioli was not alone, though Cremona was and always has been more politically alive than most parts of Italy. In 1906 the Catholic labor unions of Lombardy declared that the class struggle, condemned in principle by Catholic social doctrine, could be used as a "temporary instrument" in the ascent of the masses. Explicit participation in the class struggle, even if only for other ends, became an important distinguishing mark of the Catholic Left.[15]

Equally concrete in his political thinking was the Sicilian priest Don Luigi Sturzo. He had made his debut as an associate of Murri, but was not touched by Modernism. While Murri was being led out of the Catholic fold by his grandiose notions of a Church reshaped to serve as a protagonist in social and political strife, Sturzo sensed deeply the necessity of a definite separation between the hierarchical-sacramental Church and a political party inspired by Christian social ideals, a party that would in no way claim a monopoly of Catholic votes and would appeal to the voters on its own merits rather than as a secular arm of the Roman Church. For Sturzo the "Clerical" movement, set up to combat an absolute secular state in defense of the historical rights of the Church, was as outdated as its opponent; in fact the *historical* rights of the Church were ephemeral, and the national democratic state had firmly established itself as the necessary context of all social and political action. Catholicism would find ample freedom for development and fulfillment of its mission in the regime of democratic freedoms. "Clericalism" was a reactionary misunderstanding of the real situation that Catholics faced. By this Sturzo did not, of course, suggest any renunciation of the Pope's claims to independence.[16]

Sturzo's thought grew out of the radical Christian Democracy of the late 1890's, but rejected much of the latter's hostility to the Italian State. Sturzo also shunned the contamination of religion and politics that constituted part of Murri's heresy. Sturzo's great advantage was to have shaken off much of the encumbering inheritance of the pontificates of Pius IX and Leo XIII. From his early days in Murri's movement, Sturzo retained an appreciation of municipal and economic organization as the base for any Catholic political party.

Don Sturzo conceived of the entrance of Italian Catholics into their nation's political life as both natural and necessary: they would appear not as agents of the Papacy, but as citizens offering the contribution of Christian ideals toward the solution of the social and political problems of the age. The Roman Question would be solved in the fullness of time, and an independent Catholic party would be able to help in reaching that solution; but Sturzo was careful to add that only the Pope himself could make the final decision in this matter .

In Don Sturzo's thought the Catholic party of the future would be not only independent (*aconfessionale*) in membership but also democratic in its program. For him, democracy was a part of the regeneration of human society in Christ, which was the aim of Catholic political life; Catholic conservatives, however sincere, were in fact serving as an auxiliary force of the "moderate" parliamentary majority.

Don Sturzo's view of Italian politics was eminently concrete and practical. He served as a municipal administrator in one of Italy's backward areas and understood the importance of basic reforms. During the pontificate of Pius X he immersed himself in municipal administration; on the national scene, he contented himself with prudently opposing the conservative leadership that dominated the Catholic Congresses at which he appeared. He had one of the most important attributes of a successful Catholic leader: he knew how to wait. His day was to come under Benedict XV.

The Catholic conservatives (or Clerico-Moderates, as they were often called) were largely landowners and representatives of agrarian capital; many of them (Grosoli, Crispolti, Cornaggia) had noble titles. They controlled the bulk of the Catholic daily press through the *Società Editrice Romana,* significantly known as the "Trust," which was headed by Count Giovanni Grosoli. Their outstanding spokesman was Filippo Meda, a moderate and prudent tax reformer, and mediator between different currents, the one figure of truly national stature that they brought forth.[17]

In a general way, it may be stated that the Left and Center of the militant Catholics were the political representatives of Catholic labor and peasant unions (the *sindacati bianchi*), and that the Clerico-Moderates represented property. Yet during the pre-World War I years these distinctions were by no means as sharp as they became during the years of war and Fascism; the at least partly democratic Italian State was now accepted by almost all, and the differences between Miglioli and Sturzo, between Sturzo and Meda, between Meda and Crispolti or Grosoli were often hard to detect. Only the test of war and revolution was to bring out these differences.

It is always a mistake to write of Catholics, in Italy or elsewhere, as a bloc. Within the general limits of obedience to the Holy See there is room for all but the most radical differences. Furthermore, the "interclass" character of Catholic parties must be kept in mind: they always include both labor and property, and oscillate uneasily between conservatism and some sort of social reform. Catholic social doctrine can accommodate both. Sometimes only loyalty to the Papacy and opposition to irreligious political forces holds these parties together at all. But concrete problems, such as colonialism and imperialism, offer a touchstone for distinguishing various currents within Catholic parties, even under a cover of outward conformity.

During the pontificate of Pius X the Clerico-Moderates did not constitute the extreme Right of Italian Catholicism. On the contrary, in those years an extremist element of *ancien régime* loyalties asserted itself within the Church, opposing and condemning Christian Democracy and Clerico-Moderatism with equal fervor. To this strange group was due the alliance between the atheist Charles Maurras and those French Catholics who had never accepted the *ralliement* desired by Leo XIII. The *intégristes,* as they were called, carried along with them what was left of Italian intransigent clericalism, now represented by *Unità Cattolica* of Florence and Monsignor Scotton's *Riscossa,* which circulated in the Veneto. The *intégristes* had an Italian newspaper of their own, *La Liguria del Popolo* of Genoa, but in spite of the praise lavished upon their press by the Vatican, it was never able to compete seriously with the Trust.[18] The principal *intégristes* of France were Cardinal Billot, who later resigned from the Sacred College because of the condemnation of *Action Française,* and Abbé Emmanuel Barbier, who left the Jesuit order in 1904; their Italian center was directed by Monsignor Umberto Benigni, an undersecretary for ecclesiastical affairs in the Vatican.[19]

The Modernist heresy afforded the *intégristes* a chance to impugn the orthodoxy, obedience, and good faith of many eminent Catholics; much of the harsh, repressive character of Pius X's pontificate seems to have been due to their denunciations and attacks, which circulated in semiprivate "correspondences" and information agency "reports." The Jesuits were denounced as "traitors" because of their willingness to compromise with existing constitutional states, even though their concessions were purely practical and did not touch their absolute principles. The *intégristes* carried on their campaigns with an *odium theologicum* unusual even in clerical controversies. However, they made the one serious mistake of attacking a cardinal who was eminently *papabile*. When Pius X suddenly died in 1914 Cardinal Giacomo Della Chiesa of Bologna, a constant target of *intégriste* enmity, was elected to succeed him as Benedict XV; the *intégristes* never quite recovered.*

In this presentation of the various currents within Italian organized Catholicism, one point should be made clear. The Catholic Left was moving toward a Social-Democratic and Reformist position. It looked to small-property and cooperative ownership as its ideals, rather than to Socialist nationalization and collectivization, but the practical differences were often small. Though in theory White organizers might accept the official "sociology" of class collaboration and "vertical" corporativism as taught in *Rerum Novarum* and expounded in the writings of Toniolo, in fact they employed the methods and, to some extent, the language of reformist socialism. The "horizontal" labor union and the strike weapon were as necessary to the Whites as to the Reds, if they were to gain any following among the working masses. These methods

---

* With their accounts of betrayals, conspiracies and secret societies the *intégristes* fell into the well-known pattern of European reactionary thought, which attributes such events as the French Revolution, the Risorgimento, and the Russian Revolution to dark invisible plotters of Masonic-Semitic origins. "Conspiracy theories" of history seem always to be a symptom of social and individual stress; the *intégristes* later showed strange affinities with Ludendorff and the like. However, "conspiracy theories" have a long tradition, going back to the first explanation of the French Revolution by its victims.

came in, of course, through the back door. Just as the Church advances the thesis of a confessional state, and admits, in the special conditions of modern society, the *hypothesis* of a religiously tolerant or even neutral state, so Catholic social practice was capable of moving from the thesis of a corporative organization based on class collaboration to the hypothesis of labor union organization using class struggle as a temporarily necessary tactic; but in both cases the hypothesis is nothing more than a concession to modern life. The doctrine of religious and social unity remains intact, however far from being put into practice; the concrete social action of Catholics is largely based on compromise between a medieval ideal and a modern reality.

Catholic labor forces were and are small landholders, tenants, and sharecroppers, elements still tied to the land, not essentially revolutionary. The rural proletariat of the North, especially the wage laborers of the Po valley, gravitated toward the Socialists. To the difference in program corresponded a difference in social make-up.

In 1912 there were 817,034 organized workers in Italy, of whom only 104,614 belonged to Catholic unions. Of these, 67,466 were in industry, 37,148 in agriculture.

In the years before World War I Catholic labor was strong only in light industry and agriculture. Most of the industrial workers who enrolled in Catholic unions in 1912 were Lombard textile workers, largely women. Another area in which Catholics made some progress was white-collar labor; Umberto Tupini, later so prominent in the Popular Party and the Christian Democratic Party, began his career as an organizer of Roman white-collar workers in 1913. In the province of Cremona there were no less than 10,065 organized Catholic farm workers, evidence of Miglioli's following.[20]

The official "line" was laid down by Toniolo: Catholic labor unions, permeated with religious spirit and practice like the medieval guilds, would have more than an economic part to play in a restored Christian social order. They would eventually serve as organs of political representation for the working class, as they had in the Florentine Republic.

Such classical Christian Democratic ideals would have had little appeal for the politically active heavy-industry workers of North

Italy, or for the militant agricultural proletariat of the Po valley. *Their* aspiration was the transformation of State and society through working-class action, conceived as either reform or revolution, and they fought under the banner of the Italian Socialist Party.

THE ENCOUNTER WITH ITALIAN NATIONALISM

While the Catholic Left was thus moving toward positions somewhere between corporativism and Social Democracy, the Catholic Right, i.e., the vast conservative element in the Catholic organizations and the idealistically inclined members of Catholic University Youth, was increasingly drawn toward Italian Nationalism, a new anti-Liberal force.

At first sight Italian Nationalism does not seem compatible with any form of religion, offering as it did the Fatherland as the supreme ideal of the citizen. But in fact the youthful Nationalist movement of 1903–14 in Italy had the same lure for Italian Catholics that Maurras's *Action Française* had for their brethren in France, notwithstanding the open irreligiousness of both nationalisms.*

In the beginning, Italian Nationalism, as the heir of Republican Irredentism, had a marked democratic and anti-clerical color. In the unredeemed provinces the Italian-speaking clergy was loyal to the Dual Monarchy and slowed the progress of Irredentism among the country masses; naturally the Nationalist press lost no chance of dwelling on the traditional alliance between the Holy See and the Hapsburg monarchy and the "anti-national" history of Catholicism in Italy. The "Red Catholicism" of Murri and Sturzo fared no better: it was seen as a subversive ally of international socialism.

After 1910 Italian Nationalism partially broke with its Irredentist "Adriatic" traditions. The "African," openly imperialist aspirations of its leaders came into prominence; an effort was then made to attract Italian Catholicism. Alfredo Oriani rather than

---

* See Enrico Corradini's Florentine journal *Il Regno* (1903–5), and the essays of Giovanni Papini and Giuseppe Prezzolini dating from those years. After 1905 small Nationalist journals sprang up all over Italy; *Il Carroccio* is typical. The relations between Italian Nationalism and the Catholic movement will be examined in Chapters Two and Three.

Mazzini was the prophet of this phase of Nationalism; D'Annunzio instead of Carducci was the bard. An evaluation of the "religious feeling" as a prop of social order and a veneration of Catholicism as a great creation of the Italian national spirit was substituted for the older anti-clericalism. Willingness to sacrifice for the Fatherland would be strengthened by the consolations of religion. Christianity, some Nationalists held, was produced by the alien Semitic spirit, but Catholicism was Roman and imperial.

The nationalists' program might be summarized as regimentation at home, a "national" economy, and expansion abroad.* The class struggle would be transformed, absorbed, and directed outward in a national struggle for empire. To traditional Italian conservatives this program could be presented as the completion of the Risorgimento, the final defeat of Socialism and even the acquisition of a colonial outlet for emigration: for a long time the Nationalists kept a thin veneer of traditional Liberalism, although from the beginning they had nothing in common with the sober, moderate Liberalism of the nineteenth century, as exemplified by Cavour with his European outlook. Where Cavour had favored free trade, the Nationalists stood for protectionism, the economic counterpart of their political imperialism.

For Catholics the Nationalist appeal was evident. The "ethical State" seemed idealistic and somehow nobler than the agnostic Liberal State. Not all Catholics realized, as did (for a time) Filippo Meda, that the Nationalist "ideal" was really a narrow cult of material interests, of violence and plunder, gilded by a chauvinistic rhetoric of *romanità* and empire. The solidarity of a regimented national society, with state-controlled labor organizations, could be made to appear as the fulfillment of Catholic corporative ideals, and wars of colonial aggression could be tricked out as crusades for the expansion of Catholic Christendom. The Nationalists continually attacked both the Demochristians and some Clerico-Moderates, who had in effect joined Giolitti's parliamentary system; but they aimed at drawing into their orbit Catholic University Youth, together with the upper clergy and the vast body of conservative Catholics who were not tied to any precise political grouping. The Nationalist goal was a great party of the Right,

* After 1910 the movement can be followed in *L'Idea Nazionale* of Rome. See Chapter Two.

into which the "Clericals" would enter not as leaders but as followers. The danger of a Catholic party would thus be averted.

Toward the Vatican the Nationalists always entertained feelings of uneasiness and suspicion, as they did toward any international force.* The Papacy was often suspected, with some justice, of harboring pro-Austrian feelings: How indeed could it be otherwise? The Hapsburg monarchy towered over the wrecks of time as the last great Catholic dynastic state.

The contradictions and sources of future conflict within Italian society were laid bare in the Libyan War of 1911–12. Keen observers could see how shaky was the balance that Giolitti had managed to establish in the first decade of the new century. To redress that balance, or to weight it toward the Right, Catholic forces would be called into play.

---

* Their hostility toward Freemasonry gained them some sympathy among Catholics who often failed to perceive the nonreligious motivation for it.

Chapter Two

ITALIAN CATHOLICISM AND THE LIBYAN WAR:
FIRST CONTACTS WITH THE ITALIAN
NATIONALIST PARTY

From our vantage point in the early 1960's Italy's Libyan War of 1911–12 seems a particularly unfortunate colonial enterprise from which no good might have been expected. However, war literature and statesmen's memoirs give quite a different view. For Giolitti and his constitutional majority it was the mere foreclosing of a diplomatic and military mortgage. For opposing Liberals like Albertini of the powerful *Corriere della Sera* it was an upholding of Italian national honor and of her position as a great power. The Libyan War brought Italian Catholics nearer to full reconciliation with the State, on the one hand; on the other, it widened the breach within the Catholic camp itself and created embarrassments for the Holy See.

The two extremes of the Italian political spectrum, the Nationalists and the Revolutionary Syndicalists, found a meeting point in the Libyan enterprise, as later in the founding of the Fascist movement. That the Nationalists supported Italian expansion is no occasion for surprise, but the militaristic attitudes of a few Revolutionary Syndicalists call for explanation. The shifting, unsteady character of their political thought gives a clue; in fact they were a restless fringe element in search of violent adventure. If the promised Socialist revolution would not provide it, perhaps a war of expansion would.

No disloyalty to the final aims of Socialism was felt to be implied. The Libyan War was widely held to be an act of social justice, giving a chance for the Italian proletariat to work out its salvation on the free soil of Africa. For the last generation the Italian laborer had faced poverty and want at home. If he emigrated, he endured exploitation and the loss of national identity in his new home, and Italy lost both strength and prestige by the emigration of her workers. This "social" aspect of the new imperialism was best expressed for Italian public opinion not by

Nationalist leaders like Corradini, who had been working for years along these lines, but by the gentle poet Giovanni Pascoli in his famous oration *La grande proletaria si è mossa*. *La grande proletaria* was the Italian nation itself, the Cinderella among the nations who was at last coming into her own.

Another more influential poet put his pen at the service of a greater Italy: Gabriele D'Annunzio. This restless spirit, ever in search of new sensations and themes for his literary production, took up war with the same enthusiasm that he had taken up aviation in 1909; but the thrill of heroism was closely associated with a morbid preoccupation with death, a constant note in the poet's work. D'Annunzio's poems, sent from exile in France, were run in the great Milanese daily, *Il Corriere della Sera*. Albertini reminisced:

> Of wonderful encouragement to the nation and the fighting men were the *Canzoni della gesta d'Oltremare* which Gabriele D'Annunzio sent to the *Corriere* from Arcachon in order to exalt the enterprise and its various episodes. We too, like all the major dailies, made rhetoric. In part it was unconscious, begotten by our and the country's enthusiasm; in part it was a necessity that skeptics and those who judge events at a distance can smile at. But the newspaper is not a posthumous work of history. It is a reflection of life and a push toward action.[1]

Up to this point D'Annunzio had never accepted official Liberal Italy as it had issued from the Risorgimento. In his short term as *deputato della bellezza* he had moved to the Left of the Chamber in protest (during the constitutional crisis of 1898–1900). His contempt for the "Third Italy" of his own time was proclaimed in bitter verses lamenting the departed glories of Latin civilization and coarsely jeering at the "eyeless mole" in the Quirinal. Only Garibaldi, "giver of kingdoms," stirred his patriotic imagination. The Roman Church was coupled with the Third Italy in his scorn:

> Against the one consistory
> That chatters, grafts, and seizes,
> And the other that milks the treasury
> Of Peter for its greedy soul,
> Let us raise the ideal image.*

---

* See the poem *A Roma* in *Elettra* (1904), second book of the *Laudi*, and also the poet's view of *Roma demagogica*, Alfredo Gargiulo, *Gabriele D'Annunzio, studio critico* (Naples, 1912), pp. 222–23. The poet's notion of a political superman is expressed in the drama *La Gloria* (1899), a strange unintended prophecy of Fascism. In this chapter D'Annunzio is dealt with at length be-

But an ideal image of what? The poet was a man of sensations, not of ideas, and no ideal had offered itself to fill his inner void.

He finally found the stage upon which he could act as a Garibaldian, as a poet of real glory and death. The expansion of Italy gave him new functions, both literary and practical: he became a bard in the Libyan War, a hero in World War I, and finally a dictator at Fiume in 1919, on the examples of Napoleon and Garibaldi. His ideal image came briefly and disastrously to life.

His "Songs of the Overseas Feats" (*Le canzoni della gesta d'Oltremare*), published (with the deletion of one anti-Austrian passage) in January 1912 at the height of the Libyan conflict, were a tissue of classical and crusader reminiscences woven together with highly colored accounts of Italian heroism in the current war against Turk and Arab. The historic struggle between the cities of Italy and the forces of Islam was a theme dear to D'Annunzio, and he made the most of it. Past and present were bound together in these strange hymns of death and glory. The novelty of military aircraft, the minutiae of suffering and extinction, were described together with the Catholic piety of Louis IX and the daring of Pisan, Genoese, and Venetian mariners.

D'Annunzio did not hesitate to sound a religious, even miraculous note, as in the following recounting of the legend of the chalice of Genoa:

> In Christ King, O Genoa, I call upon thee . . .
> The Lord's blood boils in the emerald cup.
>
> Behold the vessel of life, behold the bowl
> Where Jesus poured out the last wine
> To the Twelve on Passover eve,
>
> And said: "This is my blood, which is
> Blood of the new covenant, and is shed
> For many." And He became divine, above evil.
>
> When he cried "Elohi" from a burnt-out heart,
> In the ninth hour a man of Arimathea
> Came; and in that vessel gathered the scattered blood.

---

cause of his importance in Italian life between 1890 and 1925. To a great extent the tastes and temperament of a whole generation of Italians were "D'Annunzian."

Henceforward, by grace from on high
An assembly of the Pure held in guard
The carven emerald. . . .

Just as when suddenly Embriaco* in the burning
     night of Caesarea,
Found the cup of salvation for his people
And put it on the galleasse,
Like the palladium on the trireme,
Recelebrating the glory of the race,

So perhaps a deified spirit of the seed of Aeneas
Is coming back to us with the divine mark
Of the distant sands. . . .[2]

Even when D'Annunzio, as here, uses Christian themes, in his hands they become pagan; yet an astonishing number of Catholics rallied to the "crusade" that he heralded.

Much of the Catholic hierarchy and press did more than merely support the war as a patriotic duty: from pulpits and in public meetings the Libyan conflict was actually declared to be a "holy war." The Battle of Lepanto (the 340th anniversary of which occurred conveniently in October 1911, shortly after the start of the Libyan War) was solemnly commemorated, and—another evocation of crusader memories—the Sovereign Order of Malta sent the Italians a hospital ship.[3]

Catholic enthusiasm for the war was also stirred up by the Bank of Rome. This bank, founded in 1880 by certain landed interests of Latium and always identified with aristocratic "Clerical" families, had penetrated into many areas of the Levant after 1900, and had shown a particular concern with Libya, where it had been active since 1907. Not only did the Bank of Rome carry out ordinary financial operations there, it also owned and managed a steamship line with five vessels. The Russian representative at the Vatican noted that the aggressive head of the Bank of Rome, Ernesto Pacelli, was "uncle of the rising star of Vatican diplomacy, Monsignor Eugenio Pacelli," and dryly observed that "the happy outcome of the Italian military enterprise would give to the clerical world here the possibility of joining worldly benefits with the observance of spiritual neutrality."[4]

---

* A Genoese crusader.

But in fact the Vatican's interests were far wider than the compass of any banking activities. When a cardinal of the Roman Curia, Vannutelli, who had been Apostolic Delegate at Constantinople, publicly supported the war, he was sharply rebuked; the Vatican officially "deplored" the crusading attitude of the Catholic "Trust" press and underlined its own neutrality. (This, incidentally, was a triumph for the *intégristes* and marks a high point of their influence.) Though the Young Turks were suspected of Masonic ties, a conflict between the Church and the Ottoman Empire could only have had disastrous effects for all concerned. Also, Giolitti had clearly indicated in his initial proclamation to the Arabs that Libya was to remain a Moslem domain.[5]

What the Libyan War did show most definitely was the danger of too close a link between the Vatican, with its world-wide concerns, and the Italian Catholic world, with its increasing immersion in the politics of the Italian State. The Roman Question was still unsolved, and the Holy See, if it yielded to the importunities of Italian Catholics, might easily have found itself forced into accepting the "usurpations" of the Italian Kingdom. The whole episode suggested most strongly the wisdom of Don Sturzo's proposal of a separation of the Catholic Church and the political organization of Catholics in Italy.

Although the Clerico-Moderate Catholic deputies in Parliament voted in favor of the war, there was no unanimity among Catholics as a whole. At Cremona the patriotic bishop Monsignor Bonomelli saw the war as a common cause of Church and State:

> Italy . . . will have the advantage of opening, only a few miles away from the islands, a colony for her emigrants, an outlet for her commerce, a port of defense for her coasts. . . . Alongside of the Italian tricolor I see the Cross rising. . . . Italy will certainly respect the religion of the natives; but it may be hoped that the patient labor of missionaries, upheld and protected by the majesty of the State, can work a healthy transformation there, however slowly.[6]

But the Catholic peasant-union leader of Cremona, Miglioli, and his organ *L'Azione* took quite a different tack:

> We are grieved that certain Catholic newspapers, such as the *Corriere d'Italia* of Rome, are among the supporters of our penetration into Tripoli, at whatver cost. The Radical-Gio-

littian government . . . which woefully neglects the most serious problems of our internal economic and civil life, has, it seems, no other way to follow, for the special amusement of the people, than to send its sons away to be shot by the Turks.[7]

Later *L'Azione* accepted the Libyan War as an accomplished fact and a patriotic duty, though taking care to distinguish its position from that of "warmongering" and "jingoistic" Italian Nationalism. The Christian Democrats of the Romagna also opposed the war.

In this episode of modern Italian history, brief and self-contained as it is, we have all the elements of future crises, so far as the Catholics are concerned. Italian expansionism had found collaborators and instruments in the established institutions of the Italian Catholic movement: the Catholic press (or at least that great part of it controlled by the Trust), the Bank of Rome, and even a large part of the Hierarchy. On the other hand, the Catholic Left had its first real experience of opposition, however bland. The Vatican had had to differentiate its policies sharply from those of the Italian Catholic movement. The cleavages within the Catholic bloc were marked out, and future pressures would only widen them.

One point must be put clearly; i.e., the absence of any distinctively Catholic view of the war. Miglioli's opposition was like that of the Italian social reformers toward foreign "diversions"; his bishop's support was like that of the Italian Nationalists, with their idea of an African "outlet" (*living-space,* it would be called later). Reformism on the one side and Nationalism on the other filled the vague phrases of current Catholic political philosophy with whatever concrete meaning they were capable of bearing.

CATHOLICISM AND ROMANISM: CONTACTS WITH THE NATIONALIST PARTY

Just as Italian Catholicism was being opened anew to outside influences after the long isolation of 1870–90, so the Italian secular world was showing a new interest in religious problems and a receptiveness to "Catholic" ideas.

In *Cristo e Quirino,* first published in 1897 and often reprinted, the young Syndicalist Paolo Orano attempted to redefine the whole problem of Christianity. He began with a bold antithesis

between a hopeless, individualistic, and "anarcho-mystical" East
and a progressive, socially minded, law-making, and state-building
West. Christianity arises in the East but takes root only in the
West, a paradox that Orano explains through Christ's having become a symbol to the restless and world-weary slave population
of the Empire. The masses were reconciled to a stratified society
by the Christian teaching of resignation and contempt for earthly
goods that were inaccessible anyway. Indeed, Christian religious
feeling soothed and comforted the masses, and this feeling was
used by the Church, a hierarchical, eminently Roman institution,
to maintain the fabric of the Latin world. Thus Christianity, in
this view, becomes a symptom of widespread sickness, to which the
Church provides a cure. The proletariat of the late Roman Empire
was inspired by Christian ideals, now adopted by the whole of
society, into taking upon its shoulders the yoke of Church discipline. The poor were called children of God, but they stayed poor.

In all of this Orano was very probably influenced by Nietzsche,
although he is not among the many authorities that Orano cites.
Orano certainly saw no future usefulness for the Church. Nevertheless, his distinction between Christian religious sentiment and
the Roman Church was essential for Italian Nationalists: the first
was alien to them, but the second could become an instrument of
policy. After all, was it not an emanation of Italian national gen-
ius, an expression of *romanità*?

A curiously similar state of mind existed among some Italian
Catholics, as was shown by the little magazine *La Torre* of Siena,
which styled itself the "organ of the Italian spiritual reaction."
It was put out by two young writers, Domenico Giuliotti and
Federigo Tozzi, who were soon joined by Guido Battelli. In its
first issue *La Torre* aimed to astonish:

> We profess ourselves, to the scandal of the foolish, *reaction-
> aries* and Catholics; . . . tolerance is indifference; he who be-
> lieves, wants others to believe too. We are intolerant. . . . Im-
> perialists and Catholics, we keep our eye on Rome. . . . It is
> essential that Rome, polluted by the [Radical-Democratic] *bloc,*
> go back to being *Roman.* . . . We propose to Italian National-
> ism, which has grown up in the shadow of Rome, that it boldly
> transform itself into Imperialism and confess itself to be Catho-
> lic. . . . While France is dying, Italy must arise on new wings,
> to draw everything along with her.

There were some explanations in the next issue:

> We are supremely *Italian*. As such, today in the twentieth century we adopt the mighty dream of Dante, in hatred for the democratic frenchifying of our country. . . . And keep in mind that it is from Dante that we have learned to exalt the divinity of the Church and to horsewhip false priests. If Dante was *anti-clerical in this way*, then we are anticlerical like him.[8]

The political line of *La Torre* was laid down by Giuliotti, who had an especial loathing for Giolitti's crowning reform, universal suffrage. The Italians were, according to Giuliotti, more than ever a "passive herd of idiots." In the countryside the Italians were "happily illiterate," and elsewhere they were being "turned into literate asses by the anticlericalism of their teachers," or *"scientifically* incited to revolt by lawyers, doctors, professors, and druggists in the People's Universities" (a reference to adult education, largely democratic and Socialist in inspiration). Liberalism was, for Giuliotti, simply the "doorkeeper of Socialism."[9]

Naturally this Tuscan group had little use for the Clerico-Moderates who dominated most Italian Catholic activities, and had just thrown their votes to the Liberals by the Gentiloni Pact of 1913. No "spiritual nourishment" for the masses was to be expected from such an "inorganic" alliance.

It was rather from the Nationalists that something might be hoped for. Italian Nationalism had its work cut out: "to restore to honor the moral values of our race and the traditions of the stock." Italian consciousness must be freed from "barbaric cosmo-politanism," by which was meant Masonry and Jewry, "the infected springs from which have arisen liberalism, radicalism, and socialism."

The culmination of this work would be the Empire:

> The Roman fathers carried away the Empire from East to West, just as the Church moved from East to West. The Roman eagle and the Cross took the same path.
>
> The saints said that this is God's plan. And we believe it, feel it, and rejoice in it. If for sixteen centuries a new barbarism has weighed upon Italy, we must dispel it, and rebuild that *civil and moral primacy,* which is not a rhetorical phrase, but the truth.
>
> As the pontiff is *primus inter pares,* so must Italy be *prima inter pares.*

An empire at once Italian and Catholic, then; for empire means *power* and Catholicism *truth*.[10]

In all this there was much posturing, attention-seeking, and repetition of De Maistre and Gioberti. But there was also a surprising foretaste of the phrasing and imagery of Fascism; the later careers of Giuliotti and Battelli show that this was more than an accidental parallel.* The most ominous theme of all was the appeal to nationalism and imperialism: therein the young Tuscan writers were true prophets. When the Fascist "Empire" was finally proclaimed, it did not lack religious sanctions—of a sort.

La Torre, though symptomatic of a new state of mind, enjoyed no substantial Catholic backing and it died in 1914 after only a few months of life. Yet the question it had posed—the relation between Italian Nationalism and the organized Catholics of Italy—was a real one and was taken up by a better financed and more authoritative journal.

L'Idea Nazionale was edited by five Nationalists who were all to play an active part in Fascism: Enrico Corradini, Francesco Coppola, Luigi Federzoni, Roberto Forges Davanzati, and Maurizio Maraviglia. Corradini was already the Nestor of the Nationalist movement. Coppola was a racist (a rare bird in Italy) who during the Libyan War wrote an open letter to Charles Maurras complaining that the unholy alliance of Jewish gold and demagogy, Puritan hypocrisy, and Turko-Tartar savagery was directed against Italy. Federzoni, like the rest of them, did well under Fascism, but voted against Mussolini in the Grand Council of Fascism at the last fatal session of July 24, 1943.

In 1912–14 *L'Idea Nazionale* made the first real contacts between Nationalist Party spokesmen and the official organizations of Italian Catholicism, for the most part under Clerico-Moderate leadership. In discussions with the Nationalists the Clerico-Moderates were ably represented by Filippo Meda, the balancing and mediating figure among Italian Catholics.

Meda at first saw clearly that the Nationalists' glorification of struggle, power, and production was irreconcilable with several of the fundamental tenets of Christianity, but he went on to make

* Giuliotti became one of Papini's associates in the Catholic-Fascist journal *Frontespizio* after 1931. Battelli in 1926 published St. Bonaventure's *Life of Saint Francis,* with an introduction by Benito Mussolini!

a significant admission: "In other questions—for example, those concerning the superiority of national interest over class interests, and the precedence, for a state, of foreign problems over internal problems—we can sometimes agree with the Nationalists."[11]

Implicitly, the door was left open for a practical understanding between Nationalists and Clerico-Moderates for joint action against socialism, particularly during a war.

But the Nationalists had no real hope of annexing the Clerico-Moderates or the internationally minded circles close to the Vatican. The first were devoted to the "little man" and to small property, an ideal which the Nationalists scorned as "micromania," whereas the Vatican was concerned above all with preserving the Dual Monarchy.[12] The forces of Catholic labor and the Romagna Christian Democrats were even more inaccessible. Nationalist attention was directed to Catholic university youth.

In January 1913 the Catholic University Circle of Rome held an open debate with the Nationalists. In this meeting, conducted in an atmosphere of correctness, courtesy, and even, at times, cordiality, certain lines of possible convergence were traced. The young Catholic speaker Francesco Aquilanti said:

> The Catholics recognize the degree of superiority and hence the progress of Nationalist thought over democratic thought, and happily take note of the triumph of the idea of duty over the conception of profit, the cancer of the democracies. . . . We agree with Corradini when he recognizes in democracy, in a historical sense, a factor of social disintegration, but we do not bow down before the despotic and tyrannical absolutism of civil society embodied in the nation. . . . We observe with satisfaction that the ethical State of the Nationalists is superior to the secular State of the democrats because it has a unitary and formative character; but when in matters of ecclesiastical policy the ethical State, presenting itself as secular, proclaims its own sovereignty over the Church, then we defend ourselves from it. . . . Likewise, we approve of the ethical school, which directs and shapes minds with the mallet of social order, but we wish to guard the precious flower of freedom.[13]

Meda took part in the discussion, noting that as a historical fact Nationalism paralleled Socialism: both were materialistic, but Nationalism transferred to an international plane the struggle among the classes which Socialism affirms. Meda ended by rejecting the Nationalist view of war as a normal fact of life; war was a "phenomenon of exceptional seriousness that can and should be undergone, but is not desired and called for." In a more cautious way Egilberto Martire, a young Catholic journalist, agreed. (This same Martire was one day to be a leading intermediary between Catholicism and Fascism in Italy, though his career under Fascism ended without distinction.)

In summing up, Aquilanti expressed disagreement with Meda. He did not believe that Nationalism had a "materialistic soul," but that it was deeply idealistic, "an idealism, however, that has stopped at the philosophic stage without rising to the supreme realities revealed by faith." When the discussion went on, and Federzoni asked what Italian Catholics would do if forced to choose between Church and Nation, Aquilanti answered that in such a case the Catholics would be for the true God against the idol, for the Church, however reluctantly, against the Nation.

What was especially interesting in all this was not Aquilanti's declarations in themselves, but the state of mind to which they bore witness. The rhetoric of Italian Nationalism was making definite inroads upon Catholic youth. Many Catholics, once having made certain theoretical reservations about Nationalist "ideals," could easily underwrite much of the Nationalist program. Croce, when he rejected the Nationalists' "war without faith and justice," showed a far greater moral awareness.*

The immediate aspiration of the young Nationalist movement was often and clearly stated: to head a new Italian Right, to furnish a new ruling cadre for the Italian State. Into this new Italian Right would enter, of course, the forces of organized Italian Catholicism, but as followers, not leaders. The same supporting role would be played by conservative Liberals.

These ideas were put forth most clearly by the Nationalist lawyer Alfredo Rocco in a 1914 pamphlet:

> Today there can be points of contact between Nationalists and Catholics. . . . The Nationalists believe that the State cannot be indifferent to that most important and fundamental

---

* Not all young Catholics stayed sympathetic toward the Italian Nationalist movement. In May 1914 the yearly congress of the Italian Catholic University Student Federation (FUCI) sharply noted the "absolute incompatibility" between its ideals and the doctrine of Italian Nationalism as it was taking shape, and resolved that its members could not belong to Nationalist associations. See Spadolini, *Giolitti e i cattolici*, p. 247.

social phenomenon, religion. And since the religion of the overwhelming majority of the Italians is Catholic, the Italian State cannot ignore the Catholic Church and the Catholic religion. Indeed, it should take into direct consideration the interests of Italian Catholics, insofar as they are compatible with the interests of the Nation . . . The Nationalists do not believe that the State should be an instrument of the Church [in Rocco's view this was "clericalism"]; instead they believe that the State must assert its sovereignty also in regard to the Church. Since, however, they recognize that the Catholic religion and Church are most important factors of national life, they wish to watch over Catholic interests as far as possible, always safeguarding the sovereignty of the State. And at this stage of Italian life, such protection should take the form of respect for the freedom of conscience of Italian Catholics, against the antireligious persecutions of anticlerical democrats. In the future it will perhaps be possible to go farther and establish an agreement with the Catholic Church, even if only tacit, by which the Catholic organization could serve the Italian nation for its expansion in the world.[14]

In these words may be found the germ of the whole future religious policy of Fascism, which consisted in establishing "points of contact" between Church and Regime and attempting to exploit religion for the purposes of Italian imperialism; all of this being accompanied by a consistent denial of Christianity itself. Like Orano, Rocco saw primitive Christianity as an individualistic "dissolving force," whereas Nationalism was a "national religion, the dedication of oneself, daily self-abnegation." These views are especially noteworthy, for in 1929 Rocco was the chief negotiator of the Lateran Pacts for the Fascist Regime.

Although the one concrete attempt at political collaboration between the Nationalists and a local Catholic organization in the Veneto came to naught because Catholic voters would not support Corradini,[15] all the conditions for an alliance between Nationalism and organized Catholicism existed by 1914.

Chapter Three

THE CATHOLIC ALLIANCE WITH SALANDRA, 1914–15

The organized Catholics of Italy became a prop of the existing order in 1904, when they were allowed by Pius X to support Conservative or Moderate candidates in certain key areas of North Italy; this permission was broadened in 1909 and became general in 1913, in the new conditions of universal suffrage. In the elections of that year the Moderate forces that had so long upheld Giolitti found it necessary to call in the Catholic voting masses in order to redress a balance that was leaning dangerously toward the Extreme Left. The Catholic organizations delivered their votes in 330 constituencies at a modest price, and the situation seemed "saved."[1] But this operation, conducted in an underhanded manner, did much to discredit Italian Liberalism when it became publicly known as the "Gentiloni Pact" right after the elections, as recounted in Chapter One.

In every way 1913 and 1914 were years of general uneasiness. The parliamentary majority of November 1913 was made up of 305 Liberals and Democrats of various shades, 34 Catholics (headed by Filippo Meda), and 68 anti-Clerical Radicals. Under the terms of the Gentiloni Pact 228 majority deputies had been elected with Catholic support. Any government resting on such an eclectic base would have limited possibilities; yet the situation of Italy demanded a "strong" government, capable of taking a consistent line.*

* The "Liberals" included the Nationalist spokesman Federzoni, who campaigned in Rome with Catholic support against the anticlerical Masonic bloc. His election is another indication of the practical understanding possible between Right-Wing Catholics and Italian Nationalists; in 1914 Albertini saw in the small Nationalist Party clear signs of *clericofilia*. See Albertini, *Venti anni di vita politica*, II, 291.

In Sicily, where there was no accord between local Catholics and the official Moderate candidates, Mafia methods were employed against the Catholics. Christian Democratic candidates, approved by Count Gentiloni's union, were defeated with the tacit connivance of the police: Catholic voters were terrorized, voting places seized, and socially active priests often sent into hiding. This at a moment in which much of the rest of Italy saw an officially sponsored electoral alliance between Liberal-Moderate and Catholic forces! See De Rosa, *Filippo Meda*, pp. 161–65.

First of all, the Italian economy, which had expanded so greatly since 1900, was in recession. Italian heavy industry (steel, shipping, and motors) had grown up with tariff protection and military subsidies. A hothouse plant, in 1913 it was undergoing a crisis of overproduction. The important Italian textile industry was also in difficulties. Moreover, the Libyan venture had cost far more than expected, since Arab resistance to Italian rule had yet to be overcome, and the Government was operating with a large yearly deficit.[2]

Italian labor was restless. In 1913, some 384,725 workers went out on strike, more than in any previous year.[3] In the Milanese workshops the strikes of 1913–14 took on aspects of Syndicalist violence hitherto unheard of.[4] Nor was farm labor any quieter: in the vital Emilia-Ferrara region, where thousands of acres had been reclaimed by capitalist enterprise, the new Syndicalist unions, numbering 98,000 members as against some 400,000 of the reformist CGL, carried on an uncompromising revolutionary struggle.[5]

Giolitti's hopes that Italian Socialism could be brought into a parliamentary orbit seemed dim by 1913. Instead the Italian Socialist Party had become more and more revolutionary, at least in words; its official organ *Avanti!* had become a general headquarters, where Benito Mussolini and a staff of agitators laid down the strategy and tactics of an international "class war," which was to replace the ambiguous "class struggle" of earlier Socialist formulations.

At the other extreme of the Italian political spectrum there was a disturbing growth of youthful fringe groups—Nationalist, D'Annunzian-Imperialist, and Futurist (founded in 1909)—which all rejected and ridiculed not only the democratic principles of Giolitti and the constitutional majority, but even the very foundations of the Italian State as it had come out of the Risorgimento. The prosaic Liberal *Italietta* was to be succeeded by a tri-continental empire. Like the Syndicalists, the young reactionaries and imperialists were vastly excited by the new world of steel and motors. For the Syndicalist, industry was the foundation of a new moral and social order; for the imperialist, it was the sinews of empire.

Of these groups, made up largely of thwarted, semieducated, middle-class youth, some, the Futurists in particular, were violently antireligious; others, especially the Sienese group dealt with in the preceding chapter, called themselves "Catholic" in some special nonclerical sense. As may be seen from the Aquilanti-Federzoni debate, even official Catholic youth was not altogether immune from the pre-1914 ferment of ideas and aspirations. The fringe groups were all united only by their hatred for the "bourgeois" decencies of the European Liberal tradition, including the Christian-humanitarian elements therein, and a readiness for violent action that could publicly display their talents. Such marginal elements exist in many countries; in moments of stress they are far more important than their numbers would suggest.*

The Giolitti government, rather than carry on in this atmosphere of discontent, chose to quit 10 March 1914. The immediate occasion of Giolitti's resignation was the secession of the Radicals from his majority. In addition, one of his ministers had brought in a bill making it obligatory for the civil marriage to precede the religious ceremony, at which point the Catholics rose in arms. The veteran statesman preferred to leave power rather than compose the differences within his hybrid parliamentary majority. Most observers took this as merely one of his usual strategic withdrawals. He would wait for calmer weather, it was thought, and then return to the helm, as he had done more than once before, most recently in 1909. It proved instead to be the point at which his fortunes began to wane, for he was never able to dominate Italian political life thereafter: the era of Giolitti was ended.[6]

Giolitti had resigned without an adverse vote in Parliament; consequently his successor was not clearly marked out by a parliamentary opposition. The king was advised by Giolitti to send for Sonnino, who declined for lack of an assured majority in Parliament; Giolitti then singled out the conservative-Liberal jurist Salandra, an Apulian, whose new government was then upheld in Parliament by the usual official majority.

* While the Futurists were often mere sensation-seekers, the Italian Syndicalists had some of the intensity and closeness of a religious brotherhood in the years before World War I, befitting Sorel's disciples. The figure of the Syndicalist leader Filippo Corridoni, an authentic proletarian, is re-evoked by two of his friends, Tullio Masotti, *Corridoni* (Milan, 1932), and Alceste De Ambris, *Filippo Corridoni* (Rome, 1922), old Syndicalist comrades whose ways parted during the Fascist period. By 1914 the Italian political struggle was assuming the narrowness, tension, and violence of a religiously motivated civil war. Something similar happened in Britain between 1910 and 1914, as may be seen from George Dangerfield's *The Strange Death of Liberal England*.

The cabinet crisis of March–April, 1914, was notable in that it developed and was resolved outside of Parliament—a dangerous precedent. It ended in a sharp turn to the Right, and in it the Catholics appeared, for the first time in the Kingdom's parliamentary history, as an important element. Their opposition to the Government's marriage legislation had perhaps hastened Giolitti's withdrawal, and their relation to Salandra became a polemical point for the revolutionary Socialist Arturo Labriola when he rose in the Chamber of Deputies to warn against turning to the Right.

Labriola reviewed Salandra's past and concluded that he was an *autoritario giurisdizionalista,* by which he meant that Salandra wished for a State-dominated national Church, to be arrived at by a "jurisdictionalist" concordat of the eighteenth-century type. Labriola went on:

> The Honorable Salandra interprets literally the First Article of the Statute, according to which the religion of the State is Catholic and other forms of worship are tolerated. . . . The Honorable Giolitti would have been able to say, from his own crudely empirical point of view, that he had led the Catholics into the service of democracy. Now the Honorable Salandra wants to reverse the terms and oblige the democrats to serve the Catholics! . . . This is the *giolittismo* of the *Osservatore Romano* and of the Holy See. . . . If parliamentary democracy is not solemnizing its own funeral, it should realize that the defense of democracy cannot be entrusted to those who never had confidence in it and constantly mocked its principles.

This was strong enough, but more was yet to come. The Republican Comandini reminded his colleagues that Salandra had written against "political Catholicism," but that in action Salandra had favored the Catholics, that he had opposed divorce legislation and had upheld religious instruction in public schools.[7]

Not since 1870 had an Italian cabinet come to power with so friendly a relationship with the Catholics. Needless to say, Meda and his Clerico-Moderate group voted for Salandra; it was the first of many services they were to render him.

Shortly after taking office, the Salandra government had to face a revolutionary storm far worse than any that previous governments had known since 1898. An antimilitary demonstration at Ancona 7 June 1914 led to clashes with the state police, several deaths, and a wave of disorders throughout Italy. A short general strike was proclaimed, Mussolini led a riotous demonstration in Milan (only to be knocked unconscious), and—more seriously— much of the Romagna and the Marches actually rose in revolt. The noisy rabblerousing of Mussolini and the Syndicalists in Milan could be dealt with, but the Anarchist-Republican-Socialist risings in the Romagnole countryside had a "grass-roots" character: the insurgents seized the instruments of public control—railroads, telegraph lines, police stations, municipalities—and succeeded in disarming the forces of order, including one army general and his staff. In many places the Republic was proclaimed. Though the insurrections did not last more than a week, they had a deep effect on the later course of Italian politics, for they had shown how easily the State could be set aside in certain areas of Italy, how thin the veneer of law and order really was. Yet the rising also shed a cruel light on the Italian Left: after two generations the adventurous anarchism of Bakunin still prevailed in the Italian revolutionary countryside over the sober scientific Socialism of the Reformists and the official Party. The "Red Week" of June 1914 served to put the forces of order on their guard. Mussolini, who in the columns of *Avanti!* had done so much to instigate revolution, defined the Red-Week insurrection and strike as "the most serious people's uprising that has shaken the Third Italy from 1870 to today."[*]

Among the forces of order must be reckoned the Catholics. The Church suffered heavily in the Romagna and the Marches. Church buildings were burned or sacked, priests abused and exposed to public shame, and—the most disturbing fact of all—there had been no acts of heroism or martyrdom. The Christian Democrats of the Romagna, excellent witnesses, were appalled at the weakness generally displayed by Catholics in defending their altars. Both clergy and laity had been passive victims during the whole crisis.[†]

[*] See Giorgio Pini and Duilio Susmel, *Mussolini l'uomo e l'opera* (Florence, 1953), I, 228. Mussolini was actually at Forlì, in the Romagna, when the disturbances began, though his principal role was played after he returned to Milan. (Mussolini had gone to Forlì to deliver an address on Marat!) Pietro Nenni, then a Republican leader at Ancona, supported the original Red-Week demonstration there.

[†] See *L'Azione* (Cesena), especially 19 July 1914. The parish church at Mezzano, in the province of Ravenna, was actually destroyed in the revolutionary fury of Red Week.

The official Italian Catholic Electoral Union, headed by the same Count Gentiloni who had delivered the organized Catholic vote in the elections of 1913, reacted to Red Week in a circular of June 17:

> We Catholics, who through the rage of astute and barbarous demagogues have suffered more than others the loss and reproach of our violated altars and profaned tabernacles, of our burned churches, should seriously think of our defense against those who would want to plunge our Italy into the abyss of revolution and terror.
> *Catholic voters,* the Fatherland expects of you that each will do his duty.[8]

The pro-Salandra stand taken by Italian Catholic leaders in the intervention crisis of April–May, 1915, cannot be understood unless the searing experience of the June 1914 Red Week is kept well in mind. It engendered among many Catholic notables a panic fear of revolution and a concern for order at whatever cost. The Salandra government was the incarnation of public order. A patriotic war might appear as a remedy for domestic turbulence, although it finally turned out that the remedy actually brought on a new and more virulent attack of the old disease.

The first fruits of the new Catholic policy were already to be seen in the municipal elections of 14 June 1914, when the Roman Capitol was conquered by a Right-Wing electoral coalition including both Catholics and Nationalists. Political—i.e., parliamentary —alliance between the two forces was far away, but local collaboration against a common enemy had already begun.[9]

Thus at the outbreak of World War I, Italy was going through a period of rekindled social animosities, and Giolitti's era of good feeling seemed at an end. The new rulers, enjoying their power after Giolitti's long parliamentary reign, plunged into a course of action that Giolitti himself rightly feared: they began negotiating with the Allies with a view toward coming into the war. Simultaneously, Italy was dealing with Austria and Germany, in hopes of regaining some part of the *irredenta* areas without war, although it became clear that Austria would make no really substantial concessions. On the other hand, the Allies did not hesitate to make Italy the most generous promises.

The external reasons for Italian intervention still seem, at a distance of more than forty years, strangely insufficient. Were Trent and Trieste worth the travails of world war? It seems likely that Salandra had other impelling motives to go ahead with his war plans. He was enjoying his one chance to be head of the Government, before a return of Giolitti of the sort that had always occurred in the past. However, the entry of Italy into the war would have the effect of excluding the declaredly neutralist Giolitti from the Government for an indefinite period, and would give Salandra, a statesman with a fatal consciousness of his historical role, a chance to write his name in large letters in the history of his country. In addition, Italy had adopted democratic voting procedures, and it would be only a matter of time before the old ruling class would have to yield its places in Parliament; a war would delay this doom indefinitely. Finally, Red Week had shown the possibilities of social strife: a war would offer excellent chances for repressing the Left.

From Catholic reactions to World War I, we can see how religiously and politically entangled was the situation of Italian Catholics, caught as they were between the world policy of the Vatican and the national aims of Italy.

The Holy See itself was initially pro-Austrian and remained so as long as the war could be seen as a defense of Europe's last Catholic empire. But the war soon became general and amoral. Against the murder of a Catholic archduke by Serbian Orthodox Nationalists had to be set the unprovoked invasion of a small Catholic state by Germany; the balance of wrongs clearly indicated Vatican neutrality, real as well as formal.[10]

When Matthias Erzberger of the German Catholic Centrum Party was in Rome on a wartime mission for his Government during Easter Week of 1915, Benedict XV accorded him a private audience in which one of the deepest reasons for Vatican neutrality was laid bare. "If the War lasts much longer, there will be a social revolution such as the world has never before seen," said the Pope, with undeniable foresight.[11] As Archbishop of Bologna he had been near the storm center of the June 1914 Red Week, an impressive foretaste of future "social revolution."

Neutral itself, it was natural that the Holy See should wish that Italy also remain so. Italian belligerency would endanger the Papacy's communications with much of the Catholic world, and if, as seemed possible, Italy's entrance into the war should lead to some sort of social upheaval, how could the Holy See remain unaffected thereby? Though neutralism was never officially enjoined upon Italian Catholics, it was clear where Vatican sympathies lay; hence *most* of the organized Catholics of Italy were neutralist at the outset of the war.

The general neutralism of Italian Catholics was of many sorts. The old intransigent-*intégriste* current, traditionally favorable to the Austrian monarchy, looked upon the war as a sort of divine visitation on an apostate continent. Though Belgium was a Catholic country, had she not trusted to the workings of an irreligiously conceived European state-system rather than to divine protection? But these die-hards by now counted for little; out of favor in the Vatican after Pius X died (20 August 1914), they were a dwindling conventicle in Italy itself.[12]

The attitude of another small Catholic group deserves closer attention. The Christian Democrats supported Italian intervention against Austria enthusiastically, and took their place in the democratic wing of the interventionist movement.

The interventionist movement of 1914–15 was a violent juxtaposition of incompatibles. The old Mazzinian traditions of national self-determination and their corollary, Republican Irredentism, were represented by the interventionism of Salvemini, Bissolati, and their followers. The Masonic lodges naturally rallied to the Grand Orient mother country, France. But at the same time the turbid fringe elements of the Italian Left, such as the Revolutionary *Fasci* headed by Mussolini and Corridoni, combined with the futurists and the Nationalists in an anti-parliamentary interventionist campaign that found its prophet in D'Annunzio and its proper field of action in street violence. Rather suicidally, the moderate Liberal Salandra used this movement to maneuver Italy into the war without the consent of Parliament. The propaganda, the strategy, and the "élites" of Fascism were born in the interventionist agitation of 1914–15, with the connivance of the Right Wing of Italian Liberalism.[13]

The Christian Democrats regarded Salvemini as "the apostle of political justice in Italy."[14] They shared his aversion for the policy of protectionism, favors, and local arrangements which had kept Giolitti in control of Italian politics for so long; like Salvemini, they ignored the concrete achievements of the Giolitti era. The interventionism of the Christian Democrats was, among other things, a revolt against the 1913 Gentiloni Pact, the delivering of Catholic votes en bloc to Giolitti and other moderates, against the threatened polarization of Italian political life between a revolutionary and subversive Left and an oligarchic privileged Right. The interventionist campaign offered to the Christian Democrats, as to so many other groups on the margin of Italian political life, a chance to play a national part.[15]

Yet their interventionism had profounder reasons. The movement harked back to the great Catholic patriots of the Risorgimento, Gioberti, Rosmini, Manzoni, as well as to Mazzini, with his Irredentism and his idea of a league of small European nations.[16] In many ways, the Christian Democratic movement of the Romagna was the only element of Italian Catholicism that could be called *democratic* in the common European sense. Yet so feverish was the Italian interventionist temper in May 1915 that even a Christian Democrat like Giuseppe Donati could cry out during a war demonstration at Florence: "Parliament can be corrupted, but the Fatherland will not be murdered!"[17]

As one Christian Democrat from Latium observed, interventionism found little response among the Catholic masses.[18] Unquestionably the martial attitude of the movement limited its influence at this time; after the war its chances for a national role were gone forever. Donati, the only prominent interventionist Christian Democrat who survived the war, went over to Don Luigi Sturzo after the Popular Party was organized.

The Catholic working masses were nearer to another Catholic Left, that of the Cremona peasant-union leader, Guido Miglioli. More than any other Catholic leader, Miglioli represented rural Catholic opposition to World War I. In the crisis of April–May, 1915, his organ, *L'Azione* of Cremona, was uncompromisingly neutralist from beginning to end. It branded D'Annunzio as the poet of immorality, as a coiner of sensual blasphemies. The poet's great war speech at Quarto on 5 May had ended in a striking evangelical paraphrase: "Blessed are those who spurn sterile loves, to be virgins for this first and last love," "blessed are the youths who hunger and thirst for glory, for they shall be satisfied," and finally, "blessed are the pure in heart, blessed are those who come back victorious, for they shall see the new face of Rome, the brow crowned afresh by Dante, the triumphant beauty of Italy." Nothing could be conceived more revolting to an alert Christian religious conscience.

The Christian Democrat Cacciaguerra still thought of the future Duce as an example of artless good faith,* whereas *L'Azione* of Cremona recognized Mussolini as a "criminal" revolutionary. It appealed to the "sacred" parliamentary legality which so many interventionists of democratic convictions had forgotten; it shared the peace sentiments of Giolitti and the official Socialist Party (new affinities for all concerned), and on the other hand it identified interventionism with that old serpent, international Freemasonry. It was natural, held Miglioli, that the Socialists and Catholics, who really understood the Italian laboring masses, should stand firm against the war, and that the Liberals should replace the constitutional ideals of Cavour with the turbid new imperialism of Mussolini, destroyer of Parliament. Interventionism, declared *L'Azione,* was the battle cry of the Emilian reactionaries of the *Resto del Carlino*; it was to be their revenge for the electoral defeat of 1913.

Miglioli voted in Parliament against the war measures of 25 May; an "ardent and convinced neutralist," he held that he was thereby expressing the wishes of his constituents. His convictions were strengthened by the unhappy results of the Libyan enterprise, which he had been among the few to oppose from the start. Miglioli's rejection of World War I stemmed from two fundamental beliefs: that modern war, in which a few politicians disposed of millions of lives, was deeply immoral, and that the Italian working classes were solidly against the intervention of their nation. The 1915 crisis proved to be, in many ways, Miglioli's prophetic hour.

The "conditional neutralism" of the Catholic notables was quite another thing.[19] The initial preference for peace expressed by Meda and Tovini, and their organ *Il Cittadino di Brescia,* was predicated upon a view of "national interests" that did not differ

---

* This was the line taken by *L'Azione* (Cremona) in every number of April–May, 1915. In contrast, Mussolini's sincerity and artlessness even extended to the financing of his newspaper, said Cacciaguerra in *L'Azione* (Cesena 29 November 1914. Both of these opinions concerning Mussolini were widespread in Italy. During the revolutionary Socialist phase of his career he was even called a *poetino!*

greatly from that of the other bourgeois supporters of Salandra. Once it became clear that the Government aimed at war in the late spring of 1915, the Clerico-Moderates began preparing Catholic opinion for the fatal step. Catholics were urged to put blind faith in the Government.[20] Together with this deft and patient work of persuasion was a definite need to distinguish Clerico-Moderate loyalty to Salandra (which would accompany him over the brink of war) from the vulgar interventionism of the city-street campaigns, with its clashing Masonic, Nationalist, and Revolutionary Syndicalist colors. After D'Annunzio's Quarto speech, the authoritative Catholic parliamentary leader Meda was cautious in committing himself:

> It must be recognized that, on the one hand, D'Annunzio has really taken part in the moral preparation of this hour, and in this respect the office of herald of the Italian people was his due . . . but even in the discipline of the present hour, it must not be forgotten . . . that the patriotism by which the 5 May address is certainly marked must not serve to let pass all the rest; above all, let not that patriotism, which accepts so much that is incompatible with the moral and religious conscience, be spread any further among youth, where much of it has already been spread.[21]

The Clerico-Moderates would quietly accept intervention as a necessity of state, but they would have no part of the rhetoric of interventionism. They would acquiesce in Salandra's by-passing of Parliament, but were not ready to join in any discrediting of the parliamentary order itself. Throughout, the Catholic notables were primarily concerned with national order and "discipline" (but with what sacrifice of higher religious values?).

To be fair to the Clerico-Moderates, the probable alternatives to Salandra in April–May, 1915, must be considered. A new Giolitti government, with the possible support of the official Socialist Party, might have opened the floodgates of social change and led to the real participation of the forces of Italian labor in the governing of the State. In such an Italy, the leadership of organized Catholicism might have passed from Clerico-Moderate to other hands, perhaps to a Catholic Left upheld by the Catholic rural working classes. And there were yet darker possibilities, grimly hinted at during Red Week of June 1914.

The Clerico-Moderates accepted the "strong State" of the Sa-landra-Sonnino conservative constitutional tradition, with its high evaluation of the national Catholic "moral sentiment." The Clerico-Moderates' repairing to Salandra's standard foreshadowed their rallying in 1923 to another "strong State" and their submitting to its demolition of Parliament.*

The *Cittadino di Brescia* had referred to the Catholics as the "strongest and healthiest" part of the nation.[22] And indeed a good case can be made for the basic sanity of Italian Catholics, when it is remembered how many of them in 1915 were allied with Giolitti, Croce, and even Turati, against the hysteria of World War I.

---

* Salandra later wrote in *La Neutralità italiana* (p. 241), that "among the political groups the only one that gave full and sincere help to the Government was that which had the name of Liberal without any addition of democracy. They were men of the Right, many of them tied to me personally by long-standing friendship and views held in common. Some Nationalists and Catholics stood by their side, without losing their own identity (*senza confondersi*)."

Chapter Four

WORLD WAR I AND THE FOUNDATION OF
THE ITALIAN POPULAR PARTY, 1915–19

At the verge of intervention, most Catholic deputies were ready to back Salandra. Among some 300 deputies of the old majority who had left calling cards with the neutralist Giolitti during the crisis of April 1915, there apparently was not one Catholic; and, with the exception of Miglioli, the Catholics voted for the Government's initial war measures.[1]

The war itself was a terrible shock. Though officially a "great power," Italy equaled Great Britain, France, and Germany neither in the resources nor in the social cohesion so needful for the great test of war. The Italian conscript soldier showed great endurance and sacrifice; but on the whole the war was a middle-class affair toward which much of the nation showed no spirit. The widespread sullenness of the industrial proletarian masses made itself felt more and more as the war dragged on, especially in 1917; here and there discontent took on a revolutionary turn, as at Turin. Yet in certain ways the war marked a great forward step for Italy. Most Italians felt more deeply their common destiny in a Fatherland which could never again be the creature of a narrow elite as it had been for so many years after unification. This heightening of political awareness had deep effects in the Italian Catholic camp. From the confusion of the war years came forth an autonomous Catholic Party and labor-union federation, both on a truly national level. In 1919 the Italian militant Catholic reached political adulthood.

The official leadership of Italian Catholicism supported the Italian war effort, but in varying degrees. Meda and the Clerico-Moderates upheld the successive war governments of 1915–19 and publicly stood by the Government during the dark days of 1917, while Sturzo and the rest of the new central *giunta* of Catholic

Action (a significant innovation of Benedict's XV's pontificate) were far more reserved in their attitude.[2]

Meda entered the successive war governments of 1916–19 as Minister of Finance, an unofficial representative of Italian Catholicism. His many wartime speeches show above all a preoccupation with national order and "discipline," so closely connected with the war effort; for the alternative to continued war, a negotiated peace, had become the program of international socialism, which was in Meda's eyes the great force of subversion and ruin. Meda's dedication to the war effort was a consequence of his sharing the interests and fears of the conservative Liberals who had taken Italy into the fray and intended to see it through; the war was a way not only of saving the state from Socialist pressure, but also of tearing it from Giolitti's hands. More positively, both Meda and the venerable Toniolo (who died in 1918) hoped for a postwar international order based on the federative principles so dear to Catholic tradition.[3]

More sinister was the war career of the chaplain Father Agostino Gemelli. A Franciscan and a medical psychologist, Gemelli analyzed the mentality of men in combat and showed that their courage was largely inspired by illusions that could be produced and exploited scientifically; the combined arts of pulpit and laboratory could serve the armed state. Gemelli combined with the modern ideal of a technically equipped elite the traditional paternalism of the Italian clergy, well exemplified by the General Staff Chaplain Father Semeria, who in his introduction to Gemelli's treatise *Il nostro soldato* had spoken of the "little brain" of the average Italian peasant-conscript, unable to comprehend the lofty idea of the Fatherland. The combination provided a formula by which Gemelli was to become the great educator of Italian Catholicism of the 1930's and 1940's.[4]

Such was the martial contribution of the Catholics most in view. Among the masses a different spirit prevailed. There the war was increasingly unpopular, and Benedict XV's words condemning the "useless slaughter" were closer to the mass mood than Meda's social patriotism. Miglioli continued his opposition to the war, even voting against the war ministry of "concentration" on 29 June 1916; in this he merely reflected the opinions of the Italian country-

side, much of which was passing from indifference to hostility
toward the war. Only one war slogan caught popular favor: "The
land for the peasants!" Prowar elements (such as the Bissolati
interventionist-Socialists) launched it in hopes of strengthening
peasant morale, in order to hold out a reward for wartime suffer-
ings. The slogan was in line with the general illusion that World
War I would be the last war in history, to be followed by an era
of universal democratic brotherhood. The Socialist Party, on the
other hand, propagated the same slogan in a frankly revolutionary
sense.[5]

The Catholic tenant-farmer or sharecropper was as much affected by this agitation as was the Socialist field laborer. Furthermore, Catholic social programs had always posited small landholdings as a goal. Consistently enough, Catholic peasant organizations
advanced demands for the expropriation and settlement of un-
tilled lands and for the breaking up of the *latifondi*: a new spirit
was abroad among the previously inert Catholic rural masses.

Catholic labor shot up during the war. The number of organized Catholic workers, mostly agricultural, rose from 63,000 to
162,000, almost tripling. In March 1918, the old *Unione econo-
mico-sociale,* a survival of Pius X's system of control from above,
was succeeded by a labor federation paralleling the national organization of Socialist unions. Religious qualifications were loos-
ened, and the old corporative ideal of "mixed unions" of em-
ployers and workers was buried, for the new unions were realistic
economic groups under autonomous lay leadership.[6]

At the very moment in which the Clerico-Moderates, in the
person of Filippo Meda, represented the organized Catholics of
Italy in the war governments, they lost ground within the Catholic
organizations themselves. The new Catholic leaders of 1918 were
Christian Democrats such as Gronchi and Tupini. Their unquestioned chief was Don Luigi Sturzo, who rose under Benedict
XV to be head of lay Catholic Action.[7]

At the end of the war Don Luigi Sturzo organized the Popular
Party, which launched its appeal to the nation in January 1919.
In this it became clear that he had Vatican approval. The Holy
See removed the last barriers to Catholic participation in the po-
litical life of the nation while at the same time declaring that the
new Party naturally did not represent the Holy See or the Church.

Don Sturzo resigned from Catholic Action, the old Electoral Union was dissolved, and the remaining Catholic Action organizations were directed toward specifically religious ends.*

The new Party was different from Murri's Christian Democracy of 1898–1904, in which many of its leaders had begun their careers. Whereas Murri had always conceived of the Church and its lay auxiliary organizations as the base of a Catholic mass party, Sturzo absolutely rejected any notion of a declaredly Catholic mass party resting on an ecclesiastical substructure. The new Party, as he and the other Christian Democratic leaders of 1919 conceived it, was to be independent of Catholic Action. Its program was one of democratic reform, appealing on a secular plane to millions of voters of diverse social classes; to be sure, religious liberty, including the liberty of the Church to carry out its spiritual mission, was part of the Party program, but the Party was not "Catholic." At the most, it was a party of Catholics, quite a different matter. Inspired by Christian principles, it would of course draw to it the great mass of organized Catholics in Italy, but Sturzo hoped that many voters outside the Catholic Action organizations and even outside the Catholic fold itself would rally to his program.[8]

Sturzo saw in World War I the end of Liberal-bourgeois hegemony in Europe. The *bourgeoisie* had failed to establish a just international or social order, and the excluded peoples of the world, as well as the exploited classes of society, were clamoring for admission to the privileges of modern civilization. Sturzo's past as a municipal administrator in Sicily had acquainted him at first hand with the failings of the centralized Italian Liberal State, its narrowness and detachment from the masses.[9]

By 1919 most Catholics had long since abandoned the sterile protest against the secular State, the nostalgia for absolutism that

* Gabriele de Rosa, *Storia del Partito Popolare* (Bari, 1958), pp. 15 *et seq.*, hereafter cited as *Partito Popolare*.

But the great papal Secretary of State, Cardinal Gasparri, had little love for the new Party, even though he did not oppose it. In fact, ten years later, while he was negotiating the Lateran Pacts, he wrote apologetically to a Catholic conservative senator that the Popular Party in 1919 had seemed to him less objectionable than those already in existence, *before the coming of Fascism.* So deep was the Cardinal's unavowed dislike of the Popular Party that he recollected it in 1928 as having been declaredly *areligioso,* when in reality the Party had merely styled itself *aconfessionale*; a significant lapse of memory. See his words in De Rosa, *Filippo Meda*, p. 226.

had characterized their earlier movements. Yet the long Catholic struggle against Liberalism had become fruitful when, during the crisis of the 1890's, it had stopped proclaiming itself as a religious crusade and had taken up the tasks of social reform. Whatever was really valuable in Liberalism, Democracy, and Socialism had been taken into the Catholic movement, sifted and purified by the Christian conscience, as Sturzo conceived it.

Now, in Don Sturzo's eyes, there opened before the new party of Catholics a great chance for political reconstruction. At the same time that the Catholic camp had finally been freed from hierarchical control and had come of age politically and socially, the Italian State became a consistent democracy. In the summer of 1919 a new electoral law was passed removing the few restrictions of the 1912 suffrage, abolishing the old single constituencies, and introducing a modified plural-constituency form of proportional representation. The shift was almost revolutionary in its effects, for the mass parties, both Socialist and Popular, which had naturally agitated for electoral reform since the war ended, now towered over the caucus groups of Giolitti and other Liberal chiefs. For Sturzo, this meant the advent of a new political class that was to take the place of the outworn Liberal leadership of Italy.

Yet the aspirations of Don Sturzo clashed fatally against certain hard political realities. First of all, his Party was not a reliable instrument. The traditional Clerical leading strings were far from cut. One element on the Right, headed by Cavazzoni, a Lombard conservative, the press lord Count Grosoli, and Fathers Gemelli and Olgiati, insisted on giving a Catholic coloring to the new Party, on not breaking all ties with Catholic Action, on openly championing the traditional rights of the Papacy and emphasizing the conservative function of the Catholic social doctrine. An Extreme Left group, under Miglioli's leadership, veered toward outright collectivism and class war, peasant against landlord: these "White Bolsheviks" were especially embittered by the war.

At the 1919 Congress of Bologna Sturzo's central Christian Democratic platform easily withstood attacks of this sort from both Right and Left. But they were indicative of deep divisions within the Party. A great number of affluent or middle-class supporters of the Party were probably far more Clerico-Moderate than Christian Democratic in their inclinations, and went along with

Don Sturzo only because the country was in a social ferment and conservatism was hopelessly out of favor.*

From this appeared a serious weakness: the Party had no daily press of its own and had to rely principally upon the Clerico-Moderate Trust in presenting its case to the public.[10]

Another danger arose from the very nature of Italian politics. The old Liberal system, with its restricted suffrage and single constituencies, may not have permitted the rise of a healthy party life. It certainly hindered any normal change of political leadership in the nation. An oligarchy in the 1870's and 1880's, it later turned to one-man rule under Crispi and Giolitti. Yet it *did* assure stable government, with manageable parliamentary majorities, and the constitutional façade was maintained.

The old single-constituency elections were "made" by local deals and small-scale abuses, which constituted so large a part of Giolitti's electoral magic. Much of Italian political fortune depended not upon election results, but upon how those election results were assured in advance. Even in the elections of 1913, held under a form of universal suffrage, a constitutional-Liberal majority was assured by the Gentiloni Pact. But in that election, the last one that Giolitti was able to manage, one mass political force—the organized Catholics—had to be called in to stem another, the Socialists. It was a hollow victory in 1913, a harbinger of worse to come. In 1919 the Catholics were not so docile, and elections were no longer manageable: when Giolitti, a prisoner of his old methods, tried to manage the 1921 elections, he failed utterly and benefited only Mussolini.

If the democratic system failed to produce as stable and continuous a government as the old Liberal system had for so many decades, the way was open for a new sort of dictatorship. For

---

* De Rosa, *Partito Popolare*, pp. 51–85. Of the Left-Wing Demochristians, Giovanni Gronchi doubted the sincerity of the Clerico-Moderate notables who had signed the Popular Party Manifesto, but he joined the Party anyway, in hope that the forces of Catholic Labor and Catholic Youth would outweigh the Conservatives in its councils. Giuseppe Donati, on the other hand, did not join the Party until two years later. See Donati, *Scritti Politici* (Rome, 1956), I, lxx. A young Catholic leader from the newly annexed Trentino, Alcide De Gasperi, joined the new Party at once, and was invited to preside over the first party Congress at Bologna; this was especially appropriate since Sturzo took the name "Popular Party" from the *Volkspartei* of Trent. See De Rosa, *Partito Popolare*, p. 42.

many years the old system had been in fact a bland parliamentary dictatorship, though functioning with all the constitutional freedoms. If democracy failed, the alternative was now a demagogic and terroristic dictatorship controlling the masses directly, for the Italian constitutional system no longer afforded the means of "making" elections and governments by the old covert methods.

Why the postwar democratic system ushered in a new dictatorship, why the Popular Party proved a broken reed and failed to produce the leaders so necessary to the new democratic system, are problems that will be dealt with in the next chapter.

Chapter Five

THE ITALIAN POPULAR PARTY, "SHORT FRUIT OF LONG LABOR," 1919–22

THE POPULAR PARTY IN ITALIAN POLITICS, 1919–22

The Italian constitutional State did not succeed in passing from Liberalism to Democracy after World War I. In six years it was swept away, and in its place rose a totalitarian regime based on the Fascist Party. The Fascists, in spite of their aspirations toward absolute sway, never eliminated the Monarchy and never subjugated the Church, but they governed Italy with the uneasy sanction of both. The Monarchy renounced the constitutional-Liberal traditions of seventy-four years in exchange for the pomp of empire. The Church abandoned the one mass political movement of Italian Catholics, the Popular Party, together with the great Catholic labor unions, in return for a territorial settlement of the Roman Question, and a concordat that assured the continued existence of Catholic Action, Catholic Youth (including Catholic university student organizations), and a national Catholic university in the totalitarian conditions of Fascist Italy.

Such, very briefly, was the final outcome of the postwar Italian crisis. From spring 1919 to autumn 1920 the Italian Socialist Party held the initiative; still, it failed to lead the Italian proletariat to that "Soviet" revolutionary conquest of the State, which it kept promising. From Autumn 1920 to October 1922 a violent counter-revolutionary group, the Fascist movement, having seen the impotence of the Socialists, opened a successful campaign to seize control of Italy, taking advantage of political complicity and military defections within the constitutional State itself, in the end securing from royal hands all the chrisms of a constitutional succession to power; finally between October 1922 and January 1925 a dictatorship was gradually clamped on Italy by electoral manipulations, force, and blackmail. After January 1925 a few police roundups and Blackshirt raids were all that remained to be made before

Mussolini had an absolute monopoly of all the channels of public authority and information. The leaders and spokesmen of the old parties went into exile, retirement, or prison. The shaky structure of the Monarchy and the rock of the Roman Church still rose above the flood, but everything else—parties, labor unions, newspapers—had gone under.

It is hard to assess the part played by the Popular Party in all this: the *Popolari* were a mass party, a great force in the nation and in Parliament, yet their influence was negative. In 1919 they blocked the Socialists. In 1920–21 they were an auxiliary of Giovanni Giolitti. Their great acts in 1922 were a series of refusals and withdrawals, all helping to bring about exactly that political deadlock which led to Mussolini's violent solution. A desperate effort in 1923–24 to save the Italian constitutional order caused the *Popolari* Right Wing to go over openly to Fascism, whereas the rest of the Party put up a last resistance. The Vatican deplored this division in the ranks of the faithful, but in such a way that would especially discredit the *Popolari* and prepare the way for an eventual settlement between the Church and the new Fascist Regime.[1] The history of the Popular Party is the history of its relations with more energetic and better-led parties.

Before considering more closely the Popular Party of 1919–25, let us fix two points of orientation:

The Socialists were the leading political party of postwar Italy for almost two years. They were untainted by responsibility for the war, and hence in a perfect position to profit from postwar disillusionment. Furthermore, the Russian Revolution of 1917 had shown what an industrial proletariat could do in a revolutionary situation, and the Italian working class was ready.

Yet the Socialists lost both advantages. They savagely ridiculed and insulted the sacrifices demanded by the war, instead of invoking them as the moral basis for a just peace settlement. Thereby they alienated many veterans. And, even worse, the Socialists did nothing concrete to prepare the revolution. The revolutionary temper of the Italian worker was dulled by an inconclusive planless succession of strikes and seizures. The Party talked revolution, but lacked the kind of corps of trained revolutionaries that the Russian Bolsheviks had prepared. The Leninist minority finally broke away to form the Communist Party in 1921. The real vocation of most of the Italian Socialist Party and labor-union leadership was peaceful and parliamentary.

At the other political extreme there were revolutionary or counterrevolutionary cadres, which in 1919 lacked plans and leaders. The Futurist-Syndicalist-Imperialist fringe groups that had made so much noise in 1909–15 had left their original "temple of war," the coffeehouse (this was Croce's gibe of 1915). They had gone through a genuine military training, first during the interventionist demonstrations and street fights of April–May, 1915, and then in the *arditi* (assault formations), the aviation and the torpedo-boat squadrons of World War I. The Garibaldian ideal of a heroic irregular militia served as an apparent historical precedent. The testing ground for these "elite" groups was the seizure of Fiume, where in September 1919 D'Annunzio's enterprise showed that such a militia could count on the seditious aid of many army and navy officers. For a moment, it seemed likely that a *coup d'état* would be launched from the Adriatic. When the Fiume "regency" finally went under in late 1920, Mussolini's opportunist leadership offered itself in place of the disillusioned poet's. Many of the adventurers of Fiume, abandoning Syndicalism for Fascism, began regrouping around the Duce, though the movement suffered from a lack of money. When the landowners of the Emilia-Romagna region supplied it, Fascism moved into action: first against the labor organizations of the Po valley, then against the whole Italian "revolutionary" Left, which had already let slip its great chance, and finally against Catholic economic and social organizations as well.[2]

Perhaps better than anyone else, Gaetano Salvemini has thus described the original Fascists, as he knew them through his taking part in Bissolati's democratic interventionist movement of 1915. Like most observers of the democratic Left, Salvemini failed to recognize the importance of the military training that many Fascists had gone through. In other respects his words ring true.

> Bissolati's program was not at fault in being more idealistic . . . than that which won out in our official world; . . . its incurable weakness was that neither in Italy nor abroad did the Socialists and democrats have the cultural preparation necessary for grasping it and putting it into effect. In England,

France, and Italy they were either pacifists, in which case they were hostile to the war, indifferent to the problems of peace, and led by their *a priori* pessimism to leave the field uncontested to the enemies of peace, or else they were overcome by war fury, dazzled by the mirage of the "sacred union," and fell easy prey to Nationalist propaganda, as long as it was decked out in some sort of clumsy revolutionary make-up.

This last phenomenon of Nationalists disguised as revolutionaries was especially widespread in Italy. Among the schismatic Socialists, Syndicalists, Anarchists, Republicans, Radicals, and Masons who made up the democratic intervention movement, only a part—and not the greater part—knew what it wanted, kept control over its behavior, and fought on Bissolati's side with a clear vision of its own duties. Most of them were restless spirits, belated romantics, apologists of violence, of revolt, of the bold stroke; for the intoxication of the feat of danger, rather than for the attainment of any clearly fixed and seriously desired purpose. Almost all of them came from that intellectual lower middle class in whose excessive numbers, economic, intellectual, and moral poverty and famished restlessness must be sought one of the most serious and least remediable causes of our social ills and our political crises. They sensed in the war an excellent chance to increase the disorder of a society in which they had not yet succeeded in being sure of their daily bread. It was they who invented the myth of the "revolutionary war." But no sooner did they find a secure and fairly convenient little place in a propaganda office, in a divisional command, or in a committee of the so-called home front, than they fast became jingoes, archmilitarists, ultra-bourgeois, carrying into these new activities the same noisy violence that they had once used in their revolutionary garglings. The Ministry of Foreign Affairs and the Freemasonry found in these wretched people just the right agents to entangle, disorient, and pervert the democratic movement of intervention. When Benito Mussolini in October 1914 jumped from absolute neutralism to anti-German interventionism, the confusion-spreading elements of interventionism could not fail to recognize in him their natural chief; they followed him during the war and after it. They have given to Fascism its general staff and its cadres.

And if noisy uncoordinated gesturing is revolution, then these interventionists were certainly revolutionaries. But democratic they were not. The unfolding of events has shown that their mentality was a by-product of nationalist ideologies, concealed by extremist labels.[3]

To understand the *centrist* position of the *Popolari,* these opposed extremes of the Italian political spectrum must be kept in mind. The Popular Party attempted and failed to provide an alternative to them.

In the *biennio rosso* of 1919–20 the *Popolari* did much to save Italy from socialism. As Don Sturzo said later, "the aim of immunizing the masses from Bolshevik propaganda was always pursued."[4] The revolutionary leaders of Turin at first thought that the Popular Party would unwittingly play John the Baptist for a Leninist Messiah; Catholicism would organize the rural masses, train them to a higher level of political awareness, and thus bring them within the reach of Socialist revolutionary agitation.[5] But in reality the first fruits of Popularism were unexpectedly bitter for Italian Socialism, as the Socialist leader Pietro Nenni wrote in 1926:

> The only bourgeois party to face the struggle [the national elections of 1919] with much vigor was the Popular Party, formed very recently. And from then on this party, strong in that it was supported and outfitted by the Church, disposing of a center of influence in every parish house and sacristy, performed a first-rate task of social conservation. Its chief, Don Luigi Sturzo, was not a conservative, but his wishes were overridden by those of the Vatican; on the other hand, there was no place in the country for an autonomous Center. The reactionary press has often spoken of "black Bolshevism," especially with reference to the *Popolari*'s ambiguous attitude toward the war and to the social struggles that the *Popolari* had to go through in some provinces to keep their influence over the peasants. The truth is that without this so-called black Bolshevism in 1919 no dikes would have been found to hold in the Socialist tide. The only party in condition to neutralize and combat the Reds' influence was the Popular Party, and that for three reasons: it was at the same time both old and new, that is, it did not take up the inheritance of the old clericalism and yet it used the organization of the Church; it was not compromised in the war and could profess patriotism in the city and neutralism in the country; it had made up the quarrel between old-style clericalism and modernism [it would have been more accurate to write "Christian Democracy," in the broad social sense] in a synthesis that was expressed by the motto "Libertas" on a crossed shield, the emblem of the Popular Party. In the long run the compromise was shown to be

lifeless, and the Party was tossed about between Right and Left until it finally split, the Clerical Right having seen in Fascism the Regime it had been longing for. "Libertas!" . . . The elections of 16 November 1919 were Red elections. The Socialists obtained a great success, which could have been a triumph if the *Popolari* had not succeeded in mustering the peasants behind candidates of the crossed shield.[6]

The Popular Party, with its program of fostering small farm property, kept many small landholders, tenants, and sharecroppers from going farther Left. It was entirely natural for the peasantry to prefer the Catholic social program of small holdings to the collectivization preached by the Socialists of 1919, and in 1919 the bulk of the peasant vote went to the party of Don Sturzo.

Moreover the Popular Party gave temporary shelter to many middle-class voters who feared a proletarian revolution and yet saw that conservative or moderate formulas had no effect. Gaetano Salvemini shrewdly assessed the weak adventitious character of much of the Popular Party's middle-class support.

As Salvemini saw it, the Popular Party was "interclass," just as Don Sturzo had said. Therein lay the secret of its great voting strength, its fatal divisions, and its failure to hang together under difficult conditions. Party Secretary Sturzo and his followers were Christian Democrats who had come into their own after the long silence under Pius X. The Christian Democratic group had two strong points: Catholic labor, which in 1920 numbered 1,180,000, including 935,000 on the land, and the lower clergy. The Italian parish priest had partaken of the long suffering of his parishioners in the war; as a result of the postwar monetary crisis the value of his fixed income fell to almost nothing. Now forced to live on the offerings of the faithful, the lower clergy had escaped the economic domination of the bishops. The Christian Democrats, no longer suspected of Modernist heresy, had in the lower clergy a useful ally in their work of organization and propaganda.

Dependence on the parish priests later proved to be a serious flaw in the Christian Democratic organization, for the lower clergy was still subject to episcopal discipline. An autonomous Catholic party must be as independent of the parish clergy as of the bishops if it is to play a political role of its own.

The Christian Democrats were uncompromising, observed

Salvemini, in refusing offers of alliances from the Nationalists, Fascists, and conservative landowners. But these offers found increasing favor with the Clerico-Moderates, the Party's Right Wing, who had among them the shrewdest and most prestigious Catholic politicians, including many deputies and senators. They controlled the newspaper Trust and could count on the sympathies of much of the higher clergy.

Many voters who supported the Popular Party in 1919 and 1921 were neither Christian Democrats nor Clerico-Moderates. Some were not Catholics at all. Young middle-class intellectuals, seeking a party of reform rather than of revolution, medium- and small-property owners, adventurers of various kinds, found at least a temporary shelter in this vast catchall party.

The Party's successes in 1919 and 1921 were due, said Salvemini, to "a heavy feverish work of propaganda in all social classes," in which "the peasants were promised land" but "the landlords were assured of the collection of their rents." For Liberals, the Party offered a defense of constitutional freedoms against the "Bolsheviks"; for Catholics, the Party seemed to bring closer the long-heralded Catholic reconquest of modern society. The interventionists could find a kindred spirit in Filippo Meda, the wartime minister; whereas the many who were disgusted with the war and its aftermath could share Benedict XV's sorrow over the "useless slaughter," a sentiment common to many Italian Catholics.

The Party was equally ambiguous in its views on foreign policy. A new policy of peace and support of the League was promised to the democratically inclined, but the Party joined the Nationalists in protesting against Italy's small share of the postwar spoils, especially in Dalmatia and Africa. The Popular group at Fiume upheld D'Annunzio's enterprise, in spite of the banishment of Croat priests.[7]

According to Salvemini, this equivocal, confused coalition of interests and ideals performed the classical function of a Catholic movement, providing a first line of defense for the *bourgeoisie* and the Monarchy. The Party had divided the Italian working class, especially in the countryside, by propagating a sort of "Bolshevism" of its own, even to the point of occasionally taking part in peasant land seizures and agitations. Salvemini understood that this sort of "Bolshevism" was a political vaccination against real revolution, and noted bitingly that "the Italian *bourgeoisie,* by yielding one hundred seats in the Chamber to the Popular Party, did not pay too high a price for the work of conservation that the Party performed, since it was keeping those one hundred places from being taken by genuine revolutionaries."

Yet the real links between the Party and a part of the Italian working class kept the Party on Center or Center-Left political moorings, and the conservative or counterrevolutionary *Popolari* began leaving the Party. As Salvemini put it, "a great many industrialists, landowners, shopkeepers, and professional men, to whom in 1919 the light of Christianity had been revealed, received with new enthusiasm and new electoral and financial sacrifices the revelation of Fascism." Eventually the Clerico-Moderates, too, would be tempted to disavow the "Bolshevism" of the Catholic mass party and follow many other propertied groups in openly supporting the Fascist counterrevolution. And with them was much of the upper clergy, especially at Milan, which was always inclined to use its authority against the Party at decisive moments. In fact, the Popular Party finally split along the lines indicated by Salvemini, and only the Christian Democrats stayed faithful to the constitutional order once it was under attack by Fascists rather than disciples of Lenin.[8]

The democratic elections of 1919 brought forth a Chamber full of incompatible divisions. The largest bloc of deputies was Socialist, prey to revolutionary delusions. The next in size was the *Popolari.* No government could be formed without the votes of at least one of these blocs.

Since the Socialists were not in an absolute majority by themselves and could coalesce with no other party to form a government, the *Popolari* became an indispensable part of any governmental majority. There were too many *Popolari* to be disregarded, too few to constitute a government of their own men. Under these circumstances the "Democratic" Nitti cabinet of 1919 should have made every effort to build up a consistent following among *both* Liberal-Democratic Center deputies *and* Popolari—the elements of its parliamentary majority—in such a way as to assure the distracted country a continuous stable government.

Nothing of the sort was done. Instead, Nitti tried to appease both extremes, the Socialists and the Nationalist-Fascists, although neither showed anything but contempt for his weakness. While the Socialists were pressing him with mass disorders and political strikes at home, the elite cadres of the Nationalists and proto-Fascists seized Fiume and threatened, prophetically, to march on Rome. Once ensconced in the "holocaust city," D'Annunzio jeered coarsely at the Premier's dumpy figure and his "antinational" policies, though the whole Fiume expedition would have been impossible without connivance and aid from many military and civil officials of Nitti's own government.

While Nitti tried to soften the enemies of the constitutional state, he continually slighted the *Popolari* and their labor allies. A representative of Southern landowning interests himself, he never showed any understanding of the Popular Party's proposals for land reform, the very point in which the Party came to grips with the nation's postwar problems in a democratic spirit. Even worse, the Nitti government dealt with "Red" railroad and communication labor unions to the exclusion and detriment of smaller "White" unions in the same fields, though the White unions had bravely refused to embarrass the Government by joining in political strikes called by the Reds. From the Government's course of action it seemed as if loyal Catholic workers in the State-owned transportation and communication networks were being penalized and the Socialists rewarded! In fact, the anticlerical traditions of Italian democracy still influenced its postwar exponents.

In spite of all these proofs of misunderstanding or outright ill will, the *Popolari* bore with Nitti until the spring of 1920. Then, when they revolted in May and brought down the Government, it turned out that their parliamentary leader, Filippo Meda, was unwilling to accept the King's invitation to form a government. Meda, in whom caution amounted to a vice, was a follower, not a leader; the best advice he found to give Victor Emmanuel III was to try yet another "reincarnation" of the discredited Nitti, who was now willing to promise certain reforms desired by the *Popolari*.

Meda had a fault common to so many Italian politicians of the postwar years. He had not yet learned the methods of the new democratic system and still trusted in parliamentary maneuvering of the traditional Liberal sort. Instead the new voting public needed dramatic acts of leadership. Such acts in a democracy can capture the mass imagination and carry along a reluctant or divided parliament. Leadership of this kind is essential in democratic political life. The Popular Party parliamentary group failed to provide it. Cautious, unimaginative leadership was not the least of the Party's weaknesses.*

The last Nitti ministry aborted in less than a month. When the Government tried to raise the artificial "political price" of bread, Nitti could not face the storm of protests raised by the opposition and went down for the last time.

His successor was Giolitti, who had returned to active political life the year before with a bold program of reconstruction, which was especially attractive to much of the Italian public because it included the confiscation of excessive war profits. Giolitti took into his government several authoritative *Popolari,* including the veteran Meda. It seemed as if his own plans of administrative-fiscal reorganization would be combined with the Popular program of land reform and educational freedom, two fundamental points in any Christian Democratic action; thus a securely based Center-Popular government would pull the nation out of its postwar difficulties.

Giolitti's reforming energy at first seemed to carry all before it. D'Annunzio's farcical "Regency of the Carnaro" was disposed of with a whiff of grapeshot, while the new foreign minister, Count Sforza, worked out a sensible solution of the Adriatic problem with Yugoslavia. The insurrectionary elites of the Extreme Right were for the moment bilked and disoriented, while the armed forces returned to their constitutional allegiance.

The old statesman was equally firm and skillful in dealing with the Extreme Left, during the factory "occupations" of autumn 1920 in North Italy. A threatened sit-down strike in the great industries of Turin and Milan led to a counterthreat of lock-out by the owners, whereupon the workers seized and tried to operate the plants themselves. To many middle-class Italians, this looked like the beginning of the much-heralded "Soviet" revolution.

---

* It is clear from the concluding chapter of De Rosa, *Filippo Meda,* that Meda was a used-up man, exhausted by hard service in the wartime governments and longing for respite from political battles. Hence it was especially unfortunate for the cause of democracy in Italy that after the war he was repeatedly called to the fore, as the most authoritative lay spokesman of his party.

Instead, it was the end, for a long time to come, of any possible revolution on the Russian model in Italy. The Socialist Party was taken by surprise and had nothing ready for a genuine national uprising. It weakly left any initiative up to the reformist labor-union leadership. The "occupation" in itself soon failed, since neither technicians nor clerks would work with the occupiers. In a few days the Italian Left paid the penalty for years of talk about the dictatorship of the proletariat.

Giolitti did everything possible to lessen the drama of this moment. He refused any armed intervention by the State, which might have done incalculable material damage to the industries themselves and set off a real revolutionary explosion.* Instead, the government maintained official neutrality, but behind the scenes its ministers and prefects worked to bring the two sides together. Eventually the North Italian industrialists were prevailed upon to agree to participation by workers' councils in the management of their plants;† the Government, it was understood, would submit a bill to this effect to Parliament in 1921. Though the Left had saved its face through official impartial mediation, in fact it had been worsted. At once the Socialist tide began to ebb, leaving behind it a resentful propertied class and a stranded disheartened laboring mass.

In this intricate play of forces the *Popolari* had only a supporting role. Meda, with his excellent connections among North Italian financiers and industrialists, had done much to mediate and bring the factory owners to a compromise. But the Party itself was sidetracked. Sturzo and the White unions proposed participation by the workers in the actual ownership of industry. This solution, fitting the traditional Catholic preference for a society of small-property owners, interested neither of the contenders. Sturzo's im-

---

* "On one of the very first days of the occupation [Giolitti] received the factory owners' representatives. One of them, more excited than the others, asked him to get the workers to evacuate the plants, and to use even artillery if necessary. Giolitti politely asked, 'Do you wish me to begin by bombarding your plants?' The factory owner declined." Nothing could better illustrate the dry astringent good sense that marked Giolitti out in a nation of rhetoricians. See Sforza, *L'Italia dal 1914 al 1944*, p. 83.

† The Workers' Commissions were to be the same organs that had run the plants during the occupation. Tasca, *Nascita e avvento del Fascismo*, p. 123. Tasca notes that Mussolini himself sat on the sidelines, applauding the forces of labor so long as they seemed to be winning. Fascism became aggressive *after* the occupations failed. *Ibid.*, pp. 133–34.

portant discussion with the old Prime Minister in September, during the crisis, merely sharpened a personal distaste between the two, and made clear Giolitti's determination to ignore the broad ideas of his Popular collaborators while he used their talents and their parliamentary strength.[9] (Unfortunately Meda was working at cross purposes with Giolitti's trusted lieutenant, Camillo Corradini, during the confused opening days of the crisis. Eventually Giolitti was able to put pressure on the North Italian industrialists through the banks.)

Right after the Socialist failure of 1920 the Fascists suddenly burst onto the national scene. Heirs to D'Annunzio's heroic illegality and benefiting by the same connivance in high places, they offered their militia to the landowners of the Po valley. In the early months of 1921 they set to work destroying Socialist unions and cooperatives throughout North and Central Italy. These saviors were, in fact, a little late, for the Socialist revolution had already sputtered out before the Fascist repression began, but the propertied classes wanted revenge and insurance against any revival of socialism. The Fascists supplemented this military campaign with a smaller operation directed against the Slavic minorities in Venezia Giulia, where they were helped by patriotic policemen and soldiers.

In 1921 Giolitti decided to ride the wave of reaction throughout Italy and arranged the election of a new Chamber. With the Left in full retreat, he hoped for an enlarged stable Center majority.

Giolitti did not exactly coddle Fascism, as some of his adversaries accused him of doing. But he thought that the fanatical young movement could be guided into constitutional channels. He therefore ordered his prefects to act against Fascist violence and warned police and army commanders against arming the Blackshirts or winking at their exploits; but at the same time he included Fascist candidates in the "national" bloc of parliamentary candidates which he formed to win the 1921 elections.

Giolitti, determined to find as broad a base as possible for his "national" list, was balked by the *Popolari*. True to their principles, they decided to fight the 1921 campaign in isolation. In 1913 Giolitti's candidates had secured the Catholic vote by the Gentiloni Pact, without the voters' having any idea of what had happened, but in 1921 the Premier was unable to repeat this maneuver, for Sturzo was adamant. The Popular Party would not let itself be "transformed" into a prop of the traditional Liberal order and insisted on going to the nation with a distinctive program.

Behind Giolitti's course of action was the hope that both Socialists and Fascists could be made to serve as elements in a new parliamentary system of shifting majorities, with the "intriguing little priest" and his bulky party in check. The Socialists, whose Extreme Left had seceded to form a separate Communist Party early in 1921, would be drawn into collaborating with the Center through fear of the Fascists, now brought into Parliament. The Fascists, at the other extreme of the parliamentary spectrum, would subside once they had their first taste of responsibility.

The plain failed. The Socialists, prisoners of their own propaganda, were afraid to compromise, and the Fascists merely took advantage of what they took to be weakness on the part of the Government. The "infernal" elections of 1921, held under conditions of mounting Blackshirt violence, did not lessen the Socialist bloc as much as Giolitti had thought. They returned to the Chamber with most of their old strength, and their losses went to the advantage of the Communists. At the other end of the Chamber now sat 45 Fascists and Nationalists, who resented Giolitti's compromise with Yugoslavia. The *Popolari* were slightly stronger in the new Chamber, with the heavily Catholic Trentino voting for the first time and returning such Popular stalwarts as Alcide De Gasperi.

Giolitti looked at the unmanageable new Chamber that he had conjured up, and quit. The year 1921 was worse than 1919, and his skills would have little application in a Chamber so largely made up of doctrinaire revolutionaries and timid reformists who followed what they took to be the mood of the working class, counterrevolutionary militiamen, resentful Catholics and terrified representatives of property.

Not only was Parliament unequal to the tasks of normalization and reconstruction, but the State itself was failing. In spite of orders from their civilian chiefs in Rome, many local officials and commanders went on giving aid and comfort to the Fascist bands, now organizing on an ever-larger scale. Liberal administrators found that it was much harder to count on the forces of order to fire against the Fascists—many of whom were veterans and even *arditi*—than against Socialist or Communist laborers. Giolitti's instructions were often ignored or flouted on lower levels.

Giolitti, then, had failed to judge the temper of the mass parties, Socialist and Popular, which between them spoke for the bulk of the Italian working class and many intermediate social groups. In addition, he seems not to have realized the extent to which Fascism had corrupted the organs of the State itself. Fascism was not, as he had thought, a hotheaded youthful folly, but a cleverly planned and led counterrevolution, an attack upon the socially mediating and balancing constitutional State that Giolitti had done so much to shape. Fascism was not momentary, but had deep roots in the country's past.

Giolitti's mistaken appraisal of the Fascist counterrevolution was fatal, for he was much the best that the older group of democratic-Liberal leaders had to offer the nation. He had not failed in estimating political forces, but in judging the very nature of those forces. His failure was more than personal, it was the end of a class and a system.

Above all, this was a failure of insight and imagination. Italy was in many ways an unknown country, full of surprises. Beyond the Italy that Giolitti saw in the reports of his trusted prefects or in the balance sheets of the State lay another nation, aspiring and tormented, a generation of impatient men dazzled by messianic perspectives. With this Italy Giolitti and the other old Liberals— such as Croce, Albertini, Salandra, and Orlando—had never been in close touch, and what they saw and heard of it often moved them to scorn or condescension. Mussolini's sole political gift was his perception of the new Italy, his uncanny adeptness at exploiting its weaknesses.

Mussolini came to power fifteen months and twenty-four days after Giolitti's last ministry resigned.

Giolitti's successor, Ivanoe Bonomi, was in a most unhappy position. The eclectic Demo-Liberal-Popular majority lacked all conviction, while the Fascists set about destroying the economic (labor-union and cooperative) base of both socialism and popularism in the whole nation.

What happened at Cremona was an extreme case of Fascist violence and Socialist-Popular inability to face it. There Miglioli, after some episodes of near-violence, had obtained, through an arbiter's decision, a share for his peasants in the management of the great dairy farms on which they labored, with the marked approval of Don Sturzo and other Popular leaders. Then the landlords, having failed to break the arbitral decision in court, resorted to the Fascist Farinacci and his Blackshirt squads. Catholic and Socialist peasants alike were murderously attacked. But when Miglioli joined in a common defense with the Socialists of Cremona, both parties hastened to repudiate the act![10]

From the spring of 1921 until the March on Rome in October 1922, the Socialists, *Popolari* and the "Demo-Liberal" groups of the parliamentary Center were faced with a common problem, the Fascist occupation of key areas of Italy and the expansion of Fascist military rule in city and country. Yet all efforts to form a strong government, capable of restoring elementary law and order, ended in failure. For this the Popular Party must take a large share of the historical responsibility.

Unquestionably, the Catholic element was always unwelcome to many "Democrats," who felt that Catholic or "Clerical" rule was, if anything, worse than Fascism. The *Popolari* had been compelled to lay aside much of their own program in entering coalition governments. In addition, the *Popolari* were under heavy, overt pressure from the Vatican not to conclude any alliance, however limited and unentangling, with the Socialists. Worst of all, the Socialists themselves were divided and quarreling over revolutionary notions now hopelessly outdated. In 1922 Salvemini sadly wrote that "the Demochristians cannot present any concrete program of immediate action: the Socialists' refusal of any alliance puts them outside of political reality."[11] Yet the Popular record of "vetoes" and evasions cannot be entirely explained by these unhappy circumstances: the Party itself was trapped in the prevailing inertia of Italian democracy.

THE 1922 CRISIS

In February the Bonomi government resigned when the Giolittian "Democrats" withdrew their support. It was generally supposed that this obscure "extraparliamentary" crisis had been arranged in order to bring in a new Giolitti ministry.

But when Giolitti was proposed as Bonomi's successor, the *Popolari* interposed their "veto." Though Giolitti's supporters even went to the Vatican in their efforts to remove this block, nothing availed. And without the *Popolari* Giolitti could not command a majority.

This "veto" has aroused much discussion in Italy, both during the crises of 1922 and in the post-mortem analyses of the 1940's and 1950's. The question may be summed up under two heads. Don Sturzo implicitly justified the Popular "veto" by recalling Giolitti's cynical coddling of the Fascists in 1920–21. The *Popolari* could also remember the offhand way in which Giolitti had dismissed their ideas. In barring Giolitti's return, the *Popolari* could feel that they had not only struck a blow for Italian liberty but had defended their own party program.* Yet, on the other hand, it was generally suspected that the *Popolari* opposed Giolitti above all for his tax reforms, which would have required all government bonds to be made out in the owner's name, instead of to an anonymous bearer. Since bearer bonds were favored by ecclesiastical organizations, many of which lacked "juridical personality," Catholic opposition to Giolitti's reform was understandable. To this latter and less favorable interpretation of the 1922 "veto" Benedetto Croce has lent the weight of his great name, adding that only Giolitti had the necessary qualities to save Italy at this point.

Though Giolitti's indispensability may be questioned—the man still did not understand the nature of Fascism and the necessity of uniting against it—there is no doubt that what followed was sheer disaster. The King sent for Filippo Meda, who refused to attempt to form a government. Meda, always pessimistic, would have preferred recalling Giolitti. In Sturzo's judgment, if Meda

* Don Sturzo claimed in 1921 that his party was disliked because "we have faced the problem of the agricultural contract in its social structure, tending to transform the agricultural wage laborer into a part owner, giving the greatest possible security to the tenant and the share-cropper, . . . creating the small landholder where consistent with the development of agriculture, replacing the local tax office with the cooperative, contributing to peace-making on foundations of social justice, and hence tending to greater productivity and more intense labor" (*Discorsi politici,* p. 119). The *Popolari's* discontent with Giolitti began during the last days of his ministry, when it became clear that their desires for State recognition of private (i.e., Catholic) schools ran contrary to the policies of Giolitti's supporters, and that Giolitti himself would not bring the issue before Parliament.

did not want to govern, he should have stepped aside and let some other *Popolare* try his hand, instead of letting the initiative pass from the *Popolari* back to the Demo-Liberal Center. A bold step by a *Popolare* might have broken the impasse. Instead, the crisis ended with the emergence of one of Giolitti's least-distinguished "lieutenants," Luigi Facta, a stopgap premier whom the Popular parliamentary leaders, Cavazzoni and De Gasperi, accepted out of simple weariness. The nation received this outcome with utter indifference.[12]

The Facta government, fatally unable to restore law and order, was suddenly defeated in Parliament in July 1922, after Miglioli had aroused a Popular-Socialist demonstration among the deputies by describing Fascist outrages in his own Cremona area. The crisis caught Sturzo at a bad moment, for though he had begun long and delicate negotiations with the Socialist parliamentary group, he was still far from prepared to launch a Popular-Socialist coalition government. Unready, like the other constitutional leaders, he failed to rise to the occasion. The last chance of stopping Fascism was lost in the July crisis.

The fall of Facta was largely an affair of the *Popolari*, for Catholic labor unions, cooperatives, and youth circles were suffering from Fascist violence almost as much as the Red organizations, and the Party was uneasy. A combination of the Center Democrats, the *Popolari*, and the Socialists would have been able to uphold a determined government. The Italian people, sick of violence, would probably have welcomed a restoration of order, with the total suppression of the Blackshirt squads. Whenever the Government had taken forceful measures against Fascist invasions, as at Sarzana under Bonomi's brief government, the local populations had turned against the Blackshirts with joy and relief.

Yet the constitutional parties could join in no concerted action. The Center was divided among Giolitti's followers, Nitti's supporters, and ill-defined groups farther to the Right. The notables of Italian Liberalism prudently held back, each holding himself in reserve for a better chance that never came. The situation was further entangled by old rivalries, especially between Nitti and Giolitti.

The Socialists' situation was no better. The reformist Socialists, who comprised a majority of their Party's parliamentary group, were held in check by a fear of schism within the Party itself. Deputies like Turati, who understood well the need for a joint effort to halt the drift toward Fascist dictatorship, were afraid of losing touch with their own working-class supporters, of entering the Government amid the jeers of the proletariat. Within Italian Socialism in the summer of 1922 the lame reformists were still led by the blind revolutionaries.

The July crisis burned up the last political reserves of Italian democracy. First the task of forming a new government was passed to Orlando, who refused to take power without ministers from a Liberal Right that was in effect allied with the Fascist and Nationalists. Since the Facta government had fallen just because it had offered no decisive or energetic resistance to the Fascist occupation of large parts of Italy, Orlando represented no improvement, and failed. The parliamentary mandate, it was clear, was for a really anti-Fascist government. Bonomi, the next to be called, was willing to lead a broadly based anti-Fascist ministry with the *Popolari* and the Socialists. His old friend Turati was ready to uphold him in Parliament and would even have entered his government, though without portfolio, as a representative of Italian Socialism and a guarantor of the Government's anti-Fascist character. But Bonomi was rejected by the Democrats of the parliamentary Center after Giolitti wrote his friends several hostile letters from Vichy, where he was resting. One "satanic letter" became public, with much effect. Giolitti scorned the whole notion of a Popular-Socialist government pledged to the suppression of illegal Fascist rule; any effort in that direction, he warned, would bring "civil war." Although Giolitti professed to believe that the great problem facing Italy was financial rather than political, his words suggest strongly a desire for revenge on Sturzo and the *Popolari,* who had ruined his last chance to head a government earlier in the year.

Though Giolitti's dog-in-the-manger attitude in July 1922 did not add an inch to his historical stature, it did wreck Bonomi's anti-Fascist coalition, for the Democrats of the parliamentary Center turned against both *Popolari* and Socialists. Old anti-Clerical feelings and rancor over the Popular "veto" against Giolitti's return played their part in this crisis, helping to spoil the last chance of saving democratic Italy.[13]

With no clear majority in sight, the burden of forming a government was then passed to Filippo Meda; Sturzo wired him at Milan, where he had taken refuge after the failure of Bonomi, and urged him to sacrifice himself. For Meda, who was no fighter, it would indeed have been a sacrifice to head a government that probably would have been compelled to fire on the Blackshirts; Sturzo, who was of tougher fiber, might well have done it, but he was ineligible because of his sacerdotal status. Indeed, his ineligibility was a grave handicap to his Party, of which he was much the most capable leader during these years.

Meda, called informally from Milan by the King, declined on the ground he could take no official position that would interfere with his law practice! He recommended that Victor Emmanuel call De Nava, a Right Center leader not suspected of anti-Fascism. (The Fascist *Il Popolo d'Italia* called Meda's actions a "flight"; Mussolini had a keen eye for his adversaries' weaknesses.)

The new political class that Sturzo had expected in 1919 would clearly not come from Popular leaders such as Meda, whose *gran rifiuto*, repeated three times since 1919, put the seal of passivity upon his party and condemned it to play humble supporting roles in the Italian drama. The great chance had slipped away through a failure of nerve.

The July 1922 crisis petered out. The Left, still haunted by revolutionary phantoms, declared a general strike of protest during the last stage of the crisis, thus giving the eager Fascists a chance for more of the organized violence against which the strikers were protesting! This came at a time when many Socialist parliamentary leaders were finally ready to face reality and support any government that would save the constitution; unfortunately, they too upheld the strike, thinking it would strengthen their position. Instead, the crisis ended with the general strike, which brought on a new wave of violence and cut short any further consultations.

Once again, simply to fill a vacuum, Facta was called. His eclectic government included several ministers of the "National" Liberal Right, followers of Salandra who shared his sympathy for Fascism as a force of order. During Facta's second ministry the State drifted, while the Fascists stepped up the rhythm of their military operations. Many prefects found themselves isolated in occupied territory.

The parties were as unnerved as the administration. In October the Socialists split into reformist and revolutionary splinters. After the Popular Party had clearly shown its anti-Fascist spirit during the July crisis, Fascist invaders attacked the Party's strongholds in the North Italian countryside, deposing local governments and pillaging "White" organizations. The Catholic rural masses seemed stunned by the blows that kept raining upon them. The Party had little comfort for them: both its leadership and its parliamentary representation were at sea.* The Clerico-Moderate wing of the Party, especially strong among the aristocrats of the Senate, repudiated Sturzo's policy of an eventual anti-Fascist parliamentary alliance with the Socialists, and called upon the Party to assume a decidedly religious and "national" character. In short, many of the Clerico-Moderate men of order were ready to become Clerico-Fascists, going over to Mussolini's big battalions.

One of their most influential deputies, Stefano Cavazzoni, looked toward an eventual Popular coalition with the Fascists themselves in a great ministry headed by Giolitti, which seemed a real possibility during these last months before the March on Rome. Giolitti's personal following, which included many high State officials in Rome and Milan, was dealing with Mussolini secretly, in hopes of yet another parliamentary compromise; they kept in touch with the Popular Party through Cavazzoni.

Mussolini shrewdly drew out these negotiations, while making similar offers to Salandra. Thus he held the prestigious Liberal leaders in suspense until his own master stroke was ready. In this intricate game the Duce was helped, intentionally or not, by Facta's confusing and dilatory telegrams to Giolitti in Piedmont, which kept the old statesman away from Rome. With the constitutional party representatives Mussolini kept talking as if he were the head of a parliamentary party himself, though he really acted as the commander of a private army that was fast losing its patience.

On October 28 the long-expected coup finally took place. The

---

* When the Popular Party National Council met 19–21 October 1922, the eve of the March on Rome, Sturzo still favored a continuation of the Facta government. When Giuseppe Donati proposed that a military government be formed to cope with the Fascist mobilization, he was "submerged in a chorus of protest" from both Right and Left. Donati, *Scritti politici*, I, lxxxvi.

limp Facta government, which had already submitted its resignation, was galvanized by the Fascist convergence on Rome into making a last convulsive effort. A decree of martial law was prepared for the King's signature. Some of the caretaker ministers, such as Giovanni Amendola, meant seriously to save the State.

Facta himself did not inspire confidence, and probably felt relief when the King rejected the decree. Mussolini was summoned from Milan, where he had prudently barricaded himself, by a royal telephone call, and the "Fascist Era" began.

The situation had passed beyond all possibility of remedy by normal measures, such as a regular consultation of parliamentary leaders. Indeed, some of them were not to be found. Meda's experience is instructive. He had taken an evening train for Rome from Milan on the 27th, but stopped at Pisa when he was overtaken by the Fascist mobilization. There he got out and spent a day and a night with the Cardinal-Archbishop. The next day he returned to Milan, where he was checked at the railway station by the Fascist militia and allowed to go home after his identity was established. At his house was a telegram from Facta, calling him to Rome in the King's name![14]

It is probable that the only alternative to the Fascist coup would have been a royal command to the army to dissolve the Blackshirt squads; but rather than take such extreme measures, the King preferred to legalize and constitutionalize the Fascist seizure. In so doing he was merely following the opinion of the greatest statesman of democratic Italy, Giolitti, who had earlier in the year warned against the "civil war" that would follow any repression of Fascism. Victor Emmanuel III was not a hero, but if his old ministers had really tried to make the democratic system of 1919–22 work, rallying *Popolari* and Socialists, the mass parties, to defend the constitutional State against armed subversion, the King might have seconded their labors. Instead, the King, like the ministers and parliamentary leaders, had been strained and exhausted by a feverish, inconclusive succession of crises, which had resulted in no concerted action to save Italy.

The March on Rome came almost as a relief.

Chapter Six

THE DEATH OF THE POPULAR PARTY, 1922–27

THE POPULAR PARTY AND PIUS XI

Even before the death of Benedict XV and the accession of Pius XI (January–February, 1922), the Popular Party was losing favor in the Vatican. At the conclusion of the war, when Don Sturzo had gone to the papal Secretary of State, Cardinal Gasparri, to discuss the formation of the new Popular Party, the idea of an autonomous Catholic party had seemed best to the Holy See. The Popular Party would keep the mass of militant Catholics loyal to the social teachings of the Church without compromising the Hierarchy or the Papacy itself in the twists and turns of Italian politics.

But disillusionment soon set in. The Popular Party, which had deliberately passed over the whole Roman Question and addressed itself to the urgent problems of Italian society in the postwar period, was "no better than the Liberals." Indeed, beginning with Nitti the Italian Center began to hold out to the Holy See the prospect of a definite settlement with the Italian State, if only the *Popolari* might be repudiated or kept under control. The Fascists in 1921 began to advance the same general ideas, with great publicity and with a far greater hostility toward the party of Don Sturzo.

At this point Achille Ratti, a conservative from Lombardy and "frequenter of the great houses" of Milan, was raised to the Throne of Peter as Pius XI.[1] The new Pope was no Christian Democrat, and his election opened possibilities which Salvemini was quick to see:

> Risen to the papal throne, Benedict XV continued the electoral policy of his old diocese of Bologna, which consisted in not having any policy at all. He let spontaneous forces act in the Catholic movement, without any preference, conservative or democratic; and with this abstention, he left the field free in

Italy for the democratic forces, declaring that the Popular Party acted on its own exclusive responsibility without any control by Church authorities. . . . Pope Ratti, if he should compel Don Sturzo to leave the secretaryship of the Popular Party, if he should put the electoral and political action of the Popular organizations under control of the bishops, if he should repudiate the Honorable Miglioli, would fast become a great Pope for the Lombard and Tuscan landowners.[2]

Of course the new Pope did nothing so crude, and there were no overt repudiations. But the Popular Party was left severely alone, as were the hapless labor unions of Catholic leadership, and priests were warned against participating in Italian political life. The Church directed the Catholic masses toward Catholic Action instead, which was strictly dependent upon the Hierarchy and became the Church's real line of defense in the new situation created by Fascism. The social achievements of Christian Democracy were jettisoned in favor of an understanding with the new powers. The essential point of Pius XI's policy was to face the Fascist Regime with an equally "monolithic" Catholic force, with the Catholic masses incorporated in new organizations under conservative leaders such as Luigi Colombo of Milan, hand-picked by the pontiff himself. (Cardinal Achille Ratti, Archbishop of Milan, was regarded by Mussolini as a potential friend. In the victory anniversary celebration of 4 November 1921 Ratti had permitted the bringing of Fascist banners into the Duomo of Milan; the Duce was naturally pleased when this prelate was elected Pope a short time thereafter.)[3]

Pius XI's choice was due in great part to his own authoritarian cast of mind, but in no less a degree to the extraordinary pressure exerted by Fascism. The Fascists offered an international settlement and a privileged position to the Vatican and the Italian Church, if the Popular Party and the White labor unions were left to their fate, but they openly threatened waves of violence and destruction of Catholic organizations and parishes if their advances were rejected. And these threats were put into execution, on a limited scale, throughout 1923 and 1924.

Pius XI, who was certainly not attracted by the Fascist mentality, accepted much of what Fascism offered. He preferred to deal with Mussolini personally; the Catholics of Italy were to have no

independent voice in determining their own religious-political
situation. Everything was to be settled over their heads.

By October, 1922, Cardinal Gasparri, Father Enrico Rosa of
the Jesuit organ *Civiltà Cattolica,* and other Vatican authorities
had made it clear that Catholics had no obligations toward the
Popular Party and that it enjoyed no special favor in papal eyes.
Indeed, the Party was becoming an embarrassment to the Holy See.

The Italian Church Hierarchy itself had mixed feelings. At
Milan the prevalent sentiment since the 1920 municipal elections
had been against the independent Centrist line of the Popular
Party, and in favor of Rightist "blocs."[5] In fact, the municipal
elections of autumn 1920 mark the first open break between the
line of the Popular Party and the course of Vatican politics. The
Holy See and the Italian Hierarchy openly favored Catholic support of a "bloc" of all parties against the Left, in order to keep the
Socialists from obtaining control of many North Italian city governments. The *Popolari* were torn between their desire to give
heed to the wishes of the Holy See and the Hierarchy, expressed
unmistakably in the official and semiofficial press of the Vatican
and of Catholic Action, and their party interests, expressed in the
independent uncompromising line of Don Sturzo. If the Party
had simply complied with the desires of the Holy See and the
Hierarchy, it would have lost its distinctive character as a Center
party and became a mere auxiliary to whatever the government
chose to form a united anti-Socialist bloc; but to the Vatican this
was a secondary consideration, since the immediate task of all
Catholics was to keep the Socialists from coming to power. If a
Catholic political movement should foster that aim, well and
good; if not, the Catholic voter should follow the advice of the
clergy rather than the line laid down by Catholic lay political
leaders. The outcome of the 1920 administrative-municipal elections showed that many Catholic voters in fact followed the clergy
rather than the lay party. Don Sturzo's autonomy was respected
by the Holy See and the Hierarchy to exactly the extent to which
it served their purposes, and no more, as was shown by the events
of 1924. Herein lay the contradiction that sapped and mined the
very life of the Popular Party in Italy.

Italian bishops were often susceptible to appeals for unity
against the Left, under the leadership of a newly respectable
Fascist Party; but at the same time Blackshirt violence continually

threatened to destroy Catholic organizations, even purely religious, nonpolitical, and noneconomic groups such as the Youth Circles. In North Italy the lower clergy often found itself in direct daily conflict with Fascism and its competing claims to the allegiance of Italian youth; sometimes their bishops sided with them. At Turin, for example, Catholic Action, with the evident approval of the Archbishop, was definitely anti-Fascist: when the Clerico-Moderate Trust journal *Il Momento* went over to Fascism, Catholic Action began publishing a daily of its own, with independent political views.[6]

THE CRISIS OF POPULAR LEADERSHIP AND THE
DEPARTURE OF DON STURZO, 1923–24

Just before the March on Rome, Mussolini had cast his net widely and shrewdly. Liberals and Cardinals alike had been caught in its meshes, nor did the *Popolari* escape. Although the "revolutionary" nature of Mussolini's coup was recognized by all, constitutional appearances were to be preserved: Liberals and *Popolari* entered Mussolini's first coalition government in the hope of "constitutionalizing" the Fascists. Instead, these flanking elements were simply used as a convenient governmental and parliamentary screen, behind which the real apparatus of dictatorship was being set up. Mussolini alternated truculence and blandishments, openly insulted Parliament while deferring to the Monarchy and the armed forces, observed constitutional formalities in the Viminal but carried on the old "revolutionary" line when addressing his Blackshirts, by now an official militia; these tactics bewildered and divided the *Popolari* as they did all other constitutional forces.

Against this master of pre-dictatorial politics, the old Italy was almost disarmed. Mussolini played on the ambiguity between a "national" and a "party" dictatorship. The Fascist "transformism" of deceit and violence far exceeded anything that the old wizard of political combinations, Giolitti, had ever been able to effect. Giolitti bitterly observed that Parliament—that unworkable Chamber elected at his own insistence in 1921—had got the government it deserved. He was condemned to watch Liberal Italy, which had been his life work, expire in less than three years. He did not long survive it.

The year 1923 was one of clarification for Italian Catholics, in which their political leadership was winnowed out in a succession of tests.

The first trial was the Congress of Turin of April 1923. The Party reaffirmed its centrist-constitutional character: it approved without enthusiasm the continued presence of *Popolari* in Mussolini's cabinet "in order that the Fascist revolution may be inserted in the constitution." This essentially anti-Fascist position was held by most of the Party's rank and file. Yet the cracks in the Party leadership were widening: whereas the notables of the Right were committed without reservations to support Mussolini's "reconstruction," the Party's Left faction, led by the forthright ex-president of the Catholic University Youth Federation, Francesco Luigi Ferrari of Modena, was set against any collaboration at all. "In order to collaborate," said Ferrari, "there must be two, but Fascism excludes collaboration." Mussolini seized upon the resolution of the Turin Congress as a chance for ridding himself of his Popular ministers. The Blackshirt campaign of lawlessness and violence against Catholic organizations was redoubled, and Don Sturzo became the target of a vulgar Fascist press campaign of vilification.

At this point the inner weakness of the Party was laid bare. The Center of the Party depended upon Don Sturzo: Alcide De Gasperi, the parliamentary leader, was a young Catholic activist from the Trentino, new to Italian politics, and Giuseppe Donati, editor of the courageous new Party news organ *Il Popolo*, was a Romagnole Christian Democrat whose life had been passed in a no man's land between the Catholic camp and the Democratic-Reformist camp of Salvemini.

But Don Sturzo was a vulnerable leader. His sacred character was a serious weakness: as a priest, for example, he had been unable to sit in Parliament, the way a leader of a great party ought; as a priest, he symbolized the clergy itself, a fact which held him back from following a true political vocation.

The Fascists pressed at this weak point, threatening reprisals against the whole clergy for the political opposition of Sturzo. The Holy See itself intervened. Don Sturzo was, of course, obliged to obey the Pope; had Pius simply ordered him to depart, he would have done so without a murmur. But there is no evidence that the Pontiff yielded so openly to Fascist coercion. A hint sufficed. On 25 June 1923 the Trust organ *Il Corriere d'Italia* of Rome published an interview with Monsignor Enrico Pucci, already a prominent intermediary between Fascism and the Holy See, in which Pucci implied clearly that Sturzo was creating embarrassments to the Church. It was widely held that Pucci reflected the wishes of the Holy See. On 10 July Don Sturzo removed all ambiguities or possible misunderstandings by quitting his post as Political Secretary of the Popular Party. He remained active in the Party until 1924, when Cardinal Gasparri himself arranged for his emigration to London after Fascist pressures and physical threats had made continued existence in Italy impossible.[7]

The new leader of the Party emerged after a triumviral period which lasted through the elections of 1924. Then Alcide De Gasperi was elected in Sturzo's place as Political Secretary; and his importance was to be far greater than anyone could have foreseen in the 1920's.

ALCIDE DE GASPERI, SUCCESSOR TO DON STURZO

Alcide De Gasperi was born 3 April 1881 of humble mountain folk in the Trentino, the one solidly Italian region of the Dual Monarchy; his early training was Catholic, Austrian, and therefore cosmopolitan. He studied at Vienna; afterward he came back to Trent and became almost at once a leader in the powerful Catholic organizations there.*

The Trentino was unique. By tradition it was subject to a Prince-Bishop, and although annexed to the Austrian Empire at the Congress of Vienna, after having been first a part of the short-lived Napoleonic Kingdom of Italy, it retained a stubborn spirit of local autonomy. The overwhelming majority of the Trentino was Italian, but only a few Trentini had been deeply moved by Italian national feeling. The Austrians educated their Trentine citizens in Italian, but the textbooks were simply translated from the German at Vienna. At the time De Gasperi became prominent, in the first decade of the twentieth century, there existed in the Trentino a small upper-class Liberal Party, a Socialist Party (which had under the leadership of Cesare Battisti assumed a strongly Irredentist position), and a Catholic movement that insisted on Trentine autonomy within the Austrian system. This last was by far the strongest of the three, and reigned almost uncontested in

---

* See the bibliography on De Gasperi in Chapter Nine.

the countryside, where Socialist organizers were sometimes roughly treated by the devout peasantry. The Catholic political party, which in 1911 was called *L'Unione politica popolare del Trentino*, was merely a part of a great network of Catholic economic and social organizations: Mussolini noted publicly in 1909 that "Alcide . . . editor of the [Catholic] newspaper, becomes a banker by crossing a corridor and a sacristan at the foot of the stairs."

In 1906 De Gasperi had became editor of the local Catholic newspaper, *Il Trentino*, in the columns of which he often had to fight a double battle. On the one side, *Il Trentino* bitterly opposed the aggressive pan-German elements of the Tyrol, with their "theories of race" and their plans for the "re-Germanization" of the Trentino, which they called the Italian Tyrol; De Gasperi's articles were directed especially at Austrian Catholics who sympathized with this "ultranationalism." He pointed out to these erring brethren of his that pagan pan-Germanism would ultimately work against the "Austrian idea," which was Catholic and supranational in character. De Gasperi himself advanced a Catholic political platform for the Trentino based on Christian social teachings, on "positive nationality" (defense of the Italian character of the threatened region), and on democracy. He insisted that the accusations of Irredentism that were hurled against the Catholics of the Trentino by anti-Clerical Austrian radicals were baseless: the Catholic program was one of legality and justice, of peace and reconciliation between the two nationalities.

Hence, recent descriptions of De Gasperi as an "Irredentist" are falsehoods with a clear political intent. Irredentism implied rebellion against the lawful Austrian authorities: De Gasperi, who was nothing if not a conscientious Catholic, knew well *non est enim potestas nisi a Deo*, and governed himself accordingly.

De Gasperi's group had more than mere German nationalism to contend with. On the other side, De Gasperi had to fight a continual battle against the local Socialists, in the course of which he had a passing brush with Benito Mussolini that undoubtedly affected his whole political career.

Mussolini, called from Italy in January 1909, by the local Socialists to fill the vacant post of secretary of their labor organization, and highly commended by them as an expert in anticlericalism *(versato specialmente in materia di anticlericalismo)*, arrived in the Trentino breathing the fires of Sorelian syndicalism. The young agitator generally ignored the national question as such, for he held nationalism to be nothing more than a *morbus sacer*; on the other hand, he regarded international war as a great step toward civil war and the insurrectionary general strike, which would usher in the Syndicalist reign of the proletarian elite. The Syndicalist myth would supersede Christianity: "our proud attempt to create shall not have been in vain."

The vaunted superseding of Christianity soon took shape as a coarse anti-Clerical campaign on the usual themes: the martyrdom of Giordano Bruno, Church atrocities against the Jews of Trent in the fifteenth century, and—surprisingly enough for a man who scorned the "fetish" of nationalism and made no contribution to Trentine Irredentism—accusations of lack of national style, for Mussolini continually taunted De Gasperi for writing "Italo-Austrian" like a Tyrolean janitor, instead of the Italian of Italy. Indeed, De Gasperi's prose is no model of Italian style.

Mussolini's personal attacks on the young Catholic editor began in earnest after the two met in a public debate at Untermais on Sunday, 7 March 1909. A labor dispute had broken out at Merano, in the course of which the Catholic unions had proposed that the Socialists take part in a joint action. The Socialists then invited De Gasperi to an out-of-the-way public discussion. According to *Il Trentino*'s account (probably written by De Gasperi himself), the Socialists' messenger passed by at almost the last possible moment and did not wait for an answer; evidently they hoped that De Gasperi would not come. But De Gasperi, wishing above all to avoid being accused of cowardice, went to Untermais for the short time he could spare from his other Sunday engagements.

"The new propagandist Mussolini" was the principal Socialist speaker. He expounded the doctrines of "social revolution" and "expropriation," adding that Christian Democracy, adopted by a wily pope after 1890, was mere pretense and fraud. De Gasperi, after assuring his Socialist adversaries that he was not afraid to accept invitations to debate whenever he saw fit, answered Mussolini in a tone of cold dry contempt. The "social revolution" would not come tomorrow or next month; the expropriation of capital was not an immediate problem, but the threat of a lockout against local construction workers was. Workers' unity, peaceful and legal solidarity, were the necessary goals. Political terrorism would be a betrayal of the workers' interests for the advantage of a party.

After these sharp retorts De Gasperi wished the workers success in their struggle and then left immediately to catch a train. Thereafter Mussolini never let slip an opportunity of attacking "the superficial man who consults an Austrian railroad timetable in order to escape from an embarrassing debate," and the "semiliterate" newspaper that he edited.

When in September 1909 Mussolini was arrested, held, and finally expelled from the Empire by the Austrian authorities, De Gasperi claimed that he had nothing to do with the affair. He said that, on the contrary, Mussolini's intemperate revolutionary outbursts had at least served to expose the true nature of the seemingly reformist character of Trentino Socialism. But the Austrian historian Hans Kramer has discovered that in fact the Catholic party of the Trentino had during much of 1909 been urging the imperial authorities to rid them of Mussolini. At any rate, it is not at all surprising that De Gasperi nourished a stubborn aversion to Mussolini, which was to weigh heavily in 1923–25 when so many Catholics were ready to submit to the volatile *Duce,* now presenting himself as a protector of the Church. Between the Social Catholic prose of De Gasperi and Mussolini's poetry of violence there could be no compromise or points of contact.

De Gasperi's later years within the Austrian system were eventful. A characteristic shunning of rhetoric and an insistence on specific local problems marked his successful campaign for election to the Austrian parliament of 1911. Toward the problem of militarism, which beset Europe, De Gasperi had a deeply fatalistic attitude, since he held that modern war was a direct consequence of modern industry and commerce. A true Catholic, he held that the evils of modern society sprang from unrestricted capitalism and the spirit of social revolution that it fatally engendered. He abhorred equally Viennese "Jewish Masonry" and Austrian Socialism.

The Sarajevo murder and the outbreak of World War I created a difficult situation for De Gasperi and the whole Trentino. On the one hand, he had a natural sympathy for the old Catholic monarchy; yet the clearly German national character of the war held no appeal for him. The region itself was caught between an Italy that had turned away from its old alliances and threatened to intervene on the side of the Entente, and an angry Austria now irrevocably tied to Germany.

In these straits De Gasperi confined himself to reprinting Austrian and German official bulletins, without any significant comments. The Christian character of Francis Joseph and the neutralism of Italian Catholics were stressed in the columns of *Il Trentino*. (The Catholic organ had always been reserved and often negative in its coverage of Italian news, except for reports of Italian Catholic activities. De Gasperi seems to have had a special fondness for Meda, whose name occasionally appears in *Il Trentino* as chief spokesman for Italian Catholicism.)

Although De Gasperi regarded the World War as "God's hour" (*l'ora di Dio*), he did not lapse into passivity. On the contrary, he made some vigorous efforts to forestall a war between Italy and Austria, according to the reminiscences of Guido Miglioli. De Gasperi was at Rome during the crisis of 1915 in an attempt to mediate between the Italian Government and the Central Powers; he saw von Bülow, Baron Macchio (the Austrian ambassador to Italy), Salandra, and Sonnino. At first his efforts were seconded by influential Catholics, who still favored Italian neutrality; with the swing toward war, De Gasperi found himself more and more isolated in the Italian capital. Finally he went back to Trent, on the eve of hostilities. Between September 1914 and March 1915 De Gasperi made no less than three trips to Rome. From the testimony accumulated by Gino Valori, who tries to show De Gasperi as a neutralist, and by Giulio Andreotti, a Christian Democratic minister who portrays De Gasperi as an Italian patriot, only one conclusion emerges: De Gasperi was seeking to spare the Trentino from the ravages of war. [8]

With the outbreak of war between Italy and the Dual Monarchy De Gasperi devoted himself to the problems of Trentino refugees and internees. When the Austrian parliament finally reopened, with the Empire in the throes of dissolution, De Gasperi made common cause with the other Italian deputies in defending the rights of his minority. At the end of the war the Trentino became the most solidly Catholic region of Italy, and De Gasperi was its leading representative in the councils of the Popular Party.

On De Gasperi's political life, from beginning to end, two

characteristics are indelibly stamped. The first is his national and institutional agnosticism. As a young Catholic leader in the Trentino, he was not primarily concerned with the Italian or Austrian character of his region, but rather with the predominance of Catholic ideals and organizations within a local compass. Only one outside influence deeply disturbed him: the truculent racist nationalism of the German Tyrol, which offended his convictions as a Catholic just as deeply as it menaced his Italian "nationality." Likewise in the Italian political struggle of 1943–46, he showed himself indifferent at heart to the question of Monarchy or Republic: his concern was with the construction of a certain kind of social order, and the avoidance of dictatorial solutions. The other characteristic is his *eclecticism*. In 1906 the young De Gasperi had advocated successfully the removal of "confessional" labels from the Trentine Catholic newspaper and, later, from the party, which was officially nonconfessional. His parliamentary experience at Vienna, short as it was, tended to confirm a belief that Social-Catholic aims could be achieved through hybrid political alliances on a foundation of mutual tolerance. This belief, which harmonized with the old Austrian tradition of a Catholic state quite autonomous in its relation to the Hierarchy, distinguished De Gasperi throughout his life from Catholic enthusiasts, such as La Pira, for whom politics is merely applied religion.

THE LAST EFFORTS OF THE POPULAR PARTY, 1923–24

July 1923 saw not only the resignation of Don Luigi Sturzo but also the political schism of the organized Catholics of Italy. Already at the Turin Congress of April there had been clear signs that within the Popular Party there existed a pro-Fascist tendency, represented by such prominent figures as Livio Tovini of Brescia and the former Murrian Demochristian Egilberto Martire. But the final division came during the deliberations in the Chamber concerning the Government's projected election law, which by a "premium" award of seats to the national ticket with the largest number of votes would assure a pliable and unrepresentative Chamber issuing from the next election. The Popular parliamentary group had decided to vote confidence and a provisional budget, but to abstain from voting on the election bill; proportional representation was too fundamental a part of Popular Party programs to be renounced even in time of stress.

When the vote was actually being taken in the Chamber a group of Popular deputies suddenly broke party discipline by voting for the Government's bill; naturally they were expelled from the Party in short order. In 1924 they, together with some Popular senators, formed a *Centro Nazionale Italiano* of their own and supported the "big ticket (*listone*) of Fascism in the spring 1924 elections.

What galled the *Popolari* especially in these secession movements was the constant use of the word "Catholic" in their propaganda. The *Popolari* had always on principle shunned this sort of "confessional" identification. Along with many other Italian Catholics, they were scandalized by the free use of religious labels —yet a real separation of political and religious motives in Italian life was never more distant than in the torments of the 1920's.[9]

The new Clerico-Fascists of 1923–24 were but old Clerico-Moderates writ large. To this a few important exceptions must be made. Meda stayed in the Party, as did the conservatives Montini and Longinotti of Brescia. But the great representatives of Lombard Catholic finance, together with the Catholic aristocrats of the Bank of Rome and the Trust newspaper chain went over solidly to Clerico-Fascist positions. For years these elements furnished important mediation between the Holy See and the Italian Hierarchy on the one side and the Fascist Regime on the other. Of especial significance was the defection from the Popular ranks of Senator Marquis Filippo Crispolti, confidant of several popes, of Senator Count Giovanni Grosoli, head of the journalistic Trust, and of the Roman aristocrat Carlo Santucci, scion of an old "black" papal family.[10]

The Clerico-Fascist point of view was well put by Martire in the Trust organs. At bottom, the whole liberal-democratic world was equated with Masonic anticlericalism, which the Fascist power-state (*stato forte*) was finally to sweep away. When Fascist outrages were cited, the Clerico-Fascists answered by recalling supposed persecutions suffered by Catholicism under Liberal governments (the difference between the two equalled that between a clubbing and a pinprick, in fact). But the real Clerico-Fascist case rested upon the old distinction between thesis and hypothesis so dear to Catholic political thought. The ideal *thesis* of a state permeated by Christianity is impossible of fulfillment under modern conditions; this being so, is the *hypothesis* of a Fascist state any more objectionable on religious grounds than the *hypothesis* of a democratic state? Quite the contrary, is the Clerico-Fascist reply: the nineteenth-century rift between Church and State in Italy will be healed more rapidly under Fascism. Nor does the Fascist power-state offend the social principles of Catholicism, for it is "decentralizing," and does not claim omnipotence, like the Socialist state.[11]

Martire went on to say that the Popular Party, in its failure to develop leadership of its own, was drifting into an opposition alliance with Democrats and Socialists that promised to be far more objectionable and doubtful than the alliance of the National Center with Fascism. (This was to prove a telling point.) The "national Catholics," as he called them, would go on working for the legalization and normalization of the Fascist Regime.

The Popular Party, though weakened in financial and journalistic resources and shorn of notables, waged an energetic campaign in the spring 1924 parliamentary elections. The Fascist terror, until well after the elections were over, was unceasing; for Catholics, it reached its peak in the beating to death (evidently on Balbo's orders) of the country priest Don Minzoni, a decorated former war chaplain, in August 1923, and went on through the sacking of Catholic cooperatives at Brianza (Lombardy) in April 1924, a punishment for having given a large vote to the Popular Party. Nevertheless the Popular rank and file held together well. The independent Catholic press, the North Italian organs not tied to the Trust, such as *L'Italia* of Milan, *L'Eco di Bergamo, Il Cittadino di Brescia, Il Corriere Vicentino, Il Corriere* of Turin (established under archiepiscopal auspices by Catholic Action when the Trust journal of Turin, *Il Momento,* went over to Fascism), were all anti-Fascist in varying degree. Between the conservative Milanese *L'Italia* and the Left-Popular Milanese *Domani d'Italia* of F. L. Ferrari there was fixed a political gulf; yet they were on the same side in those few vital months of 1924 in which there was formed in Italy a genuine Catholic tradition of resistance to dictatorship.

Catholic provincial journals, dull and repetitious as they are ordinarily, are indispensable for an understanding of the real situation of Italian Catholics in 1923–25. Close to the North Italian rural parish priest and the cooperative and union he so often sponsored, these journals reported the daily abuses and pressures that Catholic organizers suffered from their Fascist competitors, while the Trust journals of Rome, Bologna, and Turin reflected the point of view of the notables who financed them.

The *Popolari* of 1924 ran the range from the leftism of F. L. Ferrari to the pessimistic "collaborationism" of Filippo Meda. The veteran Clerico-Moderate spokesman had refused to run for Parliament in 1924 unless the Popular Party should renounce any intention of opposing or rivaling Fascism, which must be allowed to run its course. However, his son Luigi Meda had joined Ferrari and other "Left" *Popolari* in calling for complete abstention from the elections, since it was clear that the Regime would not allow them to be held freely.*

The Party followed neither of these desperate counsels, but rather continued along the lines of moderate legal opposition. A Center, personified by De Gasperi and ranging from conservatives such as Giorgio Montini of Brescia to Christian Democratic labor leaders such as the Tuscan Giovanni Gronchi, led a dignified and relatively successful campaign, notable for the large number of candidates who later distinguished themselves in the Christian Democracy of the post-World War II Italian Republic. For example, the future premier Antonio Segni ran in his own Sardinia.

One of the keynotes of the 1924 campaign was the Popular conception of *autonomy*. Though of Christian inspiration, the Party never called itself Catholic. When the Clerico-Fascists spoke of Catholic interests being favored by the new Regime, the *Popolari* accused their former comrades of exploiting religious motives for political-economic ends. For whatever its outward show of deference toward the Church, Fascism was inwardly pagan. De Gasperi, recalling the Second Empire, identified the *Popolari* with Montalembert in his refusal to celebrate on the tomb of freedom. Submission to dictatorship would serve no genuine Catholic purpose.[12]

While De Gasperi thus harked back to traditional Catholic "centrism," Gronchi expressed a Catholic laborite point of view. He warned against an eventual identification of Catholicism with the Regime, particularly at a time when rural working-class living

---

* Ferrari and the Popular Left published *Il Domani d'Italia*. Meda's defeatist views were known through the monthly *Civitas*, and aroused even moderates like Jacini to protest. See *Il Popolo*, 11 March 1924.

standards were suffering in the new atmosphere of repression. In the nineteenth century the Church had been estranged from the middle classes because it seemed to be an ally of absolutist reaction. The same mistake, said Gronchi, must not be made with the working classes in the present century. In Piedmont Attilio Piccioni, who would some day be vice-premier in De Gasperi's cabinet, held out Popularism to the voters as an indispensable Christian middle ground between revolution and reaction; in the new conditions of regimentation, he said, the workers had lost, although capital profits were rising.[13]

On the eve of the 1924 elections 150 Catholic notables issued a manifesto supporting the Government's ticket. Though *Il Popolo* did everything to lessen the manifesto's impact by noting sharply that many of the signers were connected with the tottering Bank of Rome, yet the blow was shrewd and well timed to throw confusion into Catholic ranks, for it suggested that the Party was somehow cut off from the Church, or at least from the high ecclesiastical circles frequented by the Catholic notables.[14]

The *Popolari* fought the 1924 campaign with two overwhelming handicaps. Not only did the Fascists use all kinds of violence and intimidation against them, particularly in the countryside where the Popular Party, like all Catholic movements, found its real strength, but also many cardinals and bishops showed definite pro-Fascist leanings. The Vatican had declared at the outset of the campaign that, as always, it was not concerned with any political party; but added official declarations of the nonpolitical character of Catholic Action were publicly interpreted by the Clerico-Fascists as a veiled repudiation of the Popular Party.[15] These tactics struck at the very base of the Party.

Certainly it is reasonable to suppose that in the Vatican the Popular Party was by 1924 regarded as an impediment to a general understanding between Church and Regime: Would such papal intimates as Crispolti have turned against the Popular Party otherwise? In 1924 Italy had, in effect, two bitterly opposed Catholic political movements. For a convinced believer in the autonomy of politics, such as F. L. Ferrari, there was nothing wrong in this. Yet political competition between Catholics raises special problems, for the tension between spiritual fellowship and political enmity is hard to endure. Furthermore, the Holy See was to show unmistakably its preference for a compact maneuverable Catholic mass in Italy.

The final crisis of Italian constitutional government developed between June 1924 and January 1925. Up to the murder of the Socialist deputy Matteotti in June 1924, there was still some hope, however slender, for a constitutional outcome of Italian political conflicts. Within Fascism itself there were clearly two tendencies, one "normalizing" and seeking to insert itself into the existing order, and the other "squadrist," aiming at a genuinely totalitarian state. Bottai, now outliving some of his early Futurist excesses, might be taken as a representative of the first element; Farinacci, the vulgar and abusive Blackshirt leader of Cremona, was certainly the most representative "squadrist." Bottai aimed at a corporative legal order, but Farinacci's sole aim seems to have been a dictatorship of the Party and the expansion of Italy. Up to the crisis of 1924 it was not apparent toward which side Mussolini inclined; his adroitness in balancing oppositions, both within as well as outside of the Party, hid his fundamental preference for the totalitarian solution.

Matteotti was done away with after a courageous campaign in the new "fascistized" chamber against the irregularities of the spring elections. His murder raised such a storm of indignation in Italy that for a moment the Fascists seemed to stand alone. Though the Chamber had been packed by an electoral law voted under circumstances amounting to disguised coercion, the country was not Fascist: from June 1924 to January 1925 it was really anti-Fascist. Matteotti's widow was received in audience by the Pope, a fitting expression of Catholic indignation.

The problem of the anti-Fascist Opposition in Parliament was grave. After Matteotti's murder, most of the Opposition deputies absented themselves from the regular sessions of the Chamber and met in an "Aventine" assembly of their own, holding that the official Parliament had ceased to have any possible constitutional function. Yet in so doing the Opposition parties made it even more difficult for a constitutional solution to be found. Since the Chamber had been packed and intimidated, the only organ of the State that might act was the Crown. The withdrawal of the Opposition deputies did not make it easier for the King to intervene, since the possibility of some sort of parliamentary solution, however improvised, was thereby made more remote. Had the Opposition minority stayed in the Chamber, the wavering official majority might have broken up. Instead, the Opposition waited in vain for Victor Emmanuel III to dismiss Mussolini. Confronted with a choice between a disarmed Opposition reflecting mass indignation and embodying the great Italian traditions of the last seventy years, and a violent Regime that still held effective control over the nation, the Crown chose the latter; the King did not dismiss Mussolini as the Opposition had hoped.*

During the six months of protest and waiting, the Opposition carried on an unceasing campaign of exposures of the accumulated lawless acts of the Regime and of prominent personalities of the Fascist Party. While an honorable place must be given to such journals as the *Voce Repubblicana,* the chief part was taken by Giuseppe Donati, editor of the Popular Party newspaper *Il Popolo.* Donati had been an anti-Fascist from the start. His Romagnole background, his early debates with such figures as Dino Grandi (before World War I), and his long association with Salvemini gave him a sensitivity toward the Fascist problem which few Catholic leaders possessed.

In June 1923 Donati had taken an unpopular stand in his own party: he had wanted to resign when De Gasperi and the Popular parliamentary group proposed an electoral law compromise. The compromise proved impossible, and the Party took a stand against Fascism as a result. With much of the Party's Right Wing now gone, Donati's position in the Party became much stronger, especially after the elections of 1924; he was its ablest journalist and most trenchant controversialist. As an old Demochristian, Donati was particularly angered by the mixture of religious and political arguments by which the Clerico-Fascists justified their new political alliance and attempted to undermine the position of the Popular Party among Italian Catholic voters.

---

* Giolitti, although he finally took a stand against Fascism, refused to join the Aventine. He held that the Opposition was failing to carry out its mandate from the voters and helping the Fascists to establish their dictatorship; the only possible appeal to the country would be from the floor of Parliament, where speech was still free. By withdrawing, the Opposition leaders had cut their last line of communication. In retrospect, Giolitti's position has obvious merits. See De Rosa, *Giolitti e il Fascismo,* pp. 25–26.

But the great novelty of the 1924 crisis for the Catholics was precisely this: the political autonomy of Catholics, which Donati and many other *Popolari* held to be an assured conquest of modern times, was flatly denied by the Pope himself. The Holy See directly and indirectly reasserted its authority in political matters, in such a way as to put the Popular Party in a particularly unfortunate position. The Party was "nonconfessional" but inspired by Catholic social principles. Could such a party take political action contrary to the express wishes of the Pope? And at what point did the Pope's wishes have the force of a command for the faithful? And for what motives can the Holy See intervene in the politics of a Catholic nation? All of these painful problems were openly raised in the crisis of 1924; only the desire of all sides not to go to logical extremes prevented schism and, perhaps, apostasy. The Party did not openly defy the Vatican (for a leader such as De Gasperi that would be inconceivable), and the Vatican did not openly and specifically strike at the Popular Party, which after all was guilty of no heresies, however its theories of political action might differ from those favored by the prevailing tradition of Catholic thought.

In the actual course of events, these abstract problems took a real and often agonizing form.

The national indignation over the Matteotti murder had an especial effect on many Catholics. The moral issue was finally joined. Filippo Meda conquered his habitual misgivings and came out against the Government. (He became lawyer for the Catholic *Giornale* of Mantua, a target of Fascist violence.) When the Government attempted to stem the mounting tide of opposition by a gag-decree, which in effect gave the State prefects, rather than the State judiciary, authority to confiscate single issues of offending newspapers and eventually to suspend them, the entire non-Trust Catholic press of North Italy protested.[16]

At this point of high tension, in July 1924, De Gasperi, now Political Secretary of the Party, attempted to present a "centrist" political formula that would hasten Mussolini's departure and prepare a constitutional restoration. He publicly outlined a possible coalition with the moderate elements of Italian Socialism, headed by the veteran Filippo Turati; he compared such a coalition to similar alliances in Germany, Austria, and Czechoslovakia. In De Gasperi's intentions, such an alliance would keep intact the essentials of the Popular program, while helping greatly in the postwar European process of Socialist "clarification"; i.e., it would winnow out the reformist "legal" Socialists from the revolutionary elements, and thereby broaden with new democratic elements the possible base of a Center government.[17]

De Gasperi and his supporters, Don Giulio De Rossi, Donati, and others, insisted that there was nothing incompatible with Catholic principles in this. If Catholics had worked with Liberals, why not with Socialists as well? Both were in equal opposition to Catholicism, theoretically. But Socialism was not a present threat in the nation, Fascism was; and the neopagan state-worship (*statolatria*) of Fascism was as deeply anti-Catholic as the "social heresy" of the class struggle or the Liberals' "agnostic state." The religious case against Fascism, which Donati pressed in 1924–25, was to be taken up by Pius XI himself in 1931![18]

Furthermore, the Popular senators and deputies who had left the Party, such as Cavazzoni, had themselves favored an understanding with the Socialists in the crises of 1922; their suggestions had been dismissed by Sturzo for reasons of principle. Now that times had changed, did they have any right to cry out against a similar arrangement as a "betrayal"?[19]

But at this delicate moment the Popular Party leadership was struck by a bolt of papal lightning.

On 8 September 1924 Pius XI took the occasion of a visit by some Italian Catholic students to make an important declaration:

> When politics draws near to the Altar, then Religion and the Church, and the Pope who represents them, have not only the right but also the duty to give particular directives (*indicazioni e direttive*), which Catholic souls have the right to ask for and the duty to follow. . . . Now, unfortunately, ideas are circulating among us that show a dangerous immaturity. For example, it is being said that any purpose of public benefit is enough to justify cooperation in evil; but this is false; such a cooperation (which of course can only be material) can be justified only by unavoidable necessity, in order to avoid a yet greater evil.
>
> Likewise the collaboration of Catholics with Socialists in other countries is mentioned; but, because of lack of practice

in making distinctions, two quite different cases are being confused. Aside from the difference of environments, in their historical, political, and religious conditions, it is one thing to face a party that has already come to power, and another to open the way for this party and give it the possibility of arriving; the matter is essentially different.

And it is truly painful to the Father's heart to see good sons and good Catholics divide and fight each other. Why, in the name of Catholic interests, oblige others and oneself to hold fast where nondenominationalism [*aconfessionalità*] is made a program, which in itself would lead to separation even from the Catholic denomination [*confessione*]?

But neither is it for Catholics to erect violence into a system or perpetuate the threat of it, and to continue the confusion and identification of the common good with some particular good, and to favor states of fact and of mind that can only lead to painful struggles, to disastrous consequences for the public weal.

Would it not be more fruitful, indeed necessary and proper, for all Catholics to put the great principles of faith and religion, which they profess and from which no part of their life can and should be exempted, at the basis of every activity of theirs, even political?[20]

This is undoubtedly one of the most important public utterances of Pius XI, coming as it did in the midst of a moral and political crisis unparalleled in the history of the Italian State.

First, it was a body blow at the Popular Party. Not only was the cautious feeler put out by De Gasperi denounced by the supreme authority of the Church, but also Don Sturzo's fundamental conception of an autonomous nondenominational party of Catholic inspiration was itself endangered. It was clear that the political autonomy of Catholics was deeply resented by the Pope. Italian Catholics, considered as a political force, should evidently be a compact mass at the disposition of the Holy See. Pursuing this line, though with fewer words and specifications, the Pope had likewise spoken against the Clerico-Fascists, who would deliver Italian Catholics to the Regime without conditions. The Pope wished to reserve to himself the political direction of Italian Catholicism, as an element useful in future negotiations with the Fascist Regime; this intention, so clear later, can already be conjectured in September 1924. Hence the characteristic lack of concrete recommendations in the last part of Pius XI's remarks.

Donati's *Il Popolo* tried to blunt the sharpness of the papal thrust with some unconvincing exegesis:

> As for Socialist collaboration, the Pope has mentioned the delicacy of the problem, which . . . puts on two clearly distinct planes the case of "finding oneself faced with a party already in power" and the other "which opens the way to this party." . . . Both cases have already occurred among the Catholics of Europe, for the collaboration of German Catholics with the Socialists corresponds to that with a party already in power, while that of the Belgian Catholics corresponds to the case of opening the way to the other party. . . . The pontiff's word . . . cannot be taken on the part of any Catholic . . . to turn it to his advantage in a political conflict.[21]

Osservatore Romano did not let this pass, but reminded its readers that Pius XI had not recommended a free examination of conscience, but had instead laid down a "positive norm," a "categorical directive": surely the *Popolari* did not mean to furnish a "pretext for disobedience"? *Osservatore Romano* quoted with approval the account of the Pope's remarks given by *La Croix* of 11 September: "the Pope must in certain cases give political directives which are obligatory for Catholics."

To this *Il Popolo* replied guardedly with another interpretation of what Pius XI had said: that the return to normality lay in preventing Italy "from falling prey to violence on one side or to bolshevizing subversion on the other."[22] The anti-Fascists of *L'Italia* (of Milan), Giuseppe Molteni and the young Piero Malvestiti, were also forced to hold a hard-pressed position with similar arguments.[23] Molteni wrote that the possibilities of collaboration between Catholics and "bolshevism" were academic, while the question of Catholic-Fascist collaboration was urgent.

Osservatore Romano caught this too: the Pope meant the extremes not only of bolshevism but also of socialism, which the Pope did not want favored "with the pretext of an opposition to Fascist violence that no Catholic can ever approve." Socialism, explained the quasi-official journal of the Vatican, is essentially "atheistic and materialistic," as well as "radically anti-Christian in practice"; Molteni was sharply reminded that Pius XI was not indulging in *accademismo,* as Molteni had "incautiously" implied, since the papal declaration included socialism and bolshevism in the same condemnation. *Osservatore Romano* made it clear that no one disputed the *Popolari's* right to conduct a struggle against Fascist violence; but the tentative move of the *Popolari* toward a constitutional anti-Fascist coalition was forbidden from on high.[24]

Perhaps the old intransigents of *Unita Cattolica* of Florence, came nearest to the mark in saying that the pontiff had criticized both *Popolari* and the "National Center." The intransigent journal held to a neutral position between the two, as if they were somehow equal masses.[25]

But even without the words of Pius XI it was clear, as the perplexed Catholic leaders of Brescia and Bergamo had shown, that De Gasperi's proposed alliance had no practical importance.[26] By late 1924 the Socialists were split three ways; the moderate Turati spoke only for the "unitary" group. A half-century of bitter competition between Socialists and Catholics could not be wiped out by a feeble gesture in a moment of desperation. The partisans of De Gasperi, such as Don Giulio Rossi, had to content themselves with pointing out that in the name of antisocialism, Catholic principles were being betrayed in the opposite direction by the Clerico-Fascists.

Whatever the reservations of the pontiff might have been, the tide of anti-Fascist opposition in Italy rose steadily in the closing months of 1924. Even the veteran Salandra finally came out against the Government. Yet the crisis dragged on unresolved. Since the Italian Parliament had been so effectively packed by the Government, only the Crown itself could act to dismiss Mussolini. The Crown had taken upon itself the fatal responsibility of calling Mussolini in October 1922, thereby committing itself to an unparliamentary course of action. Now would it take an even graver step, and dismiss him by the same sovereign act? It became clear that it would not. But in that case there was no escape from Mussolini's staying in power.

On 3 January 1925 Mussolini cut the crisis short. He announced to the Chamber that the responsibility for what had happened in Italy during the preceding months was all his, and that henceforth the Fascists would rule dictatorially. These declarations marked the end of formal liberty in Italy: the parliamentary façade behind which Mussolini had been operating was dismantled, and the real nature of the Regime became clear to all. A shell of parliament was left as a symbol of continuity, a monument to the Regime's legitimacy. As an active organ of government the Chamber was dead, and the crisis was resolved.

The great repressions took place in 1925. The Opposition parties, press, and labor organizations were silenced or dissolved. The independent Catholic press either died, like Donati's *Il Popolo* (11 November 1925), or conformed to the directives of the Regime, like *Il Corriere* of Turin, which had been founded shortly before in order to provide Catholic readers in Piedmont with an alternative to the Clerico-Fascist *Il Momento*. The Deputies of the Aventine were violently expelled when they tried to re-enter the Chamber, and then deprived of their parliamentary mandates; anti-Fascist leaders went into exile when they were able to escape imprisonment or, in certain extreme cases, murder.

Between 28 and 30 June 1925 the Popular Party held its last Congress, directed by De Gasperi. The young "Liberal revolutionary" Piero Gobetti, who was soon to die after a Fascist beating, has left this description of De Gasperi's last hours of leadership:

> Without any question, Alcide De Gasperi, who until a few months ago was only a proconsul, is today a chief. The Congress was in his hands. Tall, thin, erect, his neck made longer and solider by one of those high stiff collars that seem to give him dignity even though they are out of style, his eyes were watchful over everything. From the platform he . . . listens to all the orators . . . yet it is plain that he is holding in his impatience, that he is not happy with this oratory, that he is thinking of tomorrow's work. . . . De Gasperi is a man who knows that he has some pride. . . . He is annoyed by flattery, compliments, useless phrases. He does not know how to pretend tolerance, he has no need of showy popularity. Instead, he values the agreement and thought-out opinion of others. Yet, used to deciding for himself, he has no taste for discussion. . . . Even in a long speech or in reading a report he is cold and incisive; he gets effects not of intensity but of precision, underlining important points in a tone that is calmer, slower, more deliberate, with a lowered voice. At Rome, when the Congress threatened to become a public demonstration, he knew how to become arrogant, to forestall the worthy Degni, the heavy sentimental President, with violent outbursts, with a rigorous intolerance of any interruptions. I have seen him get angry, with the anger of a man who will not joke about an enemy who must be fought unceasingly, at a moment when the Congress was dallying in obvious sarcasms against the *duce*. He allows rest

neither to himself nor to others. . . . As a good organizer, he prefers administration to culture and criticism. . . . He uses sharpness of temperament to save time. His last report had only one central idea: to hold firm. He threw out his words like blows, without rash outbursts, but with a visible inner force. . . . De Gasperi always speaks from notes, with papers on the table, and knows how to be firm even when he is diplomatic. The evening of 28 June, answering remarks about his report, he improvised, but he was formidable. He spoke almost in a state of agitation, with nervous broken-off sentences. One could see in him the passion of an Aventine member, who has stayed at his post alone even at the risk of having no following. For in De Gasperi there is a boundless capacity for political sacrifice; this aptitude has been strengthened by a fierceness of resistance acquired in the struggle against Austria. It was natural that he should be . . . among the first after the Matteotti crime to sense the political question as a question of moral schism. . . .

The basis of De Gasperi's thought is Christian and democratic, and although in him a long practical experience dominates over culture, yet one perceives that behind certain dry attitudes of his he is not indifferent to the fascination of great ideas, and that he also conceals a sincere love of research. Then sometimes as a politician, he is ashamed of this and pretends it is not there, as if he had been caught in a lapse; he exhibits an almost crude sectarianism, he encloses himself in his party obligations. But this isolation is neither narrow-mindedness nor ignorance.

If you want to get behind this cynical energy typical of a political chief, quite capable of moving a vote of confidence in his own work in order to save time, contemptuous of any public hypocrisy, you will find a fundamental character of hidden goodness, of warm love for his humble farmers of the Trentino. . . . This country austerity and simplicity are at the base of De Gasperi's realism: and therefore in politics he shuns rhetorical ideologies in order to understand democracy in its most basic sense, as a struggle in defense of the most forsaken classes of society, that ask not for protection but for justice and independence, unwilling to submit to brute force.[27]

This Congress was De Gasperi's last public initiative for almost twenty years. In December 1925, he had to resign the secretaryship of the Party, for he had become a compromised figure: the Fascists kept accusing De Gasperi of pro-Austrian activities during the war, to which an answer was impossible under the new conditions of censorship. A target of threats and attempts at violence, De

Gasperi was arrested while trying to leave Italy clandestinely. Tried and briefly imprisoned, in spite of an indignant legal defense by Filippo Meda, he came out of jail shortly before the signing of the Lateran Pacts of 1929. By then he was a marked man, unable to find employment in Italy.

By the end of 1926 the Popular Party had ceased to exist, even as a political catacomb.

The six years of Popular struggles and disappointments in Italy had shown conclusively that Don Sturzo's ideal of autonomy, of a lay party of Catholics, was nothing more than a noble illusion. The political awareness of most Italian Catholics in 1919 simply did not permit of such a party: the affluent Right of the Party, which had a long record of nationalist sympathies, was inclined to ally itself with other forces of the Italian Right rather than embark on a social policy of fundamental reforms, while the Left found no understanding among the Italian Socialists until it was too late for any effective unity of action. Sturzo's Center lacked the concrete force to dominate the situation, for the Catholic masses, deeply anti-Fascist and slowly moving toward democratic maturity, were not really organized by the Popular Party: they remained, especially in the country, under control of the clergy, which in turn responded to the directives of the Pope.

Thus the Popular Party was an aspiration rather than a great political force. The real control of the Italian Catholic masses remained with the clergy and, consequently, with the Vatican, which used this control to achieve its own political-religious ends.

THE DECLINE OF THE WHITE LABOR CONFEDERATION

The fate of the White Labor Confederation was parallel to that of the Popular Party. Since 1919 the Confederation had been officially nondenominational, though based on Catholic principles of corporativism and class-collaboration. Some of its leaders, like Achille Grandi, were still under the influence of Toniolo's medieval reconstructions; others, like Giovanni Gronchi, were militant democrats. Though most Catholic labor leaders were personally enrolled in the Popular Party, the Confederation itself was free of party ties.

The coming of Fascism broke the 1919 equilibrium in Catholic labor, just as it did in Catholic party politics. Benedict XV had put direct labor action in the hands of an autonomous Confederation, just as he had left direct political action to Sturzo's party; Catholic Action was restricted to the formation of religious character. However, Fascist pressures, seconded by the wealth and influence of the Clerico-Fascists, had changed all this. Pius XI responded to these pressures by gathering under his own direct control, in the organizations of Catholic Action, the forces that had been freed by his predecessor. The White Confederation, like the Popular Party, was left to fight a last token battle for pure Christian Democratic ideals; the bulk of the Catholic forces was shifted to new positions and put under new commanders directly responsible to the Pope.

Leaders like Gronchi were not afraid to point out the element of betrayal in this: it was one of those rare moments in which even controversies with the authoritative *Osservatore Romano* were not shunned. Such boldness was not to be shown in Italian Christian Democracy after World War II, for the post-1945 type of Demochristian leader is a product of Pius XI's centralized Catholic Action, and has grown up under strict clerical supervision (a necessity of the Fascist era), while the old Popular and White leaders were trained in direct social action during the freedoms of the Giolitti era. The two types of leader are worlds apart.[28]

The "solution" of the Italian labor question in 1925–26 was simple. Legal recognition, as well as practical bargaining rights with the Italian National Association of Manufacturers, the *Confindustria,* was given only to the official Fascist unions; others were allowed an aimless existence as *de facto* associations. A worker could not belong to the official union if he had any other union ties.

At this point the Catholic Action organization entered the labor field, so long left to the White Confederation. Catholic Action could not, of course, organize any unions of its own, but it proposed to work on the moral and spiritual education of Catholic workers, preparing them for membership in the official Fascist unions. Although Catholic Action made clear its *theoretical reservation* about a State or Party labor-union monoply, it had no hesitations about reaching a practical arrangement with such a monopoly once in operation.

Catholic Action, which set up a special labor "institute" of its own, at first weakly defended the White Confederation's right to existence. But as it became clear that this was a lost cause, Catholic Action cut loose altogether from the Whites, declaring its own complete lack of concern for any other organizations. In plain words, the White Confederation was left to perish unlamented, and Catholic workers were encouraged by the new papally supported Catholic Action labor institute to fall in with the Fascist labor program. As if this were not enough, Catholics like Cavazzoni, now a senator, declared the new Fascist labor legislation to be harmonious with Catholic social principles.

Achille Grandi, Gronchi, and others put out between January and July, 1926, a monthly *Cronaca sociale d'Italia,* in which for the last time in many years the Christian Democratic view of political and labor freedom found expression in Italy. Characteristically, the first issue was seized by the police. The Catholic labor leaders' arguments were in essence two: first, that a State or Party labor union is *not* close to the Catholic idea of the corporation. The corporation, springing freely from the economic categories concerned and cutting across class lines, is a *source* of political power, an element of the national representation. Catholic corporativism works from the ground up, while the Fascist system works from above. Fascist corporations, warned the Demochristians, were nothing more than transmitters of State and Party directives, a means by which the State exercises control over the labor market. Nothing could be farther from the social ideals of the pontificate of Leo XIII. Second, Catholic Action, and implicitly the Holy See itself, were assuming a grave political responsibility by pushing aside autonomous unions of Catholic inspiration and authoritatively imposing collaboration with the Regime upon the Catholic workers of Italy. Since the Regime, with its repressive militarist character, was incapable of solving Italian economic problems, the working classes would fare badly under it, and a massive anti-Fascist reaction was certain. The Demochristians of the White labor movement warned the Church against committing itself to the Regime in practice, lest she too become involved in its disasters, or at any rate lose her position among Italian workers.

Furthermore, while the moderate ex-Nationalist recruits of Fascism, like Federzoni or Rocco, welcomed Catholic support, the "revolutionary" Fascist of the Syndicalist stripe, an earlier and more authentic element in the Fascist Party, hated Catholicism and suspected Catholic "conventicles" within the monolithic unity of Fascist labor; Edmondo Rossoni is a good example. What chance would Catholics have to make their ideals prevail in this atmosphere? The events of 1931 were to show how little Catholics could do.

After the middle of 1926, life became impossible for autonomous Catholic labor. The remaining 300,000 members of the White Confederation were faced with a choice of joining the official labor unions, which meant explicit withdrawal from their own confederation, or unemployment. Some leaders were arrested, and others retired. Gronchi went into business, and the other associates withdrew to private life, without much annoyance by the Regime: Mussolini must have thought them harmless. None of them was heard from publicly until World War II.

THE NEW INTELLECTUAL ATMOSPHERE AMONG CATHOLICS

Thus at the conclusion of this first part of our study, in 1927, the way was prepared for a final settlement between the Italian State, which is to say the Fascist Regime, and the Holy See. The embarrassments of Catholic autonomy were gone, to all appearances, and both sides were ready to make sacrifices in order to reach an agreement by which the Regime would obtain additional moral support and the Holy See a pledge of political security. The Lateran Treaty of 1929 was in the making.

To define the "treason of the clerics" perpetrated in 1922–29 would be the work of a controversialist, not a narrator of historical fact. It is hard to say how far universal religious concerns were in practice subordinated to the demands of a swollen national pride and to the fears of property: even the concrete benefits obtained for the Church may be called in doubt. Were the legal privileges guaranteed by the Lateran Pacts worth the moral price paid for them? This is a question outside the realm of historical judgment. But the effect of the new positions in matters literary, where practical activity and the life of the spirit touch, is open to historical and critical study.

Just before the curtain fell on Liberal Italy, the young Popular writer Igino Giordani warned that it would be fatal to identify the Church of Rome with the Bank of Rome, that Fascism was more insidiously anti-Catholic than Socialism, that fashionable postwar religiosity had little to do with the Catholicism of the ages.[29] But his book was published by the Liberal "revolutionary" Gobetti, not by a Catholic publisher. "Official" Catholic literature took quite another turn.

There was a definite pro-Fascist movement among Italian Catholic writers, culminating in the Florentine "little magazine" *Frontespizio* (1931–42). This was essentially a coming together of several distinct currents and personalities: the translator into Italian of Wagner's dramatic poetry, Guido Manacorda, the "imperialist" veteran of *La Torre,* Domenico Giuliotti, self-conscious Tuscan writers of "local color" such as Pietro Bargellini, and that embittered, thwarted "Socialist in reverse" Giovanni Papini, who had passed through Nationalism, Pragmatism, and a sort of mystical Nietzschean cult of the solitary superman, finally to arrive at a Catholicism *sui generis.* Manacorda was another "convert" of this sort. What united them all was a hatred of the dominant Italian school of thought, i.e., post-Hegelian idealism, both in its Liberal form (Croce) and in its new Fascist incarnation (Gentile). What perhaps enraged them most about Italian idealism was its positive element, its universality and insistence upon the unity of human reason. Against it they pressed the claims of a national and even a provincial-Tuscan soul, often mixing therewith an emotionally conceived "mysticism."

A lesser target of their ire was Christian Democracy and Sturzo. The priestly function was in their eyes degraded by any action in favor of the working classes, which would at best be a mere imitation of socialism.[30]

All this was truly an interpretation of Catholicism *ad usum ducis*: it served up for literate Catholics a new sort of Fascism with religious trimmings, in place of the standard philosophical justifications of Gentile, which were irreconcilable with Catholic doctrine. Such was the special task of these writers for almost twenty years.[31]

PART II

THE REVIVAL OF
CHRISTIAN DEMOCRACY IN ITALY
1929-45

Chapter Seven

THE CATHOLIC CHURCH AND THE
FASCIST REGIME

At first the Fascist government wooed the Church by restoring the crucifix and the catechism in elementary schools, by accrediting the new Catholic University at Milan, by raising state allowances and subsidies to the clergy, and by showing marked public deference to the Hierarchy. In so doing the Fascists' first objective was to isolate the Popular Party. But once the Popular Party was out of the way it became apparent that Fascism, now taking form as a "Regime," aimed at much more. Catholicism was to be a prop of the new order in Italy, an integral part of the Regime, in accordance with the prewar aspirations of the Italian Nationalist movement.

The first step toward a complete settlement between Italy and the Holy See was made by the Fascist minister Alfredo Rocco, a veteran of the Nationalist Party who had long favored making Catholicism serve Italian national interests. The Holy See showed a lively interest in the possibilities that Rocco held forth, and through the intermediation of Monsignor Enrico Pucci, a friend of Fascism within the Catholic camp, negotiations between the Regime and the Vatican were initiated in 1926. The first representative of the Vatican was Francesco Pacelli, brother of the diplomat Monsignor Eugenio Pacelli. His very name, associated with the Bank of Rome, suggested a conciliation of Italian and Catholic interests.[1] (On Rocco, see Chapter Two; Monsignor Pucci's services to Fascism are described in Chapter Five.)

Negotiations between Italy and the Holy See went on for nearly three years before a complete settlement emerged. At one point, when the Fascists suppressed the Italian Catholic Boy Scouts, it seemed as if the whole project might fail. But perseverance and the need for a settlement, a need which far antedated the Fascist Regime and the pontificate of Pius XI, eventually brought success. On 11 February 1929 a treaty and a concordat signed at the Lateran Palace resolved the Roman Question and regulated relations between the Church and the Italian State.

The Treaty, which affirmed the sovereignty and independence of Vatican City as well as the extraterritoriality of papal palaces and basilicas, generously indemnifying the Holy See and guaranteeing its communications with the Catholic world, raised few problems. The first article, which declared Catholicism to be the "sole religion of the State," merely echoed the Statute of 1848, the basis of Italian constitutional law.

The Concordat was another matter. In addition to securing the status of the clergy and regulating the appointment of bishops, the Concordat gave to the Church wide powers in areas of direct concern to any modern state. Article 34 guaranteed "civil effects" for any Catholic sacramental marriage performed in accordance with canon law. Article 35 guaranteed equal accrediting, through a state examination, of graduates of Church and State schools. Article 36 declared that "Italy considers as the foundation and crown of public instruction the teaching of Christian doctrine according to the form received by Catholic tradition." Teaching of religion was introduced into secondary as well as elementary schools, with teachers and textbooks approved by Church authorities. In short, Italy became a confessional state, unique among the great powers of contemporary Europe.

Although Mussolini, in presenting the Lateran accords to Parliament, did everything he could to lessen their impact, blustering in the style of Paolo Orano about the "Roman" character of Catholicism in a manner that Pius XI found worse than heretical, it was in fact clear that Fascism had paid a high price for a full reconciliation with the Papacy. Much of the work of the Risorgimento was undone in 1929, and the Papacy returned as a great force, at least indirectly, in the political affairs of the Italian peninsula.

The most important of the Concordat's provisions, in its ultimate political effects, was Article 43:

> The Italian State recognizes the organizations dependent on Italian Catholic Action, in so far as they carry out their activity outside of any political party and under the direct dependence of the Church hierarchy for the spreading and realization of Catholic principles, as the Holy See has directed. The Holy See takes the opportunity of the stipulation of the

present concordat to renew the prohibition for all Italian clergy against enrolling and working in any political party.

This article provided, in effect, that one carefully circumscribed area of Italian organized public life would be immune from Fascist pressure and coercion. Had there been no such solemn protection for Catholic Action, the seeds of a new Christian Democratic movement in Italy would probably have been crushed by the Fascists.

Within the ranks of Catholic Action, within Catholic schools and parishes, something of the Christian Democratic tradition survived and came to new fruition in the generation that grew up under Fascism. This revival was hidden behind the front of uniformity put up by the Fascist dictatorship, but it can be traced in retrospect, partly by reading between the lines of what was written under the dictatorship, and partly by consulting the testimonies of those who outlasted it. By putting together what appeared in the Fascist period and what was revealed after the Regime fell, the inner life of the Christian Democratic currents in Italy can be described up to the point in which they flowed together into a new party.

The Concordat thus protected the future possibility of a Catholic party, and the Party, after its public rebirth in 1943, in its turn protected the Concordat. Both Party and Concordat have become channels through which the Papacy exerts its extraordinary indirect power in Italian affairs since World War II.

These fruits of the Concordat were hardly foreseeable in the 1930's when the Fascist Regime and the Church lived together in Italy under the terms of the Lateran Pacts. In conditions of ever tighter totalitarian control, the Church was one of the few institutions in Italy that Fascism never penetrated: in the existence of this "island" lies one of the fundamental differences between the Fascist Regime and other more truly "monolithic" dictatorships of our time. However, the Church was rarely if ever a rallying point of anti-Fascist opposition: its attitude toward the Regime varied. At certain moments the Catholic world was prepared to resist Fascism, and in other circumstances the Regime received all the marks of Catholic approval. The Fascists never attained their goal, inherited from the Italian Nationalists of 1910–15, of converting Catholicism into an auxiliary of the Regime; and at moments of tension, Fascism often threatened to return to its own anticlerical origins, recalling the program of 1919. Whether it tried to soothe and cajole the Catholic world into serving Fascist purposes, or whether it showed its secular and overtly anti-Christian side, Fascism was always far from any genuine approach to the Church.

Hence relations between Church and Regime were uneven and fluctuating. Not only did Italian Catholicism embody many political and social differences, but the Regime itself was a perpetually wobbling pivot of opposing groups. For enmities within the Fascist Party anticlericalism provided an occasionally useful outlet, and the Futurists, Syndicalists, and youth leaders of the Fascist Party Left Wing were afraid of possible Catholic competition.[2] But the larger realities of world politics generally determined the relations between the Church and Fascist Italy, as may be seen from the following summary narration:

The Church and the Regime settled down to live under the Concordat between 1929 and 1931, though not without a serious quarrel. In 1929 the theoretical divergences between the Regime's and the Church's interpretations of the Lateran Pacts were stated in all their force. Then in 1931 the two authorities clashed in practice, and the Regime threatened to lay violent hands on the whole Catholic Action organization of Italy. Essentially the 1931 dispute was caused by a Fascist jealousy of Catholic labor and youth activities, however restricted, though behind the whole dispute there was a well-founded fear that the Catholics might be planning to launch a revived Popular Party should the Regime begin to falter. During the spring and summer of 1931 Mussolini unleashed the zealots of the Fascist Left Wing; the Pope responded with a series of protests culminating in the encyclical *Non abbiamo bisogno.* In September both sides came together in a practical compromise that allowed Catholic Action a genuine sphere of its own, though carefully hedged about with government restrictions.[3]

The compromise worked well for some time: 1931–38 were idyllic years. There were many points of contact between Church and Regime: education, Blackshirt and Fascist youth chaplaincies, missionary support and legal questions arising out of the status of the "allowed" Protestant forms of worship. The corporative organization of Italian economy, the "imperial" march into Ethiopia, a heretical realm, the war against the Spanish Republic, were all directly or indirectly advantageous to Catholic interests. Furthermore, Italy in those years seemed to provide a sort of guarantee for Catholic Austria and Hungary. A Catholic alliance stretching from Lisbon to Budapest, with its center in Rome, might shut out Communism, contain German expansion, and constitute a new force of balance and social order in Europe. Such hopes were in fact to be dashed by the logical unfolding of Fascism. Essentially a movement of inner repression and outward expansion, nourished on terror and war fever, it could never really settle down, in spite of the false impression to that effect which the Duce on occasion adroitly fostered.

The idyll between the Church and Italy ended with the change in Italian foreign policy. Between 1938 and 1943 the Church succeeded in disengaging itself from the Regime, as the needs of "empire" drove Fascism into full partnership, in spirit and in fact, with German National Socialism. The turning point came in the spring of 1938, when the Germans annexed Austria, putting an end to the alliance between Italy, Austria, and Hungary. Instead of leading the minor Catholic states, Italy herself was being swept into the German system along with Central Europe.

In the course of 1938 it became clear that Fascism would draw its future sustenance from German National Socialist doctrine and example rather than from Catholic tradition. The patterns of the Third Reich began to be imitated widely by the Fascist Regime, and the single aspect of Nazism most repugnant to Catholics—racial doctrine—came to Italy in the summer of 1938.* The introduction of racial lore and segregation into Italy was more serious than its farcical circumstances might suggest: to the cult of the na-

---

* Fascism in its origins was not racist, and the Duce himself showed little respect for racial doctrines in his famous conversations with Emil Ludwig. Racism began winning support among the extreme and pro-German Fascists after Ciano's visit to Berlin in October 1936. Even after the establishment of close relations with the Third Reich, Italy was officially uncommitted in matters of race, although Fascist journalists and hierarchs began a "racial campaign" modeled closely after the National Socialist lines of Goebbels and Streicher, and it was only after the 1938 *Anschluss* that Mussolini decided to apply racial measures in Italy. From the reminiscences of Ciano and Bottai it appears that the Duce actually came to believe in the racial doctrines imported from Germany; at least he showed every outward sign of taking them seriously. For a sketch of the Fascist racial campaign see Eucardio Momigliano, *Storia tragica e grottesca del razzismo fascista* (Milan, 1946).

tional state Fascism now joined the far more overtly pagan cult of race.[4]

The incompatibility between racism and Catholic doctrine is apparent. Many Austrian Catholics, such as Father Wilhelm Schmidt, had been combating German racial doctrine for years. In Italy, even the antirational "mystics" of the Florentine Catholic review *Frontespizio* scorned it. That Teutonic racial theories, impregnated with heresy and hostility toward the Roman Church, should become an integral part of Fascist teachings was a severe blow for most alert Catholics, although the expression of their abhorrence took the form of cautious qualifying statements and hints. Only Pius XI and, somewhat later, Cardinal-Archbishop Schuster of Milan, could permit themselves the luxury of open opposition: a fact all the more striking when it is recalled that both of them had been friendly toward Fascism in the years before 1938.

The reaction of the Pope was especially strong. In a series of speeches at Castel Gandolfo during the summer of 1938 Pius XI attacked "exaggerated nationalism" and modern racial doctrines at the very moment in which the Duce was attempting to root them in Italian soil. Naturally Mussolini was furious. His foreign minister, Count Ciano, explained to the Papal Nuncio, Monsignor Borgoncini Duca, that a clash between Church and Regime could not be avoided if the Pope continued attacking racism. The Nuncio himself found nothing wrong with Fascist racism, as expounded by Ciano, and revealed that he was personally "very anti-Semitic," an interesting reflection of a state of mind not uncommon in certain Vatican circles.

Nevertheless ill feeling between the Duce and the Pope did not abate, even after Ciano's explanations. The summer of 1938 was also a period of friction between the Fascist party and Catholic Action, resolved by a renewal of the September 1931 agreements. The "nonpolitical" character of Catholic Action was reaffirmed. However, the Vatican took pains to point out, in the *Osservatore Romano,* that the renewed agreement in no way affected Catholic attitudes toward racism, since this was a spiritual rather than a political issue. The Duce then indulged in another explosion of rage, declaring to Ciano that "if the Pope continues to talk, I will scratch the scab off the Italians, and in less time than it takes to say it I will make them all anticlericals again." Though Ciano and

Father Tacchi-Venturi, the authoritative Jesuit intermediary be-
ween Palazzo Venezia and the Vatican, labored together to heal
the breach between Duce and pontiff, it was clear that the idyll
between Church and Regime was ended forever. The racial legis-
ation of the Regime had inflicted a "wound" upon the Concordat,
as the *Osservatore Romano* put it, by restricting marriages between
baptized persons of Jewish race and other Catholics: here the resemblance to the Third Reich was unmistakable.[5] Pius XI even
wrote an autograph letter of protest to the King about it, though
without effect.*

Even the death of Pius XI and the election of a new pope did
not notably improve relations between the Church and the Regime. Though Pius XII (Pacelli) was smoother and more diplo-
matically expert than his predecessor, he too was horrified by the
Germans. The plain fact of the matter was that after the final victory of Franco in Spain in 1939 Italian foreign policy, now geared
to that of the Reich, no longer harmonized with Catholic world
interests. The Axis was no prop of Catholicism. For a moment,
in late 1939, it seemed that Italy might stay out of the war, with
strong encouragement from the Pope.[6] (Pius XII spoke strongly
to Victor Emmanuel III about Germany during the royal visit to
the Vatican on 21 December 1939.) But in June 1940, Mussolini,
anxious not to be left out of the division of the European and African spoils of war, intervened in the expectation of a speedy and
total German victory. The Regime launched the slogan of the
'Fascist War," a formula that recoiled against the Fascists themselves once the war began to go badly for Italy, and made it possible
for the Monarchy to repudiate the whole adventure.

The "Fascist War" in fact tied Italy to Germany's chariot
wheels, and had the consequence of loosening even further the
old ties between the Church and the Regime. Italy's new war,
unlike the Ethiopian and the Spanish conflicts, did not serve any
interests of Catholicism. Indeed, the Church had much to fear
from a victory of the Third Reich. Hence during World War II
the Church carefully "separated its responsibilities" from those

---

* See Rossi, *Il Manganello e l'aspersorio* (Florence, 1958), pp. 385, 389. The
Holy See's tactic of writing to the King may have been more than merely pro-
tocol, for the Monarchy was more powerful in Fascist Italy than it appeared
to be.

of the Fascist Regime. The *Osservatore Romano* became the pre
ferred newspaper of Italian anti-Fascists,[7] and Italian Catholics,
sensing the new coolness between the Holy See and Italy, began
drawing apart from Fascism. In other words, they shared in the
general divorce between the Regime and the Italian people, which
became final during the disastrous years of World War II.* In
common with other Italians, they could blame Fascism for an unpopular war: in addition, as Catholics they could accuse Fascism
of having taken a turn toward the most dangerous sort of modern
paganism, and allied Italy with a Moloch.

The disengagement between the Church and the Regime prepared the way for a revived Christian Democratic movement as
part of the general anti-Fascist movements of Italy. The stored-up
resentments of young Catholic university men and Catholic Action
organizers, of the lower clergy, of the countryside, gave a popular
foundation to the new policy. The original alliance between
Church and Regime had been imposed from above upon the Catholic masses of Italy between 1922 and 1929, but the turning away
from Fascism between 1938 and 1943 was spontaneous. Under the
innocent cover of a Catholic association of university graduates
(movimento laureati) the leaders of the new Christian Democratic
movement met and discussed what would be done after Fascism
finally collapsed. Typical of young Catholic intellectuals was
Dino Del Bo, who had grown up under Fascism as a convinced
Clerico-Fascist; under the impact of war and disillusionment, he
became a convert to democracy and openly expounded it in the
Florentine Fascist university press. That this could happen at all
was a symptom of the general change in the Italian atmosphere
between 1940 and 1943, and of the special changes in Italian Catholicism. During these years the war effort was failing, the dicta-

* For a lively picture of the moral decay of the Fascist Regime, see Giuseppe
Bottai, *Vent'anni e un giorno* (Milan, 1947), the testimony of an intelligent
insider who always hated the Axis tie. The Fascist Regime began breaking up
internally when Mussolini ignored his old collaborators, like Bottai and Grandi
and plunged into ever closer alliance with the Third Reich. Only the more
violent and fanatical Blackshirts like Farinacci stayed the course and upheld
the Axis cause until the end: Bottai, Grandi, and even Ciano himself finally
turned against the Duce and the Axis alliance, at the last session of the Grand
Council of Fascism on 24 July 1943, thus precipitating the crisis that ended the
Regime. See Paolo Monelli, *Roma, 1943* (Rome, 1945), pp. 160 *et seq.*, and
Achille Tamaro, *Due anni di storia 1943–1945* (Rome, 1958), I, 9, 63.

torship fell into discredit, and a new generation of Catholic militants was ready to reconstruct the Christian Democratic movement.[8]

Dino Del Bo survived to become a Christian Democratic deputy and minister in the years after the war. Another such figure, perhaps more interesting as an example of the changes that a generation of young Catholics went through in the late 1930's and early 1940's, was Teresio Olivelli. He was both an active participant in the Catholic University Youth Federation (FUCI) and an ardent Fascist. Like many young Fascists, he hoped that somehow the Fascist Party could renew itself and guide the nation; hence he remained faithful to it until 1943. He actually rose to be party representative in the High Council of Demography and Race at the Ministry of the Interior, a strange place for a Catholic. However, he sought to belittle "race" in his treatment of Fascist doctrine; for him, race was a purely empirical fact, capable of being moulded by the spirit. In his many Party relations with the Nazis, Olivelli acted with "subtle prudence," distinguishing sharply between the sociological *nation* of Fascism and the biological *folk* of the Third Reich. For him, Fascism was a doctrine of the historical state, equally opposed to liberal individualism and to racism. Though Olivelli's hopes of influencing Fascism from within were nothing more than an illusion, however noble, his personal case is an illustration of how many young Catholics could remain Fascists for years without accepting the Axis. When the choice finally came, in 1943, between anti-Fascist Resistance work and collaboration with the Germans, Olivelli chose the former, and died in a German concentration camp. He ended as a Christian Democrat, not a Fascist.*

* In 1943 Olivelli finally broke with Fascism altogether, was imprisoned by the Germans in September, escaped, and became a leader in the Resistance near Brescia, which the local Catholics in large part financed and commanded. Olivelli took part in both military and ideological resistance work, propounding a sort of Catholic Socialism to combat the inroads of Communism. In his view, the element of social justice in Communism had to be "baptized" and put at the service of a Christian social order, just as nineteenth-century Catholicism took over what was wholesome in the classical tradition of Liberalism. But in fact Olivelli's conception of liberty as an organic participation in society was ambiguous and showed little influence of any sort of Liberalism: Olivelli was far more influenced by the Fascist omnicompetent state of his youth. In this too, incidentally, he was typical of his generation.

When the Regime collapsed in July 1943 the ground was well prepared for the emergence of the Christian Democratic Party. The new party was made up of young Catholic Action leaders like Del Bo and Enrico Mattei, but led by veterans of the Popular Party of 1919–26. During the years of occupation and civil war, 1943–45, the young Christian Democrats, fighting alongside the other anti-Fascist parties, often took on something of a revolutionary coloring: however, the Party leadership kept firmly to a middle course, keeping in mind the great possibilities offered after the war to a moderate party.

The new party did not spring forth Minerva-like in 1943 as a full-blown political organization with a clearly defined character of its own. It was a coalition of young and old, of recent converts from Clerico-Fascism and ancient foes of the Regime, of theocrats longing for the days of Innocent III and Boniface VIII and admirers of French or American Church-State separatism. The various currents within it had grown up clandestinely or at least privately in the repressive atmosphere of the Fascist Regime. Brought together by a common faith, by common enemies on the Right and the Left alike, and by a common aim of social reconstruction and defense of Catholic principles, the Christian Democrats of 1943–45 were less self-reliant than the Popular Party militants of Don Sturzo's era, but they were, by training and mentality far closer to the Hierarchy and the Holy See.*

Olivelli was finally recaptured by the Germans, and died in Matthausen in January 1945. It is noteworthy that the Rector of the Catholic University of Milan, Father Gemelli, had tried to dissuade him from taking any active part in the Resistance. Gemelli, an old friend of Fascism, was little heard from in these days. The life of Olivelli, so significant as a "case history," is piously re-evoked in a study by Alberto Caracciolo, *Teresio Olivelli* (Brescia, 1947). See also Epilogue.

* During the short-lived freedom of 1943, Catholic Action publicly declared that it had nothing in its past to repudiate. Its great work, the Christian shaping of minds, had been carried on during the Fascist period in spite of official hindering and vexations, although at times papal support had been needed in order to survive. After the fall of Fascism Catholic Action could come out of the "catacombs" and carry its apostolate into new fields. See the statements of the Bishop of Parma and of Dr. Luigi Gedda, *L'Italia* (Milan), 3 and 9 August 1943. Though in August 1943 there was among Italians a general scrambling to assert anti-Fascist merits, these Catholic Action claims have a measure of historical justice.

Chapter Eight

THE CLERICO-FASCISTS AND THEIR MEDIATION BETWEEN THE CHURCH AND THE FASCIST REGIME

During the twenty years of Fascism there was one upper-class group of Catholics, for the most part Clerico-Moderates of the Right Wing of the Popular Party that had in 1923–24 defected to Fascism, that consistently upheld the alliance between the Regime and the Church. They included the Lombard magnates such as Stefano Cavazzoni and Livio Tovini, the Bank of Rome and its allies, and the press lords such as Count Giovanni Grosoli of the Trust, which dominated much of Italian Catholic journalism.*

They found it hard to tear themselves away from the Fascist cause even when prudence dictated a policy of reserve and waiting. For too long they had been the favored intermediaries between Church and Regime, their essential task during the Fascist period. Some Clerico-Moderates (such as Meda) had not passed over to Fascism, but they sank into obscurity after the suppression of the Popular Party.

Stefano Cavazzoni was among the most important mediators.[1] In the economic difficulties of the late 1920's he was charged with reorganizing the Catholic banks of North Italy, saving their original character. He was eminently qualified for such a task, since he was one of the few militant Catholics who enjoyed the Duce's personal confidence; he was also trusted by the Hierarchy and the lay leaders of Catholic Action.

From 1933 to 1943 Cavazzoni was the Government's representative on the Council of Administration of the Catholic University

---

* The political pasts of Tovini and Cavazzoni are briefly described in Chapters Three, Four, and Five. See also Igino Giordani, *Alcide De Gasperi*. Some idea of the active part in politics played by the Bank of Rome may be got as well from the pamphlet *Il Banco di Roma nell'economia coloniale, Estratto dagli atti del Terzo Congresso di Studi Coloniali* (Florence, 1937).

at Milan, a key position when it is remembered how important the University was (and is) in the training of Italian Catholic leaders.

The Rector, Father Gemelli, has said that during this period, in which the Catholic University was often attacked by certain Fascists (especially Fascist University Youth), Cavazzoni watched out for the University's welfare: "Every time that I asked him to go to Rome to safeguard the interests of our Athenaeum, he did so with great zeal."

Another Milanese Catholic leader was Cavazzoni's friend Luigi Colombo, president of the *Banca Provinciale Lombarda*. He was lay head of Italian Catholic Action during the period of *rapprochement* between the Holy See and the Regime, and claimed that during his presidency Catholic Action was neutral politically: both Populars and Clerico-Fascists belonged. "But the situation changed in 1930, when I resigned from the office of President, holding that I could not officially represent *(autorevolmente interpretare)* currents that aimed at dragging Catholic Action into the political struggle against the Fascist government."[2]

Cavazzoni did not finally accept a Fascist party card until 1940, the very point at which it began to lose its value. His motives were evidently not partisan: he had always held that Catholics could work with the old Nationalist element within the Fascist Party, such as Luigi Federzoni, and thus forestall the designs of Fascist "totalitarians." In wartime, he thought, an intermediary position had no value: the country's first need was for a strong government. No Fascist, from 1922 up to the Italian collapse, he believed that collaboration with Fascism was the best practical means of attaining higher national and religious ends; in this he stood for a whole category of Italian Catholics.

The Clerico-Fascist magnates made one notable excursion into the field of higher journalism, the *Illustrazione Romana* whose headquarters were in the Basilica of Saints Cosmas and Damian at Rome. Its first number appeared appropriately on 11 February 1939, the tenth anniversary of the Lateran Pacts. It was a lavish picture publication printed on glossy paper, full of advertisements inserted by Catholic banks and insurance companies. Its imposing list of advisers and contributors included many cardinals and senators, a Jesuit father of *Civiltà Cattolica,* a Monsignor J. P. Hurley from the United States, and many professors. At first its sole function seemed to consist in exalting the Vatican, the Monarchy, and the Regime in one breath.

The editor was Egilberto Martire, an ex-*Popolare* who had gone over to Fascism in the split of 1923.* Martire had been for years one of the leading exponents of peace between Fascism and Catholicism: hence his place at the head of *Illustrazione Romana* seemed natural. Yet his name utterly disappears after the first issue, never to be mentioned again.

The explanation came to light with the publication of the Ciano diaries (entry of 15 February 1939).³ Martire, a deputy, had said in the corridors of the Chamber that the sensitive Ciano (then Foreign Minister) had the evil eye and that he had brought Stojadinovich bad luck during his last visit to Belgrade. The bad luck held, for the well-named Martire spent the night in a cell at Regina Coeli!

In 1940 came a new publisher for the *Illustrazione Romana* (at Turin) and a new editor, Senator Livio Tovini, an ex-*Popolare* of the Clerico-Moderate group of Brescia.† Tovini saw in the Lateran Pacts an affirmation of a common ideal: "The light of Rome and the Fascist victories, the religious ideal and the anti-Bolshevik war . . . the safeguarding of the family and the purity of the race, missionary conquests, and national prestige . . . form an indivisible block." Tovini hailed "the new Italy, victorious peacemaker, Catholic and Fascist." After Italy entered the war *Illustrazione Romana* upheld the Italian war effort as a crusade par excellence, against the anti-Catholic nation, Great Britain, citadel of Puritanism and the Jews.

Tovini's principal collaborator was Gino Sottochiesa, who might best be described as a Fascist denouncer within the Catholic camp. He had embraced Fascism in the crisis of 1923–24, had served in the press campaign impugning De Gasperi's patriotism, when De Gasperi succeeded to Don Sturzo's place in the Popular Party, and had, most recently, lent his pen to the "racial campaign," one of the few declared Catholics who did so; he provided a sort of false Catholic representation in the ranks of Italian racism, though racism in Italy remained at best a sickly foreign importation however disguised. His melancholy public career was to

* See what is said of him in Chapter Five.
† See Chapters Three, Five, and Six.

continue with an appeal to Catholics to uphold the Republic of Salò in 1944.[4]

It is an interesting indication of how far the Catholic magnates were willing to go, that at a certain point even Sottochiesa was acceptable to at least one of them: the climate of Italian Catholicism in 1929–43 cannot be gauged without taking into account the public activities of the affluent Clerico-Fascists. Their services as mediators behind the scenes were important, and their influence was widely felt: their public presence on the side of the Regime helped to create a largely false impression of Catholic mass allegiance to Mussolini.

However, the lay Clerico-Fascists were not the sole mediating force between the Regime and the Church. From what has been said, the traces of a Clerico-Fascist element within the Vatican itself are clear; it is suggested in the remarks of clerics like Monsignor Borgoncini-Duca, Pius XI's Nuncio in Italy, who had found the Fascist form of racism not such a bad thing at all. This sort of Clerico-Fascist tendency was especially prevalent among the Jesuit fathers, one of whom, Tacchi-Venturi, played an important mediatory role behind the scenes; he was widely credited with being Mussolini's adviser in religious matters and even Father Confessor to the Duce. This last was not much of a task, since the Duce never seems to have been more than a reluctant and perfunctory son of the Church, little inclined toward religious practice and less toward belief.[5]

The Jesuits of *Civiltà Cattolica* offer the greatest known example of pro-Fascist sympathies within the Vatican. From the 1920's up to the war they were generally friendly toward the Regime and its chief aims, though it would naturally be absurd to suppose that Fascism had made any doctrinal inroads among these soldiers of Loyola. It was rather a deep political and social affinity that drew them to the Fascist Regime, a feeling that Church-State cooperation could best be achieved by negotiations between the Holy See and an authoritarian, paternalistic government.*

---

* See Jemolo, *Chiesa e stato in Italia,* pp. 623–33. Jemolo attaches great importance to the political attitudes of the Jesuit fortnightly which, according to him, always gives a key to current sentiments within the Vatican. Jemolo points out that *Civiltà Cattolica* has never been disavowed by any of the popes.

Like most socially conservative Catholics, the Jesuits of *Civiltà Cattolica* were impressed by Italian corporativism. Father Angelo Brucculeri, the eco-

Perhaps the most striking case of Jesuit approval of the Regime is to be found in *Civiltà Cattolica*'s comments on the Ethiopian War. As the Jesuit fathers describe it, the Ethiopians had been living under the "thousand-year yoke" of the schismatic Copts, and the promising Jesuit efforts to convert the Empire to Catholicism in the seventeenth century had ended in banishment and suppression. However, the Society of Jesus has a long memory, and quite evidently expected that Italian victory in Ethiopia would present a new chance for its missionaries: such was the implied conclusion.[6]

Much more far-reaching than these reflections on *Etiopa religiosa* were Father Messineo's doctrinal articles entitled "Necessità di vita e diritto di espansione," prompted by the Ethiopian conflict. Father Messineo, having in an earlier article refuted the widespread French theory justifying colonialism as a mission of civilization, proceeded to justify another sort of colonialism, implicitly that of Italy, as an act of social self-preservation.[7] Messineo finally declared:

We may now legitimately conclude that a state, under the pressure of vital necessity because of the narrowness of its own territories and the deficiency of the means indispensable to individual and collective life, has the faculty of appropriating a part of the earth possessed by others, in the measure required by its necessity. This power becomes even more evident if the material means necessary for freeing oneself from these straits lie inactive, in the possession of a people that does not use them, exploit them, and increase their value, whether because the extent of its territory is greater than its needs, or because of the scarcity of man power, or else because of a backwardness of its economic system. The order of nature cannot require that immense riches of the soil remain inert . . . while another nation overflows with population that it cannot nourish because of the absolute insufficiency of public and private means. . . . Vital necessity can legitimize the occupation of a part of colonial territory, in order to satisfy the needs of individual and social life.[8]

---

nomic expert of the group, praised the Fascist corporations and sought to reduce within as narrow as possible a compass the theoretical objections that Catholics might have to them. However, in this Father Brucculeri was simply following the lead of Pius XI's encyclical *Quadragesimo Anno*. See the citations and polemical remarks of Ernesto Rossi, *Il Manganello*, pp. 215–21.

Messineo went on to show that providing for the life necessities of individual members of a social organism is a *duty* of constituted authority, which must provide for colonial expansion to meet social needs, should the case be one of "extreme or almost extreme necessity."[9]

The application of these theses to Italian expansion in Africa was obvious, though it must not be concluded that Father Messineo would have endorsed the "living-space" theories of German geopoliticians. His doctrine of colonialism is hedged about with restrictions: colonial land must be underdeveloped, and more necessary to the colonizers than to its original possessors; if it is equally necessary to them both, then moral right remains with the original possessors. At any rate, Messineo's doctrines agreed well with the African aspirations of the Regime and its insistence on the rights of the "have-not" powers; incidentally, Messineo's doctrines throw light on another great meeting ground between Church and Regime, i.e., demographic policy.

In one other important respect there was a large area of agreement between the Jesuits and the fully developed Regime: Anti-Semitism. The Fascist racial campaign of 1938 did not at first disturb the Jesuits, for they had been conducting a fierce campaign of their own against Jewry since the mid-nineteenth century.[10] In Jesuit eyes the Jews were among the principal fomenters of secularism, for their original rejection of Jesus had left them with a false messianic aspiration. According to *Civiltà Cattolica,* the Jews, spurred on by dreams of world domination distilled from the Talmud and the cabala, disrupt Christian society by undermining the Faith; they spread their rule by using alternately international gold and the doctrines of revolutionary equality that had been fostered by them in the nineteenth century.[11] The Jesuits of *Civiltà Cattolica* accredited and propagated the ugliest tales of Jewish ritual murder, even during the famous Beilis case in Kiev (1911–14), accepted without question the guilt of Captain Dreyfus, and advocated the standard medieval treatment of the "Jewish question": Given the essentially perverted nature of Judaism, the only condition for Jews is segregation, a legal separation between the Jews and the nations in whose midst they are divinely destined to live. The civil equality of Jews must be revoked, and their ill-gotten wealth legally confiscated, in accordance with the maxim of

Peter the Venerable: *serviant populis christianis, etiam invitis ipsis, divitiae Judaeorum.* [12]

The Russian Revolution confirmed the Jesuits in their views, for Jews seemed to predominate in the first Russian revolutionary governments. (Incidentally, they mistakenly identified Stalin as an Armenian.) *Civiltà Cattolica* in 1922 concluded that Russia was in the hands of the Jews. Naturally Marxism was declared to be a Jewish invention, in language which *Civiltà Cattolica* never used after 1933:

> Only the perverseness of a Semitic fancy was capable of overturning all the traditions of humanity and erecting a society the foundation of which is the abolition of all property. . . . The good sense of the Aryan stock (*stirpe ariana*) would never have invented a code in which the principle of social authority was replaced by a central office of statistics.[13]

Yet the Jesuits distinguished sharply between their own religiously motivated campaign against the Jews and the extreme anti-Semitism of the twentieth century. They never gave credence or currency to the notorious *Protocols,* perhaps because similar forgeries about the Society of Jesus had been circulated for centuries.[14]

Even after the rise of Hitler the Jesuits vigorously promoted their own anti-Jewish campaign. Not only were the old themes of Jewish gold and subversions abundantly restated, but the Zionist settlement of Palestine was attacked as well. In April 1938 *Civiltà Cattolica* published yet another survey article on the "Jewish question," as the tide of officially encouraged anti-Semitic propaganda in Italy steadily mounted. The article, stigmatizing Jewry as "an equivocal nation and an equivocal religion together," called for the same old remedy, legal segregation without persecution; however, this was as far as even the Jesuits could go in the direction of Axis anti-Semitism as it was being imported into Italy in 1938 from the Reich. There remained a gap between them.[15]

When the Fascist press, especially Farinacci's provocative *Regime Fascista,* kept claiming *Civiltà Cattolica* as an ally against the Jews, the Jesuit organ decided to clear itself of any direct complicity in the Fascist racial campaign. Father Enrico Rosa wrote a short sharp note, "La questione giudaica e la Civiltà Cattolica," in October 1938.[16] Father Rosa denied flatly that the Jesuit fathers had ever called for a general confiscation of Jewish property: violence and reprisals against the Jews in the past fifty years, said Rosa, had been committed only by non-Catholics, like the Nazis. As always, the views of *Civiltà Cattolica* were in accord with those of the pontiff, though it was clear that the Jesuit fathers had nothing against a moderate anti-Jewish policy in Italy. Mussolini himself at the moment was not officially asking for much more.

The Jesuit organ did well in choosing Father Enrico Rosa to deal with Farinacci and his Blackshirt blustering, for Rosa was a conservative anti-Fascist, and had been an active participant in that odd and tragic exile-underground movement, the *Alleanza Nazionale* of 1929–31. Indeed, Rosa's anti-Fascism is in striking contrast to the line taken by most of his colleagues of *Civiltà Cattolica*, and shows how complex Vatican politics can be; however, in order to understand Rosa's position, some account of the *Alleanza Nazionale* itself must be given.[17]

The *Alleanza* was created by the critic and journalist Mario Vinciguerra, and its most active agent was the much-traveled Lauro De Bosis, a poet and son of a poet, Adolfo De Bosis. His mother was an American who had spent most of her life in Italy, where her father had been a Methodist missionary. Upon returning to Italy in 1929 for a summer vacation from the United States where he was Secretary of the Italy-America Society, Lauro De Bosis set on foot a clandestine propaganda organization. Between June and October 1929 he spread hundreds of leaflets over North Italy, traveling under the noses of the Fascist secret police without being detected. His propaganda was not revolutionary: above all, De Bosis called upon the King to remember his constitutional duties. The *Alleanza Nazionale* was unusual in that it eschewed all republican and anticlerical aims, which, De Bosis held, merely served to bind both Quirinal and Vatican to Mussolini's dictatorship. De Bosis hoped instead that both the King and the Pope could be induced to turn against the Fascist Regime once it became clear to them that the alternative to it was not red revolution, but rather a return to constitutional freedom. The army and Catholic Action, in De Bosis' view, could turn out Mussolini and prepare the way for a revival of Liberal-Democratic Italy. This was not a bad long-range conjecture, for the palace coup of July 1943 was not unlike what De Bosis had hoped for, but in 1929–31 it was a noble mirage, though it found eminent supporters here and there, especially Croce, the *pontifex maximus* of constitutional Liberal anti-Fascism, and Father Enrico Rosa of *Civiltà Cattolica*.*

Father Rosa, who felt that nothing good would come of the Church's dalliance with Fascism, sympathized with the *Alleanza Nazionale,* and through trusted friends quietly began spreading a number of *Alleanza* pamphlets among the faithful of Catholic Action. In Verona, always a strong point of militant Catholicism, there was a Catholic group following the *Alleanza Nazionale.*[18] Such sympathy was natural, for in its pamphlets the *Alleanza* urged anti-Fascists to take a friendly new approach toward the Church:

> The Pope is in continual conflict with Fascism over the fundamental problem of the education of the young and the self-styled "Catholic" but really anti-Christian character of Fascism. . . . Catholic Action is the greatest organization outside of Fascism and is covertly anti-Fascist. At the moment of crisis it will be a valuable liaison and rallying point, not only against Fascism but also against possible subversive agitations let loose by the crisis itself. It is necessary to act in agreement with Catholic Action, not against it.[19]

There is no telling how far Rosa and the *Alleanza* might have

---

* Father Rosa was an influential personage in the Italian Catholic world, a friend and adviser of prominent Fascists and anti-Fascists alike. Perhaps his most delicate role was as guarantor of the orthodoxy of Papini, Bargellini, and Giuliotti, on the dangerous border between theology and literature. As may be seen from these associations, Rosa had not always been an adversary of the Regime. In 1924 he had regarded Fascism as a lesser evil, far preferable to a coalition between the Popular and Socialist parties. Only in the controversy between the Duce and the Pope over the meaning of the 1929 pacts did Rosa show a genuinely anti-Fascist disposition. In the lead article in *Civiltà Cattolica,* 20 July 1929, Rosa drew a precise historical parallel between Napoleon in 1802 and Mussolini in 1929, illustrating the conflict between the claims of the Church and the ambitions of dictatorial rulers. The offending issue was immediately seized by the prefect of the province of Rome as containing "anti-Italian and anti-Fascist" statements, and henceforth Rosa was marked as an anti-Fascist. A few Fascist militiamen raided the offices of the Jesuit periodical the night of 27 May 1931, at the height of the Regime's campaign against Catholic Action, and there was even some wild talk of "bullets" destined for Father Rosa, though nothing came of it. The Fascists were careful not to take extreme and irrevocable steps, nor was there any reason for them to move with real violence. Father Rosa's opposition to Fascism was on purely moral-religious grounds, motivated by a loathing for the D'Annunzian cult of violence and by an abhorrence for the totalitarian state. There was in Father Rosa no sympathy for the values of Liberalism. See the panegyrical and syrup-laden biography of Rosa by Father Ambrogio M. Fiocchi, S.J.

spread these views had not the Fascist police suddenly arrested De Bosis' mother and several of his comrades, including Vinciguerra, while Lauro himself was on a trip outside Italy. Mrs. De Bosis was prevailed upon in prison to write a letter of personal submission to the Duce, which the prosecution suddenly produced when the *Alleanza Nazionale* group was put on trial before the notorious Special Tribunal for the Defense of the State. Together with Mrs. De Bosis' submission, the prosecution read a letter that her son Lauro had written the year before to the Italian Ambassador at Washington, in which he asserted his loyalty to the Regime. Although the damning letter had been written by Lauro in order to get a job representing the League for International Education in Italy, and was hence no more than a routine gesture of conformity, the whole matter reflected public discredit upon the De Bosis family and the *Alleanza*. It drove Lauro, who was staying in Paris, to a desperate resolve.

In order to redeem his honor, he decided on a one-man flight over Rome, dropping leaflets all over the capital in the face of Balbo's air force, a project he put into effect with the help of many anti-Fascist exiles, including the Popular Party veterans Sturzo and F. L. Ferrari. But De Bosis and his craft disappeared after he had successfully papered Rome with anti-Fascist leaflets on the evening of 3 October 1931. With him died the *Alleanza Nazionale* and many of the hopes of the "legal" anti-Fascists.

This episode serves to show that even in the Vatican there was an anti-Fascist current. Behind the great bronze gate were to be found not only intermediaries between the Church and the Regime, on both a theoretical and a practical plane, but also intransigent foes of the Fascist dictatorship. As matters turned out, both sides proved useful at one time or another for the purposes of the Holy See.

During the whole Fascist period one modest lay figure stood out in retrospect among the anti-Fascists of the Vatican, the Apostolic Library cataloguer Alcide De Gasperi, whose quiet "twenty-year secretariat" was an essential though hidden part of the inner life of Italian Catholicism.

Chapter Nine

DE GASPERI, THE EXILE OF THE VATICAN

Under the false surface of conformity presented by the Clerico-Fascists—a part of the façade of twenty falsified years—were seething the various elements from which emerged the Christian Democratic Party of 1943.

Unlike the other anti-Fascist parties, Christian Democracy had no tradition of exile. The few Popular Party leaders who emigrated in the 1920's never constituted a group: Sturzo was in London and New York, Donati in Paris, F. L. Ferrari in Belgium. The White peasant organizer of Cremona, Guido Miglioli, had gone over to the Communist peasant international of Moscow. Donati and Ferrari, both men of ability, died young; they had provided a tiny Catholic representation among the anti-Fascist exiles that was completely lacking in the later 1930's. F. L. Ferrari sympathized with the tragic De Bosis' "constitutional" opposition to Fascism, with its appeal to monarchical and Catholic sentiments; in a clandestine letter of 1930, Ferrari warned the president of the Italian Federation of Catholic University Students (FUCI) against commitment to the Regime. Among Belgian Catholics he represented a powerful antidote to Clerico-Fascism.[1]

But Italian social Catholicism had less need of a political emigration than did the other movements and parties. Its organizations were intact, however subject to Fascist threats and Clerico-Fascist pressures. Catholic anti-Fascists had little reason to organize a clandestine network when they could find a headquarters in parish houses and youth clubs. During the whole Fascist era there was only one small active Catholic underground.

Furthermore, a sort of Catholic political emigration was allowed to exist after 1929 in the new state of Vatican City, where some old Popular Party leaders had been given jobs in the library. They included the writer Giordani and the ex-deputy Cingolani, but the most important among them was De Gasperi.[2] After years of being shadowed by the police, he was finally left alone, as presenting no further danger, to be supported by papal generosity.

The Fascists never forgot De Gasperi altogether and during the dispute between Church and Regime in June–July, 1931, the daily *Lavoro Fascista* singled out De Gasperi as part of an anti-Fascist cabal within the Vatican. The matter is said to have reached Mussolini's attention, but nothing came of it. Again in October 1939, the Blackshirt leader of Cremona, Roberto Farinacci, a friend of Streicher, brought up De Gasperi's activities. Both of these attacks were made by extremists within the Fascist Party at moments of high tension: ordinarily De Gasperi passed without notice.[3]

De Gasperi worked on the Vatican library catalogue during the day, and at night turned out translations of books from German in order to earn extra money for his family. However, this period of penury and obscurity did not last long, for after 1933 he suddenly appears, under the pen name *Rerum Scriptor* or *Spectator,* as the bimonthly political commentator of the new Vatican bimonthly journal *Illustrazione Vaticana.* This novelty is worth considering, for in it can be seen something of the man's political development, of his long preparation for a new political career.[4]

De Gasperi began his commentaries at the moment of Hitler's accession and went on until the end of October 1938, when the *Illustrazione Vaticana* ceased, evidently a victim of the Axis. The life span of the Vatican journal is significant, for in 1933 Italy could be seen as a mid-point between two fanaticisms, as the protector of Catholic Central Europe; but by the autumn of 1938 she had become a pole of the Axis, and Catholic Central Europe was in the hands of Germany. De Gasperi's notes give a cautiously worded account of world politics in these five years and trace the decline of Catholic hopes.

De Gasperi's great theme is the "solution of the Center,"[5] of which Austria was one of the chief examples. His attention was held by the disintegration of European Socialism, in which he saw a great chance for Catholics. As the Socialists went to pieces, torn between Western Social Democracy and Soviet Communism, the other mass parties could step in and seize upon a rich inheritance. De Gasperi was aware of attempts at Socialist revival made by such French leaders as Déat and Renaudel, and followed Socialist debates with interest: he noted laconically that the Italian Socialist exile "Pietro Nenni saw in the defeat of German Socialism a final proof of the fruitlessness of the democratic program and method," a remark he may have remembered in his later dealings with Nenni.[6]

De Gasperi's middle way had a precise political sense. It followed the principles of the German Center, of which party De Gasperi wrote an eloquent epitaph after it dissolved under pressure from the National Socialist regime. The Center Party had stood for (1) nonconfessionalism, to avoid sterile religious strife, (2) a decided defense of the liberal constitution, as the only sure protection for Catholic interests once the medieval unities were gone, and (3) a welfare state that would satisfy the mass needs that had once found expression in socialism. These are the essential points of De Gasperi's Christian Democracy as well. De Gasperi made clear his own affinities within the Catholic camp; he admired the Catholics of Belgium, who had governed in constitutional freedom without accepting Liberalism and had launched an advanced social policy while combating Socialism. He preferred the French Social Catholics who finally accepted the *ralliement* to those who isolated themselves in an ambiguous alliance with Maurras.[7]

Nor was De Gasperi seduced by the vague formulas of Catholic corporative doctrine into repudiating modern political freedoms. A corporative Senate would correct the errors of a representative Chamber, but would not replace it. In Catholic thought the corporation, embracing labor and management, was a free natural growth, a part of a spontaneous return to Christianity; the corporation was not an organ of revolution (like Sorel's producers' syndicate), or of reaction (like Valois's *Action Française*), or of state control, as in Italy and the Third Reich. Corporativism in its classical Catholic form was a means of securing economic justice, varying from country to country. It was not a political formula. De Gasperi distinguished sharply between the moral imperatives of the Church in the economic-social sphere and the relative freedom that it granted in the choice of political order.

Hence De Gasperi followed with concern the political experiments of Austrian Catholicism. The Austrian Social-Democrats, with one foot in Parliament and the other on the barricades, got no sympathy from him in their hour of defeat. Their defense of the republican constitution had been coupled with revolutionary poses and a fanatical campaign against religion. No Catholic-

Socialist collaboration had ever been possible. Dollfuss, he explained, had been forced by pressures from the Right to install a temporary dictatorship: Austria's independence was at stake in 1933. But, he warned, the new regime must at once gain the trust of the now alienated Austrian working class, as a support against German National Socialism.

De Gasperi, anxious for the success of Dollfuss' new system, even excused his suppression of all but the "national" labor unions in Austria, pointing out that *Quadragesimo Anno* (the papal encyclical which served as the foundation of the new Austrian state ideology) did not enjoin freedom of labor organization under *all* conditions. At the same time De Gasperi showed his usual care in the keeping of distinctions and the separating of responsibilities. The Austrian authoritarian state was the result of particular historical circumstances, not a unique incarnation of Catholic ideals, however holy the intentions of its founders. Again and again De Gasperi fought shy of identifying Catholicism with any given political regime.[8]

Toward National Socialism De Gasperi showed the deepest apprehension. In his first political career, under the Dual Monarchy in Trent, De Gasperi had manfully opposed pan-Germanism as an aggressive foe shot through with heresy. Nazism was the same, written large. Even worse, the Nazis had found an ally in the Catholic Franz von Papen, possessed as he was by the usual "illusion of the too clever," that the Nazi revolution could be diverted into conservative channels. Papen's part in bringing Hitler to power was for De Gasperi a scandal, to be discreetly reproved in the cautious muffled tones of Vatican journalism.

Though De Gasperi prudently presented Fascism in a not unfavorable light, he always selected Mussolini's anti-Nazi and anti-Communist utterances for quotation. More important, he never likened Fascist corporative doctrine to Catholic corporativism. After the 1935 war his distinction between the two became explicit.

Thus in the first year of *Illustrazione Vaticana* De Gasperi had shown himself resolutely set against the two main principles of Catholic conservatism in Europe: (1) that Catholicism postulated an authoritarian political order and profited by it, and (2) that such an order could be set up by working with Fascism, Nazism, and other militias of "order." Of course the same could be said of collaboration with the monarchists of France. His positive political preferences are harder to trace, but they can be made out between the lines of his dispassionate summaries (and his rare outbursts of pulpit eloquence).

De Gasperi was a great reader of foreign Catholic writers and journals, such as *Commonweal* and Father Coughlin of America, Maritain and the personalists of France.[9] Against this wide background his personal conclusions sometimes stand out in sharp relief. Noting that Catholicism was flourishing at Prague and Ljubljana in spite of the fall of the Hapsburgs, he stated: "Although the cooperation of public powers is always desirable, what is important above all in contemporary life is that the Catholic Church enjoy that degree of ordered liberty that would permit her to live her own religious life publicly and integrally and to exercise her peaceful spiritual ministry."[10]

De Gasperi cited with approval Maritain's warning that the unfolding of the inner Christian life must take precedence over institutional reform, in itself a good thing but at times a dangerous temptation. All things considered, De Gasperi had in him much of the modern Catholic liberal, with all the doctrinal reservations and tensions therein implied.

But what was in fact the middle ground on which a Catholic liberal could stand? Gil Robles' *Acción Popular* in Spain, the Salazar regime in Portugal, Dollfuss' successors in Austria, were all praised warmly by De Gasperi.[11] Yet they were not ideal, and their experience was limited to small marginal nations. In De Gasperi's view the Fascist state in Italy was not really Catholic, and the Popular Front of 1936 was impossible for Catholics, since not even a momentary compromise was possible with the Third International. Ideally, social Catholicism should raise a standard to which the prudent Liberal or Social Democrat might repair as an ally. But in fact Catholic parties, when not submerged in totalitarian regimes, seemed themselves capable only of improvising stopgap dictatorships. The ground under De Gasperi was narrowing. Catholics seemed caught between an atheistic or anticlerical Left and a chauvinistic Right.

Under these circumstances it is not surprising that in 1934–37 De Gasperi looked to Great Britain and, even more, the United States for examples of Catholicism flourishing in freedom, coun-

tries in which republican freedoms carried with them no anti-
clerical tradition and in which labor organization, in unions or
in parties, implied no alliance with Marxism. De Gasperi was
especially impressed by Franklin D. Roosevelt and his friendship
with Cardinal Mundelein. The New Deal, with its undoctrinaire
concern for social justice, seemed a middle ground of exactly the
sort that Europe lacked.[12]

Unlike so many Catholics, De Gasperi understood the difference between liberal-humanitarian opposition to the Church,
limited, tolerant and even respectful, and the fanatical anticlericalism of the absolute political creeds from Jacobinism down to the
twentieth century. He mourned Masaryk in 1937: though the
Czech president had never returned to the Church, he had felt its
historical and moral importance.[13]

The Spanish crisis of 1936–37 struck De Gasperi as especially
disheartening. The extreme parties had had recourse to civil war
before the Catholic party could win a central position for itself in
the nation. Faced with a conflict, Catholics had to choose that
side which, however dictatorial, guaranteed the most fundamental
liberty of all, i.e., that of religion (which of course De Gasperi
understood in a Catholic rather than a Liberal sense).

Yet De Gasperi knew the German world too well to put any
trust in the 1937 anti-Comintern pacts. Blasted were the hopes,
cleverly fostered by Papen, that the Church could obtain from
Hitler a settlement like that concluded with Italy. De Gasperi
increasingly turned away from Central Europe to Belgium and
France, where there was still some room for the free play of Catholic forces, though in a Liberal context.

In Western Europe, he noted, Catholics were aware of the
benefits of constitutional freedoms: the Belgian bishops firmly rejected Degrelle's advances. But in France the Catholics had no
real party of their own and had to bring up the rear of other movements, often alien to them. Furthermore, the weaknesses of the
French State did not escape De Gasperi's notice, and he sharply
observed that if the French conservatives and liberals had recourse
to private militias like the Cagoulards in order to combat the Left,
then the Liberal cause was lost. A constitutional state must defend
itself by its own forces, in accord with its own laws.[14]

De Gasperi's tone suddenly rose in February 1938, with the

final German push against Austria. Ordinarily calm, he now recalled with passion the glories of Catholic Austria: "The frontier
defended at Vienna is a frontier of ideas, of aspirations, of *Weltan-
schauung*."[15] Something of the man himself comes through, for it
was his own past that was being borne away. The rest of 1938 must
have been painful in the extreme; he noted regretfully that the
last remnant of Austrian Social Catholicism, still surviving among
the German Catholics of Bohemia-Moravia, was absorbed by
Henlein.[16] Hungary now entered the German orbit. Belgian and
French Catholicism offered continued hope, but Degrelle was
making progress among the youth.

Illustrazione Vaticana had suggested that the *Anschluss* was a
grave blow to Italy, regardless of supposed affinities of regime between Italy and Germany. Though these remarks were veiled in
hypothetical and impersonal constructions, their drift was plain.[17]
At the end of October 1938 the bimonthly publications ceased for
good. In the new atmosphere of Axis Italy such periodicals had
no chance of life.

De Gasperi had shown much of his own political character in
these five years of study and comment. His "solution of the Center" was flexible. One type of Center position was the corporative-
military regime (Salazar, Dollfuss). Another was the Catholic
minority in America or England, a religious leaven in a mass of
Protestants or unbelievers, free to develop along its own lines.
However, from what he wrote between 1933 and 1938 there emerges
another possibility: a great national Catholic party working with
other constitutional parties of Liberal or Social-Democratic coloring. Collaboration with other forces would be for specific limited
ends, and mutual trust would be ensured by the observance of constitutional freedoms. By putting aside old dreams of an integral
authoritarian restoration, Catholicism would be able to expand
freely. This was De Gasperi's solution of 1943–53.

There remains a deeper problem. Was De Gasperi's evident
preference for constitutional-democratic political solutions a matter of tactics, a judgment of what was prudent for Catholicism?
Or was it rather a moral commitment deriving from a certain view
of human nature and its possibilities for self-government? Or,
rather, was his concern with freedom a consequence of an insight
into sinful humanity, an expression of the belief that no frail

human creature had the right to dictate to his fellows? Certainly to a man whose primary concern is with the salvation of souls politics cannot be an absolute value in itself. In any hierarchy of values politics would have to take a place below the inner life of the soul. But the question remained open. The encyclicals of Leo XIII and Pius XI enjoin the safeguarding of certain principles of social justice: De Gasperi always insisted that they contained no precise political directions. But is social justice possible without certain fundamental political liberties, which therefore have an indirect religious sanction?

To these problems, which are the heritage of European liberal Catholicism and some of its "social" descendants, we do not know De Gasperi's solution.

Chapter Ten

THE ITALIAN CATHOLIC UNIVERSITY FEDERATION

In the course of his work in the Vatican De Gasperi came into regular contact with the most lively part of Italian Catholic Action, the university students' federation (FUCI), from the ranks of which were to come forth many young leaders of the 1943 Christian Democratic Party.

The FUCI had passed through a postwar crisis, finally being reorganized in 1925 by a dynamic twenty-one year old president, Igino Righetti of Rimini and a new ecclesiastical assistant, Monsignor G. B. Montini. Righetti was provincial and nationalist in background, Montini a son of the Brescia Popular deputy Giorgio Montini, one of the Clerico-Moderate magnates who had *not* gone over to Fascism when the Popular Party split in 1923.*

Under Righetti's presidency the FUCI had one great task: to train "a militant intellectual elite" of Catholics in the unfavorable conditions of Fascist Italy. Righetti was never a Fascist. In 1924, when it was still possible, he had carried on a polemic against the Fascist identification of Party and State. Firm of character and utterly devoted to his cause, Righetti made the FUCI an incubation ground for Catholic leaders. Though Righetti himself never took a Fascist party card, most Catholic students joined the Fascist University Youth (GUF) together with FUCI.

The journals founded or reorganized under Righetti, *Studium,* the FUCI cultural organ, and *Azione Fucina,* its news sheet, were both free of the usual Clerico-Fascist rhetoric. What concessions they made were to Italian patriotic sentiment, as at the time of the popular Ethiopian conflict, when many Italians who were not

---

* Monsignor Montini is at present a cardinal and Archbishop of Milan. See Monsignor Guido Anichini, *Cinquant'anni di vita della F.U.C.I.* (Rome, 1947), which mentions the high offices held by Gonella, Moro, and Andreotti in FUCI between 1927 and 1944. But the most helpful book about this group is Augusto Baroni, *Igino Righetti,* with a preface by Monsignor G. B. Montini (Rome, 1948). Most of this section is based on it.

Fascists at all upheld what was felt to be a national war. In the sudden freedom of September 1943 *Studium* could look back on its own past without shame or embarrassment; it had been forced at times to take refuge in dignified silence or to speak with obvious reserve, but it had never put its pinch of incense on the Fascist altar. Furthermore, it had maintained some cultural standards, at times in which the rest of Catholic Action had been satisfied with sermons and devotions. *Studium*'s cautious political comments had followed the central Vatican line, against both Nazism and Communism, rather than the pro-Axis line accepted by so many conservative Catholics.[1]

The Righetti-Montini groups had a continual struggle for survival. The existence of a Catholic cyst within the Italian body politic disquieted the Fascists on the one side, and on the other aroused the suspicions of conservative-Clerical elements in the Catholic world itself. Movements such as the FUCI or the Catholic University Graduates (*Movimento Laureati*), fostering a lay leadership, could create serious problems for the higher clergy. Any lay leadership would have to be responsive to pressures from the Catholic masses. But in fact the young lay leadership trained in the 1930's was securely held in Clerical leading-strings all during the Fascist period, and even today its relation to the Holy See and the Hierarchy is a great problem of Italian politics. Given the totalitarian conditions of Italy in the 1930's, lay autonomy was out of the question. Indeed, Righetti and Montini succeeded in rearing a new generation of Catholic political leaders only because they had the backing of Pius XI himself.

The 1931 dispute is a case in point. Catholic youth organizations were among the principal objects of Fascist attack. The Fascists declared FUCI membership a bar to entering or remaining in the GUF and raided FUCI groups throughout Italy. Righetti and an FUCI deputation were accorded on 18 May a remarkable special audience by Pius XI, in which the Pope declared to Righetti that every Fascist outrage or abuse should be reported to him personally: the conversation between Pius XI and Righetti was carried in the *Osservatore Romano* on 21 May, heightening the tension between Church and Regime. Finally, at the end of May, FUCI and the general Catholic youth organization were dissolved by the police. The dissolution, oddly enough, struck at the branches but not at central headquarters: evidently the Fascists did not wish to go beyond a certain point. *Studium* was able to go on.

Righetti and his collaborators, dogged by the police, were told by the Holy See to take refuge in Vatican City, where they stayed for the rest of the crisis, though making a few daring excursions into Italian territory. In the sultry Roman summer of 1931 the dispute came to a halt, and in September a settlement was reached.[2]

Under the post–1931 system the whole of Italian Catholic Action lost much of its resemblance to a social movement: public rallies, standards, and membership cards were altered or restricted. More substantially, local heads of FUCI were no longer to be elected, but named by ecclesiastical superiors. Though at first it made little difference, since under Pius XI sympathetic clerics confirmed the incumbents or ratified choices made from below, this provision was clearly aimed against the appearance of any lay autonomy among young Catholics. The lay Catholic leadership of Italy, which had enjoyed considerable autonomy under Benedict XV, had brought forth the Popular Party, the specter of which still haunted many Fascists. In 1931, as a condition of the settlement of September, the Regime insisted that former Popular leaders be removed from high places in Catholic Action.

At any rate FUCI could live normally after 1931, provided that it remained inconspicuous. But a young man who was prominent in it naturally prejudiced his chances of a career under Fascism. A special police agent was always present at both FUCI and *Laureati* meetings, a witness to the Regime's constant suspicions. There was even an attempt to outflank Righetti and the FUCI by setting up chaplaincies in the GUF. Such religious facilities would have given the Regime and its Catholic allies a pretext to claim that FUCI served no further purpose. The proposal was rejected after Righetti strongly objected.[3]

But the Righetti group's problem was internal as well. It aimed at training an autonomous elite, free from any taint of the Regime and imbued with Catholic social principles. Instead, the dominant trend in Catholic Action was to leave leadership almost entirely to ecclesiastical assistants, organize devotional exercises and pious pilgrimages at the expense of cultural activity, and go along passively with the Regime. Though Pius XI himself seems to have held that FUCI students should be trained for future tasks of leadership by bearing some responsibility themselves, the Federation, at first a little restive under the post-1931 arrangements, sank into attitudes of prudence and passivity, becoming part of the conformist Italy of the 1930's.[4]

Righetti stood against the tide, with a measure of papal support. After 1934, when he left the FUCI presidency, he occupied the chair of comparative law at the Pontifical Lateran Athenaeum, a post free of Fascist oaths, and went on with his work of organization. Incidentally, it is interesting to note the parallels with De Gasperi's life in the same period. In 1932 Righetti had stepped outside the regular framework of Catholic Action to organize militant Catholic university graduates in the *Movimento Laureati*. An elite movement, the *Laureati* consisted of several nuclei that maintained informal contact through bulletins and meetings. After 1933 they took over *Studium* and gave it a serious cultural content: in early 1943 the anti-Fascist La Pira was among its contributors. After 1936 the *Laureati* held a yearly "week of religious culture" in the mystic wood of Camaldoli, to which came anti-Fascist priests like Don Primo Mazzolari of Bozzolo (Lombardy) as well as future archbishops like Montini and Siri.[5]

In these initiatives Righetti showed a certain ingenuity. When he was president of the FUCI in 1927, he had founded *Studium* in the form of an independent publishing house, which would be able to carry on if the FUCI itself were dissolved, as almost happened in 1931. The *Laureati,* as organized by Righetti and sanctioned by Pius XI, benefited from the 1929 Concordat guarantees of Catholic Action, but yet enjoyed independence from the mass organization thereof. Righetti was free to enroll Catholic university graduates who were not Catholic Action members at all, who would be repelled by the dull and conventional atmosphere of the regular Catholic Action organization.

The last years of Righetti's life passed amid new crises.[6] Up to 1938 he had the support of Monsignor Bernareggi, Bishop of Bergamo; however, as Church-Regime relations tautened in the course of that year, the Bishop himself lost ground. During the summer of 1938 Righetti had to fight for government permission to hold a national congress of the FUCI at Florence, while the cautious leaders of Catholic Action wished to renounce both FUCI and *Laureati* yearly meetings. The meetings were finally held, but

Monsignor Bernareggi was forbidden by ecclesiastical authority to attend the *Laureati* meeting, though he was their ecclesiastical assistant. The meeting itself was permitted by the same authority under severe restrictions: the general reports would be given by priests only, without any discussion from the floor. The regular Catholic Action leadership was thus able, in an atmosphere heavy with the fear of Fascist reprisals, to compromise Bernareggi and put Righetti's life work in jeopardy.

The dispute between the Righetti group and the official Catholic Action leadership lasted till the war. Righetti followed his pontiff to the grave on 17 March 1939, but Monsignor Bernareggi and the *Laureati* went on, vigorously defending their semi-autonomous position. Finally on 20 April 1941 Pius XII spoke to the assembled leaders of the FUCI and the *Laureati* of "your apostolate at the side of and at the dependence of the ecclesiastical Hierarchy," a very carefully and ambiguously worded recognition of their importance in the Catholic world.[7]

By then the Italian (and world) situation was shifting fast. The cracks in the Fascist Regime were widening, and the need for a Catholic lay leadership of some sort was manifest. FUCI and the *Laureati* were consequently re-evaluated, though the problems posed in the course of Righetti's life remained and remain unsolved. The relation between lay leadership and Hierarchy in the religious, socio-economic, and political spheres is still ambiguous: is it one of direct dependence, indirect dependence, "autonomy," or real independence? The history of the 1930's and 40's seems to shut out at least the last-named possibility; but it remains to define the degrees of autonomy and dependence.

The Christian Democratic nucleus of 1943 that gathered around De Gasperi was largely drawn from the FUCI-*Laureati* group: several of its members—Guido Gonella and Aldo Moro from among Righetti's comrades, Giulio Andreotti from among the younger FUCI leaders—rose to high place in both Party and Government after the war.

Contacts with De Gasperi began much earlier. In 1932 Gonella left *Studium*,[8] and in 1933 appears as *direttore responsabile* of the bimonthly *Illustrazione Vaticana*, the vehicle for De Gasperi's political comments. Gonella's own political reportage appears there over the transparent pen name *Gog*. From 25 December

1936 to 10 November 1938 Gonella also edited a bimonthly supplement to *Illustrazione Vaticana,* called *Rassegna internazionale di documentazione,* a wide survey of world political journalism, remarkable for its anti-Nazi "slant." It died with its parent organ.[9]

The Fascist police had an informer within the administrations of *Illustrazione Vaticana* and the *Osservatore Romano,* and Gonella was eventually arrested at a particularly tense moment.[10] In the autumn of 1939 Catholic opinion prevalently favored Poland as against Germany: there was a clear divergence between the balanced political line of the Holy See, almost equally hostile to Berlin and Moscow, and the Clerico-Fascist acceptance of the Axis, with its totalitarian consequences. Fascism had won over some significant Catholic elements: the Catholic University of Milan, the Lombard and Roman magnates, the Papini literary group of Florence. But the bulk of Catholic Action, however timid, had not rallied to the Axis, and isolated elements within it, especially the La Pira group in Florence, were clearly opposed. Even Cardinal-Archbishop Schuster of Milan, who in 1937 had gone so far as to celebrate the *mistica fascista,* late in 1938 came out against the "Nordic heresy" from over the Alps. The organ of Milanese Catholic Action, *Italia,* critical of Papini in July 1938 and revolted by the German pogroms of November 1938, was openly pro-Polish in September 1939, even quarreling with the "fascistized" *Corriere della Sera* in defense of the Polish bastion of Catholicism.[11]

At this moment of stress, on 5 October 1939, the extremist *Regime Fascista* of Cremona revealed that "the notorious Professor Gonella," by now assistant editor of *Osservatore Romano,* had been arrested on charges of working against the Regime, though later released. Further, Gonella and his chief editor, Count Dalla Torre, were now at work to obtain Vatican City citizenship for De Gasperi, so that he could join their staff and prepare for the return of Don Sturzo (!). *Regime Fascista* implied that Monsignor Montini, son of a Popular ex-deputy, was part of the plot. Though FUCI was not mentioned, it was the FUCI group that had been singled out.

This sensational glance behind the scenes was part of Roberto Farinacci's personal campaign within the Fascist Party for an ever more "totalitarian" line, in accord with the Axis policy. However, this note of his does furnish the only public mention of this obscure period in the careers of Gonella and De Gasperi. De Gasperi was now silent, while Gonella wrote the *Acta Diurna* of the *Osservatore Romano* anonymously. Their publications had been cut off and their persons threatened; in 1939–40 the Regime seemed strong and intransigent, riding the German wave.

But the wartime disasters of 1940–42 and the inner crumbling of Fascism in those years would allow De Gasperi, Gonella, and their collaborators to take up anew their slow and patient work of propaganda and organization.[12] The young leaders trained in FUCI were to be initiated into political life by their veteran leader, De Gasperi, who had done so much during the Fascist period to link the Popular Party of the 1920's with the new generation raised in Catholic Action.

Chapter Eleven

SCATTERED CHRISTIAN DEMOCRATIC MOVEMENTS

LA PIRA AND THE CHRISTIAN DEMOCRATS OF FLORENCE

Before the final collapse of the Regime in 1943 De Gasperi and his FUCI-*Laureati* associates of Rome had come into close contacts with two notable anti-Fascist Catholic nuclei, the La Pira group in Florentine Catholic Action and Malvestiti's Guelf movement in Lombardy. Both groups suffered Fascist reprisals, both rallied to the reorganized Christian Democracy of 1943 and to the Resistance struggle, both entered De Gasperi's postwar governments.

The La Pira group operated in one of the Italian regions most deeply permeated with Fascism, often in its most violent forms. Even Mussolini's "Social Republic," the last and darkest of his political incarnations, attracted many young Tuscans.

Much Florentine anti-Fascism was itself of Fascist origin, for in the late 1930's the Regime began losing its grip on much of the educated youth of Tuscany and Rome. The nonconformist "little magazines" of 1930–36, heirs of Futurism, were cheerfully Fascist, occasionally pro-Soviet, and perpetually anticlerical, all at the same time. Within Fascism their young editors represented, however confusedly, an aspiration toward progress and freedom, together with scorn for the oppressive pseudo-Roman trappings of the Regime and for its use of Catholicism as an instrument of political conservation.* Bottai was their only real patron in the higher ranks of the Party. For a while they were tolerated, but with the shift toward a stifling totalitarian imitation of the Third Reich, which began 1936–38, they were silenced one by one. Eventually most of them passed to Communism or the revolutionary democratic Party of Action.

The Catholic environment itself took on some Fascist coloring.

---

* See especially *Il Cantiere* (1934–35). Of the *Cantiere* group Giorgio Granata became a Left Liberal and Romano Bilenchi a Communist after they became disillusioned with Fascism.

Its intellectual life was represented in large measure by *Fronte-spizio,* the organ of Giovanni Papini, Guido Manacorda, and Piero Bargellini.[1] The editors' backgrounds lay, respectively, in thwarted nationalism, a turbid antirational "mysticism," and a cult of provincial folk art, whence they had all come to a sort of Catholicism that did not exclude open contempt for Catholic Action. Though *Frontespizio* balked at German racial doctrine and scorned its Italian missionaries, it was nevertheless thoroughly Fascist in tone and content. Papini was a favorite of the Ministry of Popular Culture, especially during the war.*

In this atmosphere of Fascism tempered by disillusion there was suddenly heard a new Catholic voice, an "ascetico-mystical" review of "spirituality," which came out once every two months at the Dominican convent of St. Mark (Savonarola's home). *Principî,* published from January 1939 to February 1940, with approval of the Order, was principally the work of Professor Giorgio La Pira, who taught Roman Law at the University of Florence. The journal proposed to examine social problems in the light of pure Christian doctrine, at the same time appealing to "the healthier natural-law tendencies."

In fact *Principî* was an evangelical protest against the prevailing political systems of Europe in 1939, put largely in pertinent passages from the Fathers and Doctors of the Church. The choice of doctrinal passages revealed clearly La Pira's unexpressed intentions: indeed, this was an excellent way of publicly dissenting,

---

* See Papini's unsympathetic observations on the British in *Il Ragguaglio 1940–1941,* pp. 192–93. Papini's role as a friend of Fascism among Italian Catholics was constantly in evidence. During the racial campaign of 1938 Papini wrote *discorsetti* scolding Catholics for their unsatisfactory attitudes toward Fascism (*Frontespizio,* July 1938). Mario Luzzi in *L'Italia* of Milan, 29 July 1938, accused Papini of "defamation of organized Catholics" at a difficult moment, to which Papini replied in *L'Avvenire d'Italia* (4 August 1938), that his "innocent words" had been misunderstood!

The other *Frontespizio* Catholic writers were equally philo-Fascist in these years of the Axis. In *Frontespizio* (December 1937, pp. 883–90), Piero Bargellini denounced French rule in Corsica, a prime objective of Fascist expansion. His colleague Guido Manacorda, writing one month later, ridiculed democracy as practiced in America, France, and Britain. As he saw it, a liberty that put the Church and Father Divine on the same level was nothing more than spiritual chaos: America had a corrupting influence on Catholic faith. See *Frontespizio,* January 1938, pp. 3–11. Yet even *Frontespizio* was opposed to the importation of racism into Italy. See *ibid.,* p. 25.

since the Regime could hardly object to orthodox theological texts, however subversive their possible implications.

Principî began by examining the words *hierarchy* and *mysticism,* words current in Fascist writing for many years.[2] La Pira's articles restored their original religious-philosophical meaning. All hierarchies, including those of human society, culminate in God. The temporal world, politics, is subordinate to the spiritual world, the Church. The doctrines of the bull *Unam Sanctam* of 1302, as refined in later Catholic thought, established that "this lawful power of command of the Church in the fundamental affairs of the Christian nations constitutes a truth which has the firmness of a truth of Faith." Not only does the Church have supreme political powers, in any true hierarchy, but also the general interests of the "universal human family," and indeed the specific interests of Christian Europe, take precedence over the interests of any single nation.

As for *mysticism,* it simply refers to the union of the soul with God. The "strange and irrational" meanings that it had acquired in Italy in the 1930's (by which was meant the *mistica fascista)* should be unacceptable to Catholics, or to men of ordinary good sense: to La Pira they smacked of blasphemy.*

Principî singled out three false mysticisms of the twentieth century. The attributes of God are given to the State, to the Race, or to the Proletariat, which have become the objects of an idolatrous and inhuman worship. Hegel is at fault, as well as Communism and National Socialism, and, implicitly, Italian Fascism.

Principî had another polemical theme: the unjust sinful character of modern war.[3] Catholic moralists, especially Vitoria, forbid even a just war when it is bound to harm the general welfare of Christendom. The very evocation of war psychology by a ruler is a grave sin. How much more then should Catholics abhor a war of aggression, which under modern conditions is not only unjust in itself but also a threat to the Christian civilization of Europe. The destruction of Poland in autumn 1939 was, according to *Principî,* a twofold crime.[4] First it was a crime in that the na-

---

* Yet on 26 February 1937 Cardinal Schuster of Milan, speaking to the students of the School of *Mistica fascista,* compared Mussolini to Augustus and Constantine! Not all Catholic hierarchs shared La Pira's delicacy in such matters. See Castelli, *La Chiesa e il Fascismo,* p. 501.

tions of Europe, grown up in the shadow of the Church, each have
an individual personality and vocation: this is as true for Poles
and Bohemians (the examples are significant) as for the greater
nations. An attack on any historical European nation injures a
member of human society and of the Church herself. But second—
and here lay the sting—the attack was a crime because Poland had
been a dike separating two "non-Christian worlds."

Of course *Principî* does not deny the possibility of a just war:
a crusade against the "new Turks" threatening Europe, the National Socialists and the Communists, would be just and holy!
A war of this sort, recalling the traditions of such Popes as Gregory
VII, would put new life into Christendom: "Our time, so tragic
in so many aspects, is by now ripe for reconstituting around the
See of Peter that unity among the nations vainly sought elsewhere."[5]

It is surprising that the review lasted as long as a year before
being silenced. Presumably its theological character at first disarmed suspicions. However, the Florentine Fascists finally awak-
ened to the enemy within the gates, "a little magazine" recalling
the Liberalism of Gobetti, no less. "The criticism of Fascism is
not explicit but implicit, Fascism is not named, but is masonically
and jesuitically 'understood,'" declared *Il Bargello*, organ of the
Florentine *Fascio*, and concluded: "We advise the badly camou-
flaged compilers of *Principî* to quit stacking Masonic-Christian-
Liberal cards, mixing St. Thomas with Liberals and free traders;
they would do better to put a stop to it, because such foolishness is
too ridiculous, and for the sake of public decency is not tolerated
in the year XVIII."[6]

Of course La Pira was far from Liberal, either in economics
or in politics. But by the time this attack was published, 12 May
1940, no answer was possible, for *Principî* was no more.*

---

* La Pira went on writing against totalitarianism. See his extraordinarily
outspoken "Crisi della morale," in *Il Ragguaglio 1940–1941*, pp. 269 *et seq.* By
1943 La Pira had become a symbol of Resistance. See below, Epilogue.
   La Pira's attitude toward politics was never better put than in a short article
published in *Studium*, II–III, 1943, on the eve of Mussolini's fall. La Pira,
picking up and transforming a Fascist catch phrase, said: "Politics, with its
juridical orders and administrative instruments, has forgotten that it has as its
goal the watchful guardianship of the material and spiritual 'living space' of
the human person . . . The structure of civilization built upon Christian

With La Pira we have none of the problems of lay autonomy raised by Sturzo, De Gasperi, or even Righetti. He is an "integralist" pure and simple, to whom politics and economics are really ancillary to theology, and his career in the postwar Christian Democratic Party has been little more than an application of those beliefs. In most situations such a personality, defiant of economic realities and political calculations, would be kept on the edges of political life, but La Pira is different. He has had a real base in Florentine Catholicism, where extreme integralist tendencies have a past reaching back to Savonarola and beyond. And La Pira, though Sicilian by birth, has always shown a keen understanding of the Florentine environment, shot through with communal pride and pique, harsh and yet susceptible of mass emotion. Around La Pira, within the usually secure precincts of Catholic Action, was formed a Tuscan Christian Democratic group alien to the autonomous traditions of the old Popular Party, but imbued with a militant social-Christian spirit.

THE GUELF MOVEMENT OF MILAN

In Milan there was a Catholic anti-Fascist group far more militant than any other in Italy, the Guelf movement. Since it operated clandestinely, it could be outspoken in a way that Gonella and La Pira could not. (It must also be borne in mind that Milan, with its great industrial and professional populations, is politically far livelier than Rome and more to the left than Florence.) On the other hand, because of the movement's underground character much of its work has perished, and a documentary study is hard to carry beyond a certain point.

By a curious chance one early Guelf manifesto has been preserved complete. It was denounced as a horrible example by *La Liguria del Popolo,* an "integrally papal" political weekly that pursued autonomously minded Catholics—especially those who had belonged to the Popular Party, the "green serpent" of Masonry (and its instruments such as Esperanto, Boy Scouts, and Rotary), and the Elders of Zion—all alike, with a zeal recalling the pontifi-

---

foundations has in great part crumbled . . . One has only to think of the thorough expulsion of the Church from the political life of the State." It is not surprising to find La Pira concluding that medieval civilization, with all its deficiencies, was "Christian in its fundamental inspiration," in contrast to the modern world.

cate of Pius X. *La Liguria del Popolo* spoke for a "fringe" of Catholic opinion which accepted Fascism above all because it had put an end to Catholic lay autonomy.* It is from this unlikely source that some rare information on the Guelf movement can be obtained.

On 23 May 1931 *La Liguria del Popolo* said:

> We have before us the little manifesto of a self-styled *Committee of Guelf Action among Italian Catholics,* directed *to the Christian Democrats gathered around the Chair of Peter on the Fortieth Anniversary of Rerum Novarum,* which is something revolting. It begins thus:
> "Brothers of the Faith, citizens of the Universal Catholic City, listen to us. You have come from every part of the world to repeat before the Successor of Peter the social creed that Leo XIII's genius wishes to give to modern man.
> "You have surely sensed the fascination of Rome, walked among the glorious tombs, trodden on soil sacred to the Church and to Civilization. But perhaps you have asked yourselves: where are the Italians, where are the Italian Catholic laborers? We want to answer you.
> "The direct representatives of the Italian Catholic laborers are not among you. The political tyranny, notwithstanding all the good will of the Vatican, is holding far away from your sessions even those few that prison or exile have spared. Those few, with heartfelt passion, freely and boldly, want to tell you that you are not walking only among tombs; that the people is keeping its lamps lit; that the Italians are worthy of their past and of themselves. You will feel us among you in spirit, you will hear the beating of our hearts when you make of your breasts a crown for the Holy Father."

La Liguria del Popolo asked:

> Who are these men, who affect such love for the Pope and betray his wishes? Who are they? How many? What do these authentic Demochristians want? . . . renegades and rebels!

The Regime found the answers to these questions in 1933, when the Guelf leadership was arrested, together with other anti-Fascist underground workers in Genoa and Milan.

The prosecutors of the famous Special Tribunal for the Defense of the State found that there were three associations involved,

---

* *La Liguria del Popolo* was the last of the *intégriste* publications which had made so much stir in the pontificate of Pius X; see Chapter One.

one Socialist, one Republican ("Young Italy"), and the Catholic "Guelf Party," all of them linked with the exile movement *Justice and Liberty* (GL). They had composed, printed, and distributed pamphlets "inciting the commission of acts directed toward changing the constitution of the State and the form of the Government by means not allowed by the constitutional order of the State."[7]

Though the police had been following closely the activities of the exiles and their partners inside Italy, the final break in the case came by accident. A letter, sent by an illegal group in Milan to allies in Genoa, was delivered by mistake to a lawyer, who saw its anti-Fascist character and turned it over to the police. Following this track, the police arrested the Socialists and Republicans, and from them were led to their Catholic associates.

The police seem to have been rather surprised by their discovery that

> new on the scene of the anti-Fascist coalition but not less contemptible, insidious, and aggressive, had arisen in Milan a group of dissident Catholics calling itself "Guelf Party"; this group, ruled by a triumvirate composed of Malavasi, Malvestiti, and Rodolfi, had at its disposal a printing press . . . that of the aforesaid Ortodossi, who, helped by the young printer Ettore Bassani, had printed anti-Fascist pamphlets with the title "Christ King and People," widely spread especially in December 1932; that the said triumvirate had succeeded . . . in putting itself in contact with Ballabio, who had communicated abroad the joining of the Guelfs in the GL movement.

While some anti-Fascists, once arrested and subjected to police interrogation, could be got to appeal to the Duce for mercy, the principal Guelfs stood firm, "pseudo-Christians who have used this name to attempt to re-evoke in a totalitarian State phantoms of a past of factions, by now definitely buried."

In their investigations the police found that

> quite apart from pressures from abroad, indeed, through the sole initiative of Catholic dissidents, insidious anti-Fascists, doubly rebels, there had arisen in Milan the above-mentioned clerical group, which had as its fixed aim to carry on an activity directed toward obstructing the triumphal march of Fascism. . . . The aforesaid group had arisen by the will of exponents of Catholic Action, who, in contempt of every elementary duty

of discipline, in opposition to contrary higher orders, hoped to find right in the field of Catholic youth a "formidable platform" for the struggle undertaken against the Regime.

The prosecution made two important points in drafting the indictment against the Guelfs: (1) the Guelf group had not *actually* joined the GL organization; (2) it was clear from their pamphlets, distributed in the thousands, that the Guelfs proposed an anti-Fascist campaign of education but not revolutionary action as such. They simply planned to counteract the effects of Fascist propaganda and schooling.

Since Fascism "is identified with the Nation," the prosecution finally accused the Guelf leaders of conspiring to "weaken or destroy national feeling," a charge much less serious than outright sedition.

The trial itself was held before the Special Tribunal 30–31 January 1934. The Guelfs were defended by Luigi Meda, son of the old moderate Popular Party chief Filippo Meda, and the Catholic lawyer Clerici. Two leaders, Malvestiti and Malavasi, were condemned to five years of imprisonment each. Rodolfi, who had been caught while leaving his office with three thousand pamphlets in his possession, got three years; the printer Ortodossi got two. These were the only sentences against Catholic militants ever pronounced by the Special Tribunal, a fact noteworthy in itself.[8]

From the later accounts of Malvestiti the nature of his movement is clear enough. Malvestiti himself was a war veteran and bank accountant, who occasionally contributed articles on politics and economics to *Italia,* the Catholic Action daily of Milan. In disgust at the way Italian Catholics had yielded to Fascist threats and blandishments, he had set up in 1928 a secret propaganda organization to work against the Regime. Had it not been for reluctant and unfortunate contacts with the secular anti-Fascists, the Guelfs might well have worked quietly for years in a narrowly Catholic environment. Unquestionably their attitude found wide sympathies in Lombardy among the lower levels of Catholic laity and clergy alike, as the bitter words of the Clerico-Fascist Monsignor Luigi Cornaggia-Medici showed.[9] The anti-Fascist sentiments of much Lombard Catholicism found expression in the 1930's in the anonymous letter of protest sent to the Clerico-Fascist Cardinal Schuster (who later became much cooler toward the Regime),* in the celebration of the memory of Don Albertario, and finally in the 1940's it sought a practical outlet in the Resistance.

Malvestiti's movement harked back to Don Albertario's intransigent Christian Democracy of the 1890's, with its religious-social protest against a usurping absolute State. Indeed, the two movements were linked in the venerable person of Don Ernesto Vercesi, a veteran of the 1898 suppression. At heart Malvestiti was no more of a revolutionary threat than were his predecessors of 1898 in Milan. A forthright but unarmed opponent of the Fascist dictatorship, as Don Albertario had been of Humbert I's conservative monarchy, Malvestiti suffered the same brief imprisonment. He was released on special parole (*confino*) toward the end of 1935, and it is worth noting that he benefited by the personal intercession of Senator Stefano Cavazzoni, the Lombard Clerico-Fascist.[10] In some ways Catholic solidarity was more important than any political divisions, even those insisted upon by a totalitarian regime.

The Guelfs began to revive after 1938. During the war years contacts were made with Giovanni Gronchi of the old Popular Party Left-Center, with Achille Grandi of the long-disbanded Catholic labor unions, and with De Gasperi himself. Ex-*Popolari* such as Stefano Jacini and Achille Marazza, together with younger men such as Luigi Meda, formed part of the Milanese nucleus. The reconstituted Christian Democracy of 1943 found its Milanese recruits in the enlarged Guelf movement, which thereby fulfilled its mission in Italian history, merging into the new national party.†

---

* See Fausto Fonzi, "Don Davide Albertario," *Quaderni di Cultura e Storia Sociale*, June-July 1954, pp. 387–89, and *Italy Today, Monthly Bulletin issued by Friends of Italian Freedom*, May 15, 1930, p. 2. Don Davide Albertario's strenuous resistance to the Italian State of 1870–98, with his constant appeals to mass discontent, made any celebration of his memory anathema to the Clerico-Fascists, who were always fearful of anti-Fascism among the parish clergy and *local* units of Catholic Action.

There were Lombard peasant priests who remembered their Christian Democratic organization work in Liberal Italy, and did what they could to win the youth of their parishes for Catholic rather than Fascist social groups, much to the discomfort of the local Blackshirts. See De Rosa, *Filippo Meda*, pp. 146–47.

† Malvestiti himself became a Resistance leader in the short-lived partisan "republic" of Domodossola in 1944, afterward crossing the border into Switzerland, where he represented the Christian Democratic Party in the Swiss deputation of the North Italian Committee of National Liberation. After the war he served as a Christian Democratic deputy and minister.

Chapter Twelve

FATHER GEMELLI AND THE CATHOLIC
UNIVERSITY OF MILAN

In the last few pages we have been dealing with Catholics who felt inwardly severed from Fascism and lived in the slightest possible outer contact with the Fascist Regime. But in fact a good part of the Italian Catholic world lived in continual contact with the Regime, and its inner life too was deeply touched by Fascism.

These contacts were of varying sorts. When Fascism had come to power it professed to be at once revolutionary and a force of order. To give substance to the latter claim Fascist officials ostentatiously deferred to prelates, took part in public religious processions and ceremonies, and set up chaplaincies in Fascist militia and youth organizations.

Don Carlo Gnocchi, chaplain of the II University Legion of Milan, wrote in 1934 that organized Fascist youth (the Balilla)

> is a mighty army, which in July of this year touched the numerical level of 4,327,000 enrolled members. . . . It is an immense unbounded diocese, with 1,425 priests and a bishop of its own. A magnificent field of modern apostolate, which can put the priest in contact with vast zones of souls, ordinarily unapproachable. Let us not forget the specific mark of this movement, as it concerns us: all of its members are obliged to attend religious instruction.[1]

The yearly program for every member consisted in twenty lessons, imparted by the chaplain. On Sundays and those feast days named in the Concordat the young were left free to perform religious duties—until ten in the morning.[2]

Not all Catholics were impressed by this sort of apostolate. The forthright *Liguria del Popolo* complained on 15 August 1931 that Blackshirt squads sang indecent and blasphemous songs as they marched to mass, an eloquent indication of the inner contradictions of Fascism. The sharp-eyed Irish observer Daniel Binchy feared that this religious instruction was contradicted by the rest of the Fascist youth program: how great, he asked, were the effects of Fascist instruction upon young Catholics?[3]

Nevertheless there were real benefits to be had from the Regime. Not the least of them was the officially recognized Catholic character of the Italian State and the conception of "religious unity," "one of the great forces of a people," as an essential element of the Regime. This last had been stated 18 March 1934 by Mussolini himself.

Little wonder then that the influential Catholic monthly of Milan, *Vita e Pensiero,* could attack Protestantism in Italy as politically subversive and call for the Regime to curb it:[4]

> How is it possible to imagine propaganda of the individualistic-religious virus in Fascist Italy? . . . Not only in the name of the Faith but also in the name of the Fatherland is it a duty to react against a low sort of proselytizing, which . . . is an atrocious insult to all our finest glories and our holiest memories.

Orio Giacchi, professor of law at the Catholic University of Milan, showed that the freedoms granted legally to Protestant sects did not in fact include freedom of proselytizing.[5] A Protestant "temple" could be opened, with government authorization, in a place where a number of professing Protestants asked for it. It should not be allowed to open, said Giacchi, if intended primarily as a center for proselytizing among Catholics, in places where almost no one was already Protestant. Priests had the special duty of appealing to local government authorities to forbid such activities.

This is the gist of Giacchi's argument: Italian law favors religion in general, but there are some restrictions on non-Catholic sects. They are free in so far as they do not harm "the essential principles of the life of the State," among which must be numbered the profession of the Catholic religion. Therefore Protestant propaganda and proselytizing enjoy no legal protection. On the contrary, Catholics should urge the authorities to take discretionary measures and police action against the public spreading of Protestantism.

Of course it is not the Liberal legislation of united Italy to which Giacchi appeals, but rather the Regime's religious laws of

1929–30, in which, he claims, a new alliance of Altar and Throne has been established. More than a point of contact, it is a link binding Church and Regime in a common purpose.

Two other links of this sort must be briefly noted. First, the population policy of Fascism, though conceived as a justification and instrument of imperialism, harmonized with the morality of the Church. The demographic works of Corrado Gini were favorably received by Catholic critics, and priests were urged to be vigilant in reporting violations of the provisions of the new penal code, which forbade dissemination of birth-control information.[6] Second, the Fascist quest for empire in Africa led to a natural fusing of aims between Regime and Church. The Italian authorities repressed foreign Protestant missionary activity in Ethiopia early in 1937, and encouraged Italian Catholic missions among the heretical natives. Catholic missionaries themselves were delighted at the favorable prospects opened by the conquest of "Italian East Africa."[7]

However, the strongest link between Regime and Church was forged through the Catholic University of Milan, a fact especially relevant to this study, since much of the new Christian-Democratic leadership of the 1940's grew up there.

The University itself was the crowning work of the Milanese "neo-scholastic" group, headed by Fathers Agostino Gemelli and Francesco Olgiati. Their *Vita e Pensiero* publications, begun on the eve of World War I, had made a great impression on the Italian Catholic world. The neo-scholastics, combining Thomist principles with new scientific methods, seemed to represent a new sort of Catholic mind, capable of dealing with modern problems.

Father Agostino Gemelli had had an unusual career as doctor, experimental psychologist, and Franciscan; during wartime service as a General Staff chaplain he had learned techniques of mass psychology and control, an experience that must have influenced him greatly. At all events, he was a man of extraordinary energy, one of the outstanding figures of the Italian Catholic world. His initiative made possible the rise of the Catholic University, and he had been its Rector since it opened in 1922. The whole institution reflected his leadership.

For a university in Italy to award recognized degrees, for its graduates to pursue a profession, it must meet requirements set by the Government, and submit to inspection by the Ministry of Public Instruction. Before World War I, it would have been hard for a Catholic institution to attain such a status, since the laws on higher education had been restrictively interpreted by Liberal (or Masonic) administrations. And the Catholics themselves had previously lacked the energy and personnel for so ambitious a plan. But new developments, such as the postwar crisis, Gemelli's personal campaign (aided by the great Catholic land and banking interests of North Italy), and the coming of Fascism had changed all that. By the end of 1924 the University of the Sacred Heart had reached its goal. It had eventually attracted help from almost all elements of the Italian Church and profited greatly from the educational reforms of Mussolini's first government, achieving full official recognition at Rome. Gemelli and his associates now headed the University, an affiliated Teachers' Institute, the great publishing house *Vita e Pensiero,* with a chain of periodicals for laity and clergy, and the periodical founded by Toniolo, the *Rivista internazionale di scienze sociali.*[8]

This whole system was bound up with the Fascist Regime, upon which it depended for its continued existence. The Church-State condominium over which Father Gemelli presided was actually written into the Lateran Concordat, which provided (Article 35) that candidates from Catholic schools would be admitted to official professional examinations on an equal footing with State-educated candidates, and (Article 38) that professors appointed to the University of the Sacred Heart and its affiliated Teachers' Institute would have to receive the *nihil obstat* of the Holy See. This provision was simply to safeguard the religious and moral character of these institutions. The legal status of these professors, once named to their chairs, differed in no way from that of other Italian university professors.

Father Gemelli and the members of his staff took a political line best summarized under three heads: (1) wholehearted acceptance of the Fascist corporative system as a real application of Catholic social principles, (2) participation in Fascist "imperial" programs, with their doctrines of living space and geopolitics, (3) justification of the Fascist racial campaign on the ground of Catholic tradition. There was a consistent tendency to belittle or overlook the harsh features of the Third Reich: given Gemelli's closeness to the Regime, it is hard to see how it could have been otherwise. An example will suffice for the moment: when in March 1939 the *Rivista internazionale di scienze sociali* recalled the declarations of the recently deceased Pius XI, it referred to "atheistic Communism, Mexican abuses," and, with a notable lowering of tone, "the erroneous conduct of Germany." In the same issue Fanfani referred to the "unwarranted interventions of the German state authorities, disrespectful of sacred rights and signed covenants," without suggesting that Nazism was somehow fundamentally anti-Christian.[9] It is interesting to compare the attitudes of Fanfani, then a professor at the Catholic University, with those of anti-Fascists like De Gasperi or La Pira. When once Fanfani and De Gasperi met by chance in the Vatican Library during these years, they seem to have found little to agree on.[10] (De Gasperi later bore no grudge against Fanfani for his youthful Fascism, it seems.)

So far as Fascist corporativism is concerned, the Milanese University and its journals had some striking things to say: Professor Gino Arias even went so far as to identify it with Thomist social thought:

the corporative order, harking back to the tradition of Italian and Christian thought, answers the universal needs of our moment in history and should be received by modern states in the criteria that inspire it, as the Duce declares. Would that the invitation to a close collaboration in every field of civil life, which Catholic Rome and Fascist Rome have alike extended to the nations, might be accepted.[11]

Alberto De Stefani and Luigi Amoroso saw in Fascist corporativism

a principle of coordination and moderation. . . . In this way the block of moral principles which for a millennium had been the deep substratum of European civilization, sundered in the seventeenth century [*sic*] by the Reformation, has been restored. . . . Fascism has destroyed the idolatry of Mammon. It has smashed every monopoly and abuse of groups and categories, in the field of labor as in that of industry and finance.[12]

Gemelli himself went further:

there are events that must be explained at their first appearance. . . . From . . . the year of this periodical's foundation, only three such events have occurred in the social field: they are the promulgation of *Rerum Novarum,* of *Quadragesimo Anno,* and today the resolution and address of the Head of the Government concerning the establishment of industry-wide corporations *(corporazioni di categoria),* as the completion of the Italian corporative system. Three connected events. The first marked the condemnation of laissez-faire disorganization, the second marked the confirmation of this condemnation and its extension to the latest Socialist formulations. In the third are proclaimed the principles by which a modern state, Italy, is rising above Liberalism and Socialism. . . . It is the Fascist conception of the State, as the Nation organized, that led to corporativism. . . . The new doctrine and the new system rest, more than might appear at first sight, upon a conception of the world particularly dear to us, and true, according to our way of seeing things: the primacy of the spiritual.[13]

Amintore Fanfani, in his popular *Il significato del corporativismo, Testo ad uso dei licei e degli istituti magistrali* (1937 edition), found the same happy parallels:

It is just because the State reserves for itself the right to intervene in production when private initiative is lacking or insufficient, that it reserves for itself the right to replace that property-owner who keeps his goods unfruitfully, either through incapacity or ill will. These concepts, which have already inspired some laws on the cultivation and drainage of country landholdings, bring out the profound moral character of the Fascist corporative doctrine and rightly approach, in these demands, the doctrine on the use of goods which the Catholic Church has been preaching for centuries. The coincidence should not serve to lessen the originality and the merits of Fascist corporativism, but to show how deep is the sense of justice that animates the new doctrine.[14]

The substance of these identifications and analogies is *moral.* Fascism vigorously denied any derivation from Catholic corporativism, and even the most infatuated Clerico-Fascist had theoretical reservations about Fascist social views, but a rhetoric of morality and ideals served to cover these cracks in the imposing structure that housed both schools.[15] The gaping difference between the ideals of the two worlds was hidden by political expediencies, calculations, and an apparently real enthusiasm for the Fascist Empire.

The Catholic University group was in fact committed to Axis imperialism. This was more than the generic patriotism that had rallied so many Italians, whatever their doubts about Fascism, to support their Government against Britain and France: it was "ideological." When Haushofer's geopolitics was introduced into Italy, Ernesto Massi, Catholic University professor of economic geography, became an editor of the authoritative new monthly *Geopolitica* (January 1939), and his colleagues Marcello Boldrini and Amintore Fanfani served on its "scientific committee." Fanfani had long since accepted living-space theories. In 1936 he wrote that an empire for Italy was not a luxury, but a necessity for her continued existence.[16]

The Catholic University group and the *Vita e Pensiero* publications had already gone far in supporting earlier expansions, on *religious* as well as economic grounds. Characteristically, Fanfani wrote in the *Rivista internazionale di scienze sociali* (May 1936):

> Fourteen years were enough for our people to cover the intermediate stages on the way of Empire, which others crossed in centuries. Political pacification, reorganization of economic and social life, military might, conciliation with the Church, Roman Catholic and Fascist education of youth: these are the conquests that have tautened wills and prepared the victory. . . . The last, alone, shall become the first. The reappearance on earth of Roman virtue, strengthened by the consecration of Christianity, gives certainty of it.[17]

The popular monthly *Vita e Pensiero* carried the same thought even further in an article by another Catholic University man, Paolo Emilio Taviani (June 1936):

> Today Italy has in East Africa . . . her Empire, because she is putting into action down there also Mussolini's principles of "living dangerously," . . . because she places upon the Acrocoro, heart of Africa, a standard of that civilization which is, in its positive essence, Christian civilization, because she intends to bring social equality and brotherly charity among peoples habituated until now to arbitrary distinctions of race and class.[18]

What brotherly charity and social equality might mean in the new empire was made clear by the racial campaign of 1938, which affirmed the inferiority of Africans as well as Jews in its biological theses; this inferiority was implied in the Fascist marriage legislation of this period, which banned miscegenation.

Fanfani explained the racial policy of Fascism to the readers of the *Rivista internazionale di scienze sociali* in the most disarming terms, as the "separation of the Semites from the national demographic group," and went on to say that "for the power and the future of the nation the Italians should be racially pure, as well as numerous and constitutionally healthy."[19] In a later number of the same year, 1939, he reviewed Fausta Casonini's *Bernardino da Feltre, il martello degli usurai* (a *Vita e Pensiero* publication) and casually noted that the book was "of particularly current interest where it recalls the position assumed by the man of Feltre with regard to the Jewish problem."[20] In fact Bernardino was one of the bitterest enemies the Jews ever had.

Some strange racial interpretations of Communism were offered to Italian Catholics by Guido Manacorda's *Il Bolscevismo,* published in 1940. Manacorda, who was, incidentally, one of Papini's group, found that "the Soviet revolution, heir of the traditions of Byzantium, deeply contaminated by Semitico-Satrapico-Mongol influences, cannot fail to rise against the European West, especially against Rome and the Mediterranean." In March 1941 Taviani reviewed the book for the *Rivista internazionale di scienze sociali,* quoted this passage, and wrote: "We underwrite these conclusions without any hesitation, indeed with enthusiasm."[21] German racism was unacceptable . . . but a racial doctrine exalting Rome was a different matter.

The monthly *Vita e Pensiero* rejected as spurious the *Protocols of the Elders of Zion,* which had been circulated by Fascist propagandists. But not all of its writers showed a like caution when it came to racial theories. For examples, Dr. Luigi Gedda was opposed on *scientific* grounds to crossing races of markedly different character, such as Aryans, Hamites, and Semites, thus accepting the tenets and terms of Fascist racial doctrine, although he too found German race theories unscientific.[22]

But the most outspoken Catholic supporter of the Fascist racial campaign was Father Gemelli himself. On 10 January 1939 he spoke at the University of Bologna about the "deicide people," tragically unable to belong to Italy "because of their blood and because of their religion." These remarks were quoted in full by Mussolini's *Il Popolo d'Italia,* but left unmentioned by the *Osservatore Romano*: the meaning of this omission was not lost on Farinacci, who made much of it in his anticlerical *Regime Fascista.* In racial as in other respects—his contempt for the western democracies, especially the United States, and his persistent admiration for the Third Reich—Gemelli was far closer to the Regime than any other Italian Catholic of comparable authority and prestige.[23]

During the disillusioning years of World War II many things changed in this group. The younger professors, such as Taviani and Fanfani, turned away from Fascism. While Fanfani's political evolution is undocumented, as are so many important things in Italy which happened under the dictatorship, Taviani wrote a little book in 1943, *Prospettive sociali,* in which the transition from Fascist corporativism to a Christian Democratic position is evident.[24] For Taviani Fascist corporate structure had shown itself to be a sham. Beneath a façade of class collaboration it had really perpetuated the rule of capital. Like so many Left Christian Democrats, Taviani upheld a partial "socialization" as the only way to economic progress and freedom.

During the critical years 1943–45 Gemelli's network was silent. Almost nothing was put out by *Vita e Pensiero* aside from a little tract in 1944 by Professor Francesco Vito of Catholic University. Its aim was only to prevent Catholics from being attracted by Communism, which had become a power in North Italy in the course of the Resistance. The tract made no reference whatever to Fascism.[25]

Fanfani and Taviani had both passed over to the Resistance. Fanfani was a refugee scholar in Switzerland, and Taviani became chief of the Christian Democratic Resistance forces of Genoa; for both of them, the Resistance was a prelude to distinguished careers in the Christian Democratic Party and governments of postwar Italy.

Chapter Thirteen

CATHOLIC PARTICIPATION IN THE RESISTANCE

The Catholic movement in Italy on the eve of the war was, as we have seen, a composite of various groups differing in background and training. The war crisis of 1943, when the Italian State collapsed, gave these groups a chance to form a party of their own, a spontaneous expression of the political views of Italian Catholics. However for our purposes the Resistance has other points of interest.[1] In it we see the Catholic masses of North Italy as they really are, no longer smothered by the Fascist cope of lead and publicly spoken for by Clerico-Fascists like Senator Cavazzoni and Fathers Gemelli and Cornaggia-Medici. These masses, most numerous in the countryside of Lombardy-Venetia, but present in Piedmont and Tuscany as well, played an important part in the Italian Resistance. The local parish priest and peasantry usually helped partisan detachments and escaped prisoners of war, whereas the Catholic soldier often joined them. And in the postwar Italian Republic these masses became the bedrock upon which the Christian Democratic electoral plurality rested.

A minor but symptomatic role was played 1943–45 by dissident Catholic movements of the Left. However, they indicate more a state of mind than any possibility of mass action.

In this concluding section we shall take up successively the Resistance roles of the upper and lower clergy, Catholic partisan action, and the Catholic political movements, ending with a few general considerations on the postwar Christian Democratic Party.[2]

Between 1943 and 1945 the prelates of central and upper Italy had diplomatic responsibilities of a high order. On the one side, they dealt with the German occupying army and its collaborator, Mussolini's Italian Social Republic; on the other side were the various local Committees of National Liberation, set up by the united anti-Fascist parties as organs of provisional government. The most important of these was the great Committee of National

Liberation of Upper Italy (CLNAI), with headquarters at Milan.[3]

The Cardinal-Archbishop of Milan consequently became a central figure in an intricate game played between the Germans, their embarrassing Fascist allies, the Anglo-Americans and *their* Italian government, and the anti-Fascist parties represented in CLNAI, backed by partisan forces. The Archiepiscopal See of Milan was in direct touch with the Apostolic Nuncio at Berne.[4]

The Cardinal led the other prelates of occupied Italy in protesting against the reprisals of the Axis forces and in interceding for the oppressed population. The Social Republic was given the barest *de facto* recognition by the ecclesiastical authorities, and the Fascists could get no help from them in conscripting recruits and enrolling labor. The bishops freely permitted their clergy to minister to partisan forces, even as chaplains, and allowed church property to be used for clandestine meetings. The Holy See itself made the extraterritorial Lateran Palace available as a refuge and meeting place for the anti-Fascist party chiefs of Rome during the months of German occupation.[5]

In vain Farinacci, a pillar of the Italian Social Republic, set afoot a schismatic Catholic movement under Don Tullio Calcagno, editor of *Crociata Italica*; the priest was suspended and his journal banned by the Hierarchy. The successor of Saint Ambrose could hardly be swayed by the threats of a desperate Blackshirt.[6]

On the other hand, Cardinal Schuster did everything possible to ward off a popular insurrection in North Italy, as projected by the Committees of National Liberation. Such an insurrection, in his view, would be a disaster whether it succeeded or failed. Success would lead to Communist rule in the Po valley, while failure would bring with it mass destruction of the power plants and industry of North Italy, thus creating a fertile ground for the spread of the "tubercular" Bolshevik infection. Already, warned Cardinal Schuster and his negotiator, Don Bicchierai, the Allies had lost sympathy among the North Italian population because of their indiscriminate air attacks, while the Soviet Union was becoming dangerously popular.

To meet the Red peril the Milanese See had proposals of its own, in which the Germans had expressed interest. The evacuation of the German forces and the consequent disappearance of the Social Republic must not leave a void which would be filled by the insurrectionary Committees of National Liberation. Power must be transmitted at once to the Anglo-Americans, if necessary by means of the ecclesiastical authorities, who would use their moral authority to ensure a peaceful transition from German to Allied control.

When these plans fell through because of steady opposition from the anti-Fascist parties, Don Bicchierai went to the Anglo-American representatives in Switzerland. But the Allies had other methods of warding off a revolutionary regime in North Italy, consistent with their demands for unconditional surrender.

After this failure the Cardinal did not cease in his efforts to hinder Axis "scorched-earth" measures and partisan insurrections in North Italy, but he could not get any commitments from the Germans, who at the last minute negotiated a surrender directly with the Allies in Switzerland. With the expiring Fascist regime the Cardinal had no better luck. So successful in dealing with Arnaldo Mussolini during the dispute of 1931, he found his brother Benito a much more slippery sort. The Cardinal's naïve religious exhortations were lost upon the cynical, trapped dictator, while Schuster was still intent upon mediating between Mussolini and the Committees of National Liberation, the Duce suddenly fled toward the Swiss border and summary partisan justice.[7]

What is notable about the negotiations of the Milanese See, aside from their total failure, is that they were carried on without much help from the Christian Democrats of North Italy. Though Don Bicchierai was in contact with the Christian Democratic representative on CLNAI, Achille Marazza, the latter made no effort to advance any of Bicchierai's projects for ecclesiastical mediation. The Milanese Christian Democrats of this time, "Guelfs" or other veterans of anti-Fascism, were vaguely republican and not at all opposed to a climactic popular insurrection.

In fact the Hierarchy held itself above the parties. It condemned "crimes against human life" and "fratricidal strife," words that applied to partisans as well as Germans and Fascists. Cardinal-Archbishop Dalla Costa of Florence in his pastoral letters of 1943–44 implicitly denounced both Communism and Fascism, calling for a higher unity. Yet the many protests of the Hierarchy, especially the strong statement of the Veneto Bishops' Conference of 20 April 1944, hurt the Social Republic deeply, as the Fascist reply shows.[8]

The lower clergy was overwhelmingly for the Resistance: it had borne Blackshirt arrogance and official Fascist pressure far more than had the prelates.* Furthermore, the North Italian country priest often shaped or interpreted the attitudes of his parishioners. The countless examples of parish priests hiding fugitives, recruiting partisan fighters, furnishing aid and comfort spiritual and temporal to the Resistance, gave an at least implicit guidance to the Catholic masses. In the Mantua and Verona areas parish priests, such as the anti-Fascist veteran Don Primo Mazzolari, took the lead in organizing partisan forces.[9] These activities in the very stronghold of Italian Catholicism did not pass unnoticed by the Fascists: on 3 May 1944 Farinacci published in *Regime Fascista* a threatening letter to Cardinal Schuster on his failure to condemn parish priests who aided fugitives and partisans in escaping.

On the other side, few Catholics threw in their lot with Mussolini's Social Republic. *L'Italia Cattolica* of Venice chronicled faithfully the doings of a few Fascist Republican chaplains and recalled happier days when the Patriarch of Venice had lauded the Axis struggle against the Bolshevik hydra, but it attracted little attention. In Florence some young artists and intellectuals raised in the atmosphere of Fascism tried to continue the *Frontespizio* tradition of Catholic Fascism in a new periodical of their own, *Italia e Civiltà,* an expression of political immaturity without serious effect; Papini himself shunned all politics, withdrawing to his villa.† The La Pira group, rather than Papini, represented Catholic Florence during the Resistance.

* In the Emilia partisan "Republic of Montefiorino" one of the councillors was a priest; in this zone the Resistance was aided by an "anti-Fascist clergy, poverty-stricken, sharing the misery and needs of its parishioners." See *Emilia, Rivista Mensile di Cultura,* April 1955, pp. 103–7.

† See the clandestine edition of the Christian Democratic organ *Il Popolo* (Rome), 20 February 1944. Florence, though intended as the "Athens" of the Social Republic, was soon a prey to ruthless partisan warfare on the one side and Axis sadism on the other; the Florentines took their politics in dead earnest, and repeated many of the bloody scenes of their ancient republic. Not only was the city a center of Italian anti-Fascism, but the Florentine *Fascio* too was especially ardent and fanatical. As Vasco Pratolini said after the war, only at Florence did the Social Republic save its face. After the assassination of Gentile in 1944 cultural life languished in an atmosphere of antique Tuscan ferocity. See Carlo Francovich, "La stampa clandestina a Firenze," *Il Ponte,* September 1954.

Like other Italian partisans, the Catholic partisan soldier was often either a veteran of that Royal Army which had gone to pieces in September 1943 or else a young fugitive from the Fascist draft and the German labor roundups. While some of them found their way into Communist or Party of Action political-military groups, which were by far the largest and most efficient party forces, most Catholic partisans served in the so-called autonomous units. These were nonpolitical military groups, often fragments of the old army, dedicated exclusively to a war of patriotic defense against the German invaders and the Fascist usurpers. The principal formations of this kind were the *Di Dio* groups of Piedmont, the *Fiamme Verdi* of the Lombard mountains, and the *Osoppo* brigades of the Friuli region, bordering on Yugoslavia. Except in Tuscany, where they were especially militant and well organized, the Christian Democrats did not have many party troops of their own until late in the war; however, by the end of hostilities in 1945 some 65,000 Christian Democratic partisans were serving under the command of Enrico Mattei.[10]

A comparison between the autonomous units and the party formations shows one essential difference. The Communist *Garibaldi* formations were perhaps the only forces of World War II that had both political commissars and chaplains. Their political commissar was responsible for morale, discipline, and political orientation, explaining to the troops all political problems, conducting small group criticism and discussions, maintaining good relations with other partisan units regardless of their political color, and spreading the democratic ideals of the Resistance among the civilian population. In the *Di Dio* units, on the other hand, there was a political commissar whose exact task it was to see that there be no talk of politics among the troops. Indeed, politics were forbidden. The commissar was to be simply the representative of the Committee of National Liberation; propaganda, of an unrevolutionary character, was a command function. The units openly refrained from partisan feats having a political rather than a military purpose, in clear contrast to the practice of the party formations.[11]

Yet there were distinctively Catholic partisan forces of some weight, especially in Lombardy. For example, there was the

Fiamme Verdi Tito Speri division, which operated in the Brescia area. Organized by Catholic Action members and headed by a Catholic University graduate, though its affiliations were autonomous, it was financed by local industrialists using a parish priest as intermediary. Recruits took their oath before the altar on which the chaplain celebrated mass. The graphic and widely read *Fiamme Verdi* press was openly religious.[12]

In the disputes between this formation and the two Communist-led *Garibaldi* brigades of the area a civil war was foreshadowed. The Communists accused the *Fiamme Verdi* on 15 January 1945 of pursuing a political line contrary to the orders of the Committees of National Liberation and the "aspirations of the masses," "a mixture of ecclesiastical and reactionary politics." Other accusations from the same source were more precise: the *Fiamme Verdi* were said to have negotiated a "free Zone" and a winter armistice with the Germans (there was some truth to this), to have engaged in joint police actions with them, to have murdered, in collusion with the S.S., an Italian Lieutenant-Colonel, and to have tried to ambush several *Garibaldi* brigade commanders. The *Fiamme Verdi* command, on its part, accused the Communists of looting, of slander and public indiscretions calculated to reveal *Fiamme Verdi* military secrets.[13]

What would have happened had the Catholics and Communists fought? The *Fiamme Verdi* enjoyed Anglo-American support in the form of airdrops, military missions, and financing from Switzerland, and probably could have defeated the small *Garibaldi* brigades. By all accounts, the Brescia situation was an extreme case of what happened in much of the rest of the war area, a schism between Right and Left within the Resistance itself. At a later point Liberals and Socialists of various hue might have had to choose between Communist and Catholic mass forces. Instead, there was no military clash, for the Allies occupied North Italy in good time, and the conflict shifted to the political plane.

In the Friuli area the only forces of resistance to an exceptionally brutal Axis occupation were either Communist or Catholic in leadership. Liberals and Socialists often joined the autonomous *Osoppo* brigades, which were in fact a creation of priests and *Laureati cattolici*. Of course both the Brescia and the Friuli situation are extreme. In other parts of North Italy the minor parties sometimes had strong forces of their own, with a democratic political orientation.

Nor were relations between Communist and Catholic partisans always tense. Indeed, at Padua a young FUCI member actually became commander of a *Garibaldi* brigade.[15] The Communists often showed good political sense in shunning all appearance of anticlericalism.

One small group of Catholic students sought in vain to break down the barrier between the Communist and Catholic worlds.* The Catholic Communist movement of Rome held that Catholicism as a religious doctrine of man's last end was not in conflict with dialectical and historical materialism. On the contrary, the love for mankind engendered by the preaching of the Gospel could find its only modern social expression in the workers' revolution, which would break the chains of big capitalist domination and inaugurate a new era of human freedom. Nineteenth-century Catholic social theory, with its archaic ideal of small property and class collaboration, had no real application in an age of centralization and was in no sense a part of the Catholic religion as such.

Dialectical and historical materialism, on the other hand, was only a method of analyzing society scientifically. Its pretensions to metaphysical finality, its atheism, were illegitimate, going beyond its rightful province. Indeed, modern instrumental analysis of society had projected a false metaphysics precisely because Catholicism had, after the high Middle Ages, lost itself in abstract schemes and fallen into the blindest social conservatism. Its word had not reached the "atheists of good will" who were constructing the modern world. But in the revolutionary crisis of the twentieth century these two severed trunks could be joined together in the restored wholeness of a humanity at one with the world and with God.†

* All of our statements about the Catholic Communist movement are based on its newspaper *Voce Operaia*, published clandestinely in Rome 1943–44. See particularly the articles on ideological problems published January 1944. The movement made some headway in Rome; one priest wrote that "the Communist party is blessed by God because it is made up of the poor, who are living representatives in society of the only begotten Son of God." See Don Pacifico V. Bok, *Lux in tenebris* (Rome, 1946), a pamphlet put out by the *partigiani ferrovieri, Ufficio cultura e propaganda*.

† The Young Catholic Communists recalled their scuffles with Fascist University Youth (GUF) when they were members of FUCI themselves. Their

Such an attempt was bound to fail. The Catholic Communist movement, although recognized by the anti-Fascist parties of the Roman Committee of National Liberation as a junior associate, had no chance of competing with the Christian Democrats. It had its significance as pointing to a possible line of cleavage in the Catholic bloc, a symptom of widespread Catholic "Leftism."[16]

Another such minority was the Christian Social movement of Leghorn. Catholic Action at Leghorn had long been anti-Fascist, the city was proletarian in character and lacked the usual class of Catholic landowners and bankers to support an official Christian Democratic organization. Some local Catholics, inspired by Mounier's *Esprit* and by personal contacts with De Gasperi's colleague in the Vatican Library, Gerardo Bruni, set on foot an autonomous Catholic movement with associates in other parts of Tuscany.[17]

Unlike the Christian Democrats, the Christian Socialists were resolutely republican. They favored socialization of key industries and banks. However, they distrusted any sort of Left dictatorship, being allied with the Socialists and Republicans (not the Communists) in the Leghorn Committee of National Liberation, where the Christian Social movement was the sole representative of Catholicism. But the Christian Social movement never rose above a regional level, and its voice was soon drowned out by the mass parties of Italy.

The Christian Democratic Party came to life all over Italy in 1943,* and profited by the "semi-legality" of party life under Badoglio (July–September, 1943). The ground had already been prepared by the *Movimento Laureati*. In Rome the party was constituted by old Popular leaders, De Gasperi, Gronchi, Scelba, Spataro, by Gonella from the *Osservatore Romano,* and by Moro and Andreotti of the FUCI group. The Lombardy-Veneto Christian Democrats were especially active, finding a mass support in the parishes, schools, and Catholic Action circles of the country-

---

starting point was Catholicism, not Communism. See *Il Comunismo e i Cattolici, Edizioni di "Voce Operaia" movimento Cattolici Comunisti Roma, stampato alla macchia, Maggio, 1944,* a clandestine pamphlet in the collection of the Library of the Senate at Rome.

* The Resistance program of the new party was presented in the widespread pamphlet by *Demofilo* (De Gasperi), *La parola dei Democratici Cristiani.*

side and small towns.[18] In Florence the La Pira group formed the nucleus of a Christian Democratic Party that spread over Tuscany.*

During the Badoglio interim (July 25–September 9, 1943), La Pira edited a political sheet significantly called *San Marco*, a conscious reference to the Savonarola tradition. *San Marco* urged the workers of Florence to accept Catholic social ideals of universally held small property, an "armature of the human personality" making for the "abolition of the proletariat." Collaboration among various elements of the "hierarchy" of production was set against the Communist thesis of class struggle. Though *San Marco* had an almost Mazzinian democratic fervor, its paternalistic language must have weakened its appeal to a militant proletariat.

The Florentine Christian Democrats of the Resistance were eloquent when they accused their Communist colleagues and rivals of totalitarian aims,[19] of ignoring the struggles of the individual conscience in its search for purity and truth, but they themselves were unconvincing when they claimed to have a social-economic program of any depth or precision. The La Pira group has never really passed from the moral to the practical plane. It has projected appealing mirages on the Italian political horizon, but it has had no solution for real problems.

In the front of anti-Fascist parties two distinct and often opposed party groupings developed: the Liberal and Christian Democratic parties, which were satisfied at heart with a return to the constitutional state of 1922 and disposed to compromise with the Monarchy, at least for the duration of the war; and the Party of Action and the Socialists, who were bent upon an immediate revolutionary change in state and society. The Party of Action was a middle-class professional movement, Laborite and New Deal in inspiration. It was revolutionary by virtue of its profound anti-Fascism, of a republican and even Jacobin color; in another coun-

---

* The Christian Democrats of Florence, under determined leaders like Adone Zoli, an old member of the Popular Party, had a good capillary organization; they were able to take advantage of parishes and convents, an advantage that Catholic clandestine groups had over their more exposed colleagues in the Resistance in general. Zoli was arrested only once, and held only briefly. Particularly impressive were the variety and circulation of the Party press; the Florentine edition of *Il Popolo* was spread in editions of 9,000 copies. See the reports of Avvocato Francesco Berti mentioned in footnote 10 of this chapter.

try or another situation it would have been reformist.[20] The Socialists were, as ever, "proletarian" and verbally extreme.

The Communists belonged to neither current, but maneuvered very freely. After the return of Togliatti to Italy in the spring of 1944 the Communists suddenly agreed to accept the monarch temporarily, as the Allies had been insisting, thus initiating a policy of compromises that was to last through the Constituent Assembly of 1946–47, when the Communists went so far as to help the Christian Democrats write the Lateran Pacts into the new Constitution (Article 7).

But the Communists combined a compromise tactic in Rome with revolutionary militancy in the North Italian Resistance and in the organization of labor, a double policy that they carried on through 1947. Flexible Communist strategy in Italy was part of a world-wide struggle, the needs of which must often have escaped the Party militants of North Italy; much was sacrificed to maintain this wartime "front" of six parties. Yet the Italian Communist Party kept their trust, for its record of anti-Fascism and its Marxist teaching left no doubt that any compromise would be provisional.

In this situation the Christian Democrats under De Gasperi's leadership naturally took a central position.[21] At times, particularly during the war, their statements had a radical tinge, but it must be remembered that they were competing with the revolutionary Left. They clearly represented reform rather than revolution, a policy of social benefits without widespread socialization, and they cannily refused to commit themselves to the Monarchy or the Republic, an example of De Gasperi's political agnosticism.* Like the *Popolari* in the first postwar crisis, the Christian Democrats could bring a great mass of rural and small-town voters to bear against the revolutionary parties of the Left. Unlike so many Liberals, the Christian Democrats had a keen sense of the mass mood, and (thanks to the "White" tradition revived by Achille Grandi) a labor organization. At the same time, as proven anti-Fascists, they could appeal to those who had kept some Liberal values. Already in the Resistance debates of 1943–45 it was clear that the Christian Democratic Party was an ark of salvation for much of bourgeois Italy, the party of restoration and moderate reform.

* The clandestine *Il Popolo* (Milan), 15 January 1945, in discussing the problem of Monarchy versus Republic, refused to take sides, excluding both

Up to this point we have been concerned with how the Christian Democratic leadership of 1943 grew up under dictatorial rule, and how its character was formed. In considering the old Populars, the FUCI-*Laureati* group, the Florentine and Milanese anti-Fascist nuclei, and the Catholic University group, we must keep two questions in mind. First, what were their political traits and their relation to the Regime? Second, what was their political position *with respect to ecclesiastical authority*? Almost all the elements that went into the making of the new Christian Democratic Party lacked the autonomy of the old Popular Party. Leaders of the older party had built organizations by themselves, sometimes with little encouragement from the Hierarchy. Instead, the new leadership, except for Malvestiti, had grown up under the supervision and protection of the bishops and the Holy See, a necessary condition under the Regime. The Resistance had not entirely altered this, for the Hierarchy had gained in prestige, remaining at its posts when the State and the army failed under circumstances recalling the Dark Ages.

Few of the new leaders were as outspoken as La Pira in proclaiming the political primacy of the pontiff, but fewer still were those who had not experienced his real power in their own careers. The question of Fascism is probably passing from the realm of politics to that of history, but the question of Catholic lay autonomy in politics, as opposed to clerical "theocracy," is very much with us.

The question arises of itself at the end of our account of the Resistance: How did such an equivocal party succeed in gathering up the inheritance of Italian democracy, and rebuild the State? Any answer is bound to be complicated, but some facts leap to the eye and suggest at least a partial explanation of the emergence of the Christian Democrats as rulers of Italy.

The Christian Democratic Party was the only *mass* party not committed either to an immediate revolutionary transformation of Italy or to alliance with the Soviet Union. The Party of Action, essentially made up of a militant elite drawn from the professional-intellectual middle class, saw its political future in 1944–45 as

---

impossible reactionary returns to the past and new "leaps in the dark," though deploring the "shameful dyarchy" of the 1922–43 Monarchy; this sort of language settled nothing.

resting with the North Italian Committees of National Liberation, in which its men were especially active. One of the outstanding political partisan commanders of North Italy, the anti-Fascist veteran Ferrucio Parri, was the Party's revered head. The Party of Action envisaged the Committees as the organs of a revolutionary regime in which Actionist cadres could play a role of the first importance. On the other hand, any return to constitutional rule would soon bring to light the Party of Action's numerical weakness. The Socialist Party, although a mass party, had similar ideas, since it aimed at a workers' revolutionary regime borne up by the insurrectionary "wind from the North"; hence the slogan of Nenni, "all power to the Committees of National Liberation." Both parties of the Left balked at Premier Bonomi's efforts to maintain the Rome government in the line of continuity of the Italian State, with Prince Humbert as Lieutenant-General, under conditions of political truce.[22]

The Communists upheld the revolutionary character of the Committees of National Liberation, but at the same time took part in Bonomi's 1944–45 cabinets, accepting the political truce within the Rome government. Yet their compromise was clearly determined by the wartime needs of the Soviet Union, and their overtures to De Gasperi for a coalition rule of the three mass parties—Communist, Socialist, and Christian Democrat—remained fruitless.

The Christian Democrats at Rome played a waiting game, working with Bonomi and committing themselves as little as possible either to the Right or to the Left.[23] In the Committee of National Liberation at Milan, where one of their representatives, Falck, was an important industrialist, they rejected the revolutionary proposals of the Party of Action and stood with the Liberals for an early restoration of State authority in North Italy.[24] The State, they held, should be constitutionally reformed, but not transformed by revolutionary committees that represented party cadres rather than the express will of the Italian voting public. After the war, during the short-lived Parri cabinet (June–November, 1945) that seemed the high point of the Resistance movement, marking the conquest of legal Rome by revolutionary Milan, the Christian Democrats were able to take a central position from which they could spring to power once Parri fell.

The Parri government was the product of an uneasy compromise. In April 1945 the Milan Party of Action leaders had proposed a democratic "consultive assembly" of North Italian Committees of National Liberation delegates to keep check on the postwar government's policies. The Communists, instead, proposed to settle the problem of the future government by dealing between the party secretaries at Rome; in this they naturally found themselves in full agreement with the Christian Democrats and Liberals. During the critical insurrection period of April–May, 1945, the Christian Democrats and Liberals in turn succeeded in blocking an effort by all the Left parties in the North Italian Committee to decree the end of the Royal Lieutenancy; the "institutional truce," backed by the Allies, remained in force. Thus the "democratic" revolution called for by the Milanese Party of Action leadership foundered against the opposition of the mass proletarian parties on the one side, and of the Catholics, Liberals, and Allied occupiers on the other. Achille Marazza, the Christian Democratic representative on the Milan Committee, was personally in favor of radically democratic measures, but he was bound to moderation by the Party leadership in Rome, headed by De Gasperi.*

When the representatives of the Milan Committee went to Rome on 5 May to confer with the national party leaders on the formation of a new government, the three parties of the Left quarreled endlessly with the Liberals over the purging of Fascists, whereas the Christian Democrats held back. De Gasperi did not even attend the May conferences, alleging illness. There was a reason for this: the Americans obviously preferred no change in the Bonomi government, in which De Gasperi was foreign minister.

When the Rome political secretaries visited Milan shortly thereafter, De Gasperi showed himself in protracted Committee of National Liberation meetings to be the one party leader endowed with a "sense of the State," standing head and shoulders above the Socialists. His sober realism contrasted sharply with the

---

* See the incisive eyewitness account by the Party of Action Resistance leader Leo Valiani, *L'Avvento di De Gasperi* (Turin, 1949), pp. 1–39. Valiani underscores especially the part played by the Communists, in most ways the foremost party of 1945 Italy, in thwarting the democratic transformation of the country. Togliatti staked the postwar role of his party on a collaboration with the other "mass parties," to which he was willing to sacrifice any understanding with the Party of Action.

revolutionary agitator's rhetoric of Nenni, who was quietly excluded from the succession to Bonomi. When Bonomi resigned in June, the Party of Action scored one last success by proposing Parri as his successor, a proposal accepted by the other parties as a compromise.

However, the Parri government, in spite of the combined talents of Ministers Nenni, Togliatti, and De Gasperi, never quite came to grips with the problems of postwar Italy. Nenni recklessly told the Italians that this was *not* the government of the working class, and talked of speedy elections, although the administrative reconstruction of the State, a necessary precondition of any new election, was lagging. Parri had the misfortune to govern Italy before the arrival of large-scale American aid; there was a dangerous ambiguity between "democratic" and "social" revolution among the parties of the Left; Communist-Socialist pressures kept the Parri government from unfreezing factory labor and restoring North Italian industry to private financing and control. The government was unable to follow either a private-enterprise or a Socialistic economic policy, and had to stay on an unsatisfactory, stationary middle ground. The democratic unity of the Resistance, symbolized by the Party of Action leaders themselves, threatened to break up as a result of clashes between bourgeois and working-class economic demands, the later militantly championed by the Communists. Many anti-Fascist veterans, when they had to administer rather than fight or conspire, proved inexperienced and unable to get things done. Outside the Government coalition, forces of the Right reappeared on the political scene, protesting against the purges of small-time Fascists from public service, the influence of the Communists, and the special treatment accorded industrial labor. The government seemed slow and hesitant in taking up the necessary work of reconstruction.

The fatal crisis of the Parri government in November 1945 marked the end of the Resistance period in Italian politics.[25] The Christian Democrats, who had played a moderating role in the Government, prudently let the Liberals provoke the crisis, while De Gasperi stayed in the background and attended to foreign affairs. The Liberals, embodying a great bourgeois tradition in its most conservative form, quit Parri's government, accusing it of inadequacy and weakness in carrying out the primary task of the postwar months, i.e., to restore law and order throughout the nation. The Liberals charged that in many areas of Italy Leftist partisans were ruling illegally, while the Government, in its effort to ensure pure anti-Fascist administration, was appointing untried officials without the training and determination necessary for their difficult job. The Liberal attack ended the Resistance period of unity and collaboration among the major anti-Fascist parties, all of which were represented in Parri's cabinet.

At this point Parri, in an unaccustomed burst of vigor and decision, announced that he would carry on without the Liberals. But he was too late, for De Gasperi then gave the tottering Government the final push by resigning and declaring that the Parri government had lost its "mandate," which had been based on unanimity among the parties. Thereupon Parri called a Committee of National Liberation press conference and denounced the crisis to the assembled journalists as an attack on the democratic conquests of the Resistance by the same conservative forces that had once brought Fascism to power; the departing premier spoke darkly of a "coup." Among the participants, De Gasperi, stung to the quick, rose to his feet and urged the foreign correspondents present not to report literally Parri's bitter words. This embarrassing occasion put an end to Parri's career as a minister, though he continued to stand in Italian political life as a symbol of the republican virtues of the Resistance.[26]

In opening the crisis of November 1945 the Liberals had no chance themselves of obtaining the succession, for they were an elite group of the Right, although in this moment they reflected a widespread mood in weary postwar Italy. Nevertheless the Liberals were dwarfed by the three great parties that shared the leadership of the Italian laboring classes. The succession would have to go to one of them, and there could be little doubt as to which, for neither the Liberal *bourgeoisie* nor the Allied occupiers could accept a government headed by revolutionaries. De Gasperi was given the task of putting together a new coalition cabinet, which he succeeded in doing after prolonged negotiations and haggling over ministries among the parties; in his overtures to the Liberals De Gasperi emphasized the return to legality and ordinary administration, and he managed to bring them into the new Government after tortuous delays.

Therefore the Christian Democrats, who had ostensibly judged the November crisis to be "premature," finally gathered its fruits. Alcide De Gasperi came to power on 10 December 1945, and the postwar reconstruction of the Italian State began.

Many factors in the final crisis of 1945—the part played by the Anglo-American authorities, the attitude of the Vatican, the motives of the Communist Party—are still unknown. But one fact stands out clearly: the notable character of the man De Gasperi. During the long 1945 crises the austere Christian Democratic secretary had established his personal ascendancy over the other Italian political leaders, except for Togliatti and the nobly intentioned but quarrelsome and ineffectual leaders of the Party of Action. As Foreign Minister, De Gasperi had borne no responsibility for the economic stagnation and fumbling "de-Fascistizing" of 1945 Italy; on the other hand, he had achieved a rapport with the Americans that was to stand in good stead any future government of his. Though his Catholic ties were unquestioned, De Gasperi had given the universal impression of being able to rise above considerations of party and class when the situation of the Italian State demanded it; this was not the least of the reasons for his emergence as premier at the close of 1945.

Epilogue

THE TRIUMPH OF CHRISTIAN DEMOCRACY
IN ITALY AFTER 1945

Italy came out of World War II in a truly revolutionary situation. The State's prestige and authority had touched bottom, the reigning dynasty was discredited, and the three parties of the Left —the Communists, the Socialists, and the Party of Action—were ready to govern the nation through the Committees of National Liberation, the organs of the Resistance. Only the Western occupying powers and the Catholic movement upheld what was left of the State and kept it from falling into the hands of the Left. From 1945 to 1947 an uneasy shifting coalition of the parties of the Left and the Center ruled Italy under Allied supervision. The mass parties—Christian Democratic, Communist, and Socialist—dominated postwar politics, though the Liberal elite contributed many distinguished jurists and economists to successive assemblies and cabinets.*

What thwarted the revolution of the Left? The Western powers, the Church and the vast middle groups of Italian society joined forces behind Alcide De Gasperi, one of the few Italian Catholic leaders with an acute "sense of the State," who improvised a solution to the immediate political and economic problems of postwar Italy. For the the first time since the era of Giolitti, an Italian statesman found a formula by which the democratic process, instead of leading to deadlock and recurring crisis, could be made to bring forth a stable, moderate succession of governments. A judicious combination of American economic aid, Catholic electoral weight, and rural reforms favoring small property brought

---

* In addition to the previously cited works of Tupini and Andreotti, see the collection *Dieci anni dopo 1945–1955* (Bari, 1955), with essays by De Rosa and Leo Valiani on postwar politics. In this Epilogue we are presenting a sketch of this postwar Christian Democratic Party without claims to historical finality.

Italy through her postwar uncertainties.* Instead of government
by revolutionary committees backed by partisan militias, the old
Italian State reappeared. The Monarchy, compromised by Fascism
and the 1943 flight from Rome, was sacrificed to popular resent-
ment, but the traditional apparatus of ministries, prefectures,
Carabinieri, and magistrates was saved and strengthened under
the new Republic.

Less than a year after a national referendum established the
Republic, the Italian State completed its return to normality when
in May 1947 the Communists were ejected from De Gasperi's government. Under Togliatti the Communist Party had followed a
double policy of collaboration within the government coalition
and revolutionary agitation among the laboring masses, carrying
both tactics to an extreme. On the one hand, the Communists in
the Constituent Assembly joined the Christian Democrats in
voting to write the Lateran Pacts into the new constitution; on the
other, Communist squads did not stop at using armed violence
against Christian Democratic organizers. But the Communist
revolutionary tactic failed when faced determinedly by De Gasperi,
who was bent on re-establishing law and order through the State
police; and any serious political collaboration between the two
mass parties was doomed by Togliatti's obligatory anti-American-
ism, accentuated at the very moment in which De Gasperi was obtaining grants of aid from Washington. The long partnership
between Christian Democrats and Communists and its final dissolution probably worked to the detriment of the Communist
Party, confusing its adherents and allies, while giving De Gasperi
breathing space in which to begin his restoration of the Italian
State. Certainly by 1947 the whole Italian Left was disoriented,
largely because of ambiguities in the Communist party line.

Indeed, it is doubtful that De Gasperi's middle ground would
have proved so firm had not the Italian Left split. The postwar
policies of Stalin and Tito did much to estrange anti-Fascists of
the Italian middle and professional classes, who in the wartime
Resistance had willingly worked with the Communist Party. The
bitter question of Italy's Adriatic borders, the examples of "people's democracy" in Poland and Czechoslovakia, and the Zhdanov

* It will be remembered from Chapter Nine that De Gasperi had an *intrinsic*
sympathy for the United States.

policy within the Soviet Union all did much to discredit Togliatti's efforts at maintaining a common front. Though many anti-Fascists remained in individual opposition to the Christian Democrats, they respected De Gasperi's sincere faith in democracy and distrusted Togliatti's party.

On a concrete political plane the agonies and schisms of the Italian Left had immediate results. The Right Wing of the Italian Socialist Party broke with Nenni's majority and joined De Gasperi as a minor secular party in his government coalition. The bourgeois revolutionary Party of Action, torn between its aspirations toward Socialist equality and its concern with traditional Liberal freedoms, between its sympathies for Moscow and for Washington, broke up and disappeared. The parties of Nenni and Togliatti remained, with their great proletarian followings, a mighty force of opposition and protest, but after 1948–49 they no longer presented an immediate revolutionary threat, for De Gasperi had succeeded in restoring the Italian State.

De Gasperi accomplished this by breaking with the revolutionary traditions of anti-Fascism and the wartime Resistance, but at the same time reaffirming the constitutional and democratic character of his government. He saved the State bureaucracy from the "purges" demanded by the Left, thus attracting much support from those who had in a routine way collaborated with the Fascist Regime and feared above all a revolutionary reign of terror and revenge. Instead of the puritanical harping on the sins of Fascism by which Leftist intellectuals antagonized so many ordinary bourgeois Italians, De Gasperi and his ministers were willing to draw a veil over a past that had, after all, compromised the whole nation. Perhaps nothing else he did was more popular with those millions who had been neither convinced Fascists nor opponents of the past Regime.

Another and even more important point in which De Gasperi showed a political wisdom ripened by bitter experience was in his relation to his own party and to the Catholic world. For many years he had seen that a Catholic reconquest of secular society could not come in the form of a "clerical" regime controlled by the Holy See or the Hierarchy, that civil life had its own problems and needs of which the Roman clergy was often little aware. A reconstruction of Italy along Christian lines would be possible only if the Christian Democrats had an autonomous, constitutional-democratic program permitting alliances with other moderate democratic parties, the Liberals, Republicans, and Social Democrats. For De Gasperi, the alternative to his center policy was not an integrally Catholic Italy, but rather a united laic front against the Catholics and an eventual triumph of the Left; instead of blind opposition to all forms of Liberalism and Socialism, however moderate, Catholics must learn to distinguish and make use of what is essentially Christian in these movements. In this lay De Gasperi's great and original moment of discernment, but also the source of his loneliness within the Party and the Italian Catholic world.

Hence De Gasperi, though backed by an absolute majority of Christian Democratic votes in the Chamber between 1948 and 1953, never dispensed with the collaboration of the three constitutional Center parties, frankly preferring a democratic coalition to a one-party confessional regime. In so doing, this successor to Giolitti braved persistent opposition from his own party, which was hungry for power and position and obsessed by visions of a solidly Catholic Italy. The Christian Democratic Party had during the crusades against the Left become even more of a political catchall than the Popular Party had ever been, and proved extraordinarily restless. Many veteran leaders, such as Piccioni and Segni, who had worked with De Gasperi in the 1920's, esteemed highly the man's restraint and sense of balance, but the younger generation of Christian Democrats, trained in Catholic Action and, often, in Father Gemelli's university, were impatient to take over and impose some sort of integral political solution in place of De Gasperi's compromises.

During the years of De Gasperi's successive ministries the Party developed anew within itself the old divisions of Right and Left that always existed among Italian militant Catholics. However, the factions were far livelier than in the past, for they were now contending for real political power. The Right aimed at a new regime based on a union of all conservative forces of the nation, letting Monarchists and Neo-Fascists into the governmental coalition and jettisoning the constitutional democratic baggage that De Gasperi clung to. As ever, the Right saw a single enemy, Communism, against which an authoritarian Catholic-Nationalist regime was the only safeguard. Pressures on De Gasperi's Center from the Right were strong, for the Party had picked up many new adherents from the propertied classes, particularly in the South, concerned primarily with the defense of their social position and willing to support any anti-Communist leader, be he Liberal, Christian Democrat, or Fascist. The Right also included many important figures of Catholic Action, like the national president Dr. Luigi Gedda and the Jesuit radio priest Father Lombardi. In this lay the real strength of the Christian Democratic Right, for through the dynamic "civic committees" Catholic Action controlled a large part of the Christian Democratic vote. Thus through the channels of Catholic Action the conservatives of the Vatican were able to maintain a constant check on the Party. But even when pressures from the Right were at their peak, in the spring of 1952, De Gasperi and most of his party refused to join with the Fascist-Monarchist forces in any national alliance.[1]

The Left of the Italian Christian Democrats was and is hard to describe. Perhaps the one characteristic common to all of it in the years after the war was an impatience with De Gasperi's middle way and his insistence on political democracy rather than Catholic social doctrine as the central concern of the Party. The Party seemed to its various Left Wings to be a more fundamental reality than the parliamentary State, and capable in itself of leading Italy to a Christian rebirth. Much was said about the role of the Party in the wartime Resistance.[2] The doctrinal Left of Dossetti and La Pira believed seriously that Catholic social teachings could prevail over Marxism-Leninism among the Italian proletariat; in practice this proved to be a pious illusion. The Catholic trade-union leadership aimed at turning the Christian Democratic Party into a genuine labor party, in defiance of its "interclass" function and character. De Gasperi was always able to stem these currents, for their political inadequacies were evident.

However, the Christian Democratic Left had more than illusions to its credit. A lone figure among the veterans of the Popular Party, Giovanni Gronchi, broke away from De Gasperi's Center and took a "Left" line of his own, calling for an independent Italian foreign policy within the West European group of nations and an "opening" toward Nenni's Socialist Party, in spite of its seemingly everlasting ties with the Communists. Gronchi seemed to favor an equivocal neutralism in foreign affairs and a "Left" regime at home, based on the combined strength of the Catholic and Socialist working masses. The ruling Center group in the Party kept him away from the real levers of power by making him President of the Chamber of Deputies, but in 1955 he was unexpectedly hoisted into the presidency of the Republic by the combined votes of Communist, Socialist, and Left-Wing Christian Democratic members of Parliament. President Gronchi was for some time the attractive, ambiguous maverick of Italian Christian Democracy, a symbol of vague, fascinating possibilities.

Eventually the discontented younger generation of Christian Democrats gathered around the figure of Amintore Fanfani. In spite of his Fascistic past, the young professor had gained De Gasperi's favor by his energy and talent as an administrator. Many of the De Gasperi government reforms were drafted and executed by Fanfani, who by 1954 loomed large as De Gasperi's heir, first in the Party secretariat and then in the premiership itself. Fanfani carried his organizing talents into the affairs of the Party, and in large measure his current prevailed. But in the course of his rise to power some of Fanfani's flaws had also come to light: a dictatorial temperament and a vein of demagogy that lost him trust and sympathy within the Party and perhaps ultimately hurt his popularity in the nation. Somehow the rules and customs of parliamentary and party democracy never seemed entirely congenial to him.

Against Fanfani's bid for control stood the Christian Democratic "notables," each with a powerful position within the Party and in their own regions. Some of them, like Scelba, Segni, Piccioni, and Spataro, were veterans of the Popular Party. Others, like Gonella, Andreotti, and Moro, were Catholic Action men, veterans of FUCI who had thrown in their lot with De Gasperi and served in his cabinets. After the retirement and death of De Gasperi in 1954 Fanfani proved unable to control the Party effectively, in spite of his position as political secretary, for the "notables," drawing on support from outside the Party organizations that Fanfani's current dominated, stayed on top. The "notables," together with such independent figures of the Center as Taviani and Del Bo, keep turning up in each new Christian Democratic ministry like cards in a reshuffled deck. And behind the whole apparatus of Party and Government stand certain shadowy figures of great power, such as Enrico Mattei, head of the State Oil and Gas Trust. With the concentration of power in Catholic hands, the inner life of Italian-organized Catholicism has become intense and complex, far beyond the fathoming of a foreign observer. The Party is merely part of a whole Catholic world, and what happens on the level of Party organizations, as Fanfani's early failures have shown, is often not politically decisive. Fanfani was strong in the Party, but not in the Italian Catholic world as a whole.

The rapid changes in the Italian political balance since 1953 are current events, not yet history. De Gasperi's system, a sapient dosage of Catholic and Center-party voting strength, maintained by support from the Hierarchy and Catholic Action on the one hand and by prudent reforms and foreign assistance on the other, holding at bay a Monarchist-Fascist Right and a "Social-Communist" Left by appealing to a widespread desire among the Italians for constitutional parliamentary rule, was essentially a skillful balancing act worthy of Cavour or Giolitti. Since 1953 this system has been crumbling little by little. The whole nation, now largely freed from the phantoms of a monarcho-Fascist past as well as from the threat of revolution, has been showing unmistakable signs of impatience with a ruling party worn down by years of uninterrupted tenure of power, of factional strife, of heavy and overt confessional pressures. The Italian Left has recovered its force and freedom, now that the Socialists have definitely broken with the Communists. The meaning and significance of Italian politics can no longer be compressed into a mold of any sort—Clerical, Stalinist, or Fascist—and the ideological war or crusade is no longer the only form which political struggles in Italy must take. In the circumstances of Italy in the 1960's the traditional human values of Liberalism and Socialism, with their ancient and partly Christian roots, have a new chance to prevail, and a serious democratic alternative to Christian Democratic rule might be in the making.

The history of the Italian Catholic movement throws light upon one of the great problems of world history, that of the relationship of the Roman Church and the pontiff to the modern State and to civil society in general. From the promulgation of *Unam Sanctam* through the eras of Counter Reformation, Absolutism, Revolution, and Restoration, the direct, political power of the Pope waned, and the age of Liberalism put an end to it, except for the Vatican itself. The Papacy has come to depend on alliances with rulers, from Francis I to Mussolini, which assured it a substantial indirect power. However, in our own time this method has been visibly failing, and the Church has begun to exert its indirect power in complex new ways. The Catholic lay militant has been pressed into service as a twofold intermediary between the Papacy and the modern State: as a member of Catholic Action he responds to the Hierarchy and assists it, but as a Christian Democrat he assumes direct political responsibilities that the Hierarchy must shun. Through him, a new figure in the history of the Church, the Papacy learns much about the modern world and how it can be influenced. But in sponsoring or at least permitting lay Catholic parties with some degree of political autonomy, the Papacy has renounced no part of its claims to a rightful empire over the minds of men, but has rather chosen a new method, in harmony with the mass organization of the modern world.[3]

CONCLUDING NOTE ON CHRISTIAN DEMOCRATIC PROGRAMS, 1899–1948

Catholic party programs tend to be generic, like all such documents, leaving their authors uncommitted in specific situations. The first of them, the program of the "young Christian Democrats" of 1899, was corporative, in the best style of Toniolo and Murri. The corporations envisaged were *vertical,* according to profession and industry.

The Christian Democrats of 1899 advocated a radical departure from classical Italian Liberalism: "We want the proportional representation of the parties in the councils of the Communes and of the Nation, as a higher form of political fairness, and as making for the proportional representation of social interest, which will be the result of corporative social organization." These words should be understood in the context of their time: in the political crisis which the Italian State was going through in 1899, certain banal statements of the Christian Democratic program concerning political and civil liberties had the effect of putting these young Catholics squarely against the conservative, militaristic Italy of Humbert I, and foreshadowed the later development of the Popular Party.

In their points concerning agriculture, always one of the most serious parts of any Catholic social program, the Christian Democrats of 1899 laid emphasis upon the development of small holdings, through appropriate legislation providing for state aid, instruction, and arbitration.

Finally, the Christian Democratic program called for peace between Italy and "the Catholic Church and the Roman Pontificate, which are the historico-moral and political center of the Italian Nation"; the true greatness and prosperity of Italy lay in her working with the Papacy and becoming the center of "a universal renewal of humanity," along Christian and popular lines. The glory of the twentieth century, predicted these overeager disciples of Leo XIII, would be "international Christian Democracy," as if there were room in the Catholic world for more than one international authority.

The January 1919 program of the Popular Party expressed no such messianic confusion of the ecclesiastical and the political, which was the root-error of Murri's movement: Point 8 called simply for the "freedom and independence of the Church in the full unfolding of her spiritual mission, liberty, and respect for the Christian conscience, considered as foundation and bulwark of the life of the Nation, of popular freedoms and of the rising conquests of civilization in the world." The Popular Party program emphasized freedom of labor organization rather than vertical corporativism, and parliamentary political democracy rather than corporate political representation: these were the advances of Don Sturzo over Murri.

Like the 1899 Christian Democrats, the *Popolari* attached fundamental importance to the formation and legal protection of small rural holdings, on a family basis. In the social and political struggles of 1919–22, agricultural reform was the point at which the Popular Party most clearly separated itself from the parties of Italian conservatism: this particular part of their program had real political consequences.

The Christian Democratic party programs and resolutions of 1944–48 present, in many ways, a cautious return to early "integral" ideas on Church and State. In 1944 *Idee ricostruttive della Democrazia Cristiana,* the first party statement, declared that "a free regime will be strong only if based on moral values," and that the State should therefore "watch over morality, protect the integrity of the family, and aid parents in their mission of educating the new generations in a Christian way." "It is in the particular interest of democracy that the Christian leaven ferment the whole life of society," which meant concretely, among other things, that the State should recognize religious marriage and assure "freedom" to Catholic schools. The Popular Party's severely expressed autonomy was gone. Instead, De Gasperi's successor party showed its Vatican and Catholic Action origins in accentuating its programmatic confessionalism.

Carried along by the proletarian-revolutionary spirit of 1944, the Christian Democrats spoke of worker participation in the profits, management, and capital of industrial enterprises. In this the Party was seeking an impracticable middle ground between socialism and capitalism and its ideas bore no fruit, since they failed to interest the proletariat itself. The Christian Democratic agricultural program, on the other hand, actually found expression in Article 44 of the new constitution and in postwar agricultural legislation. In the middle and rural sectors of the nation Christian Democracy has found its true support.

The Party called for the partial expropriation of large estates, where economically and technically feasible, the compensation of landlords, and the creation of numerous small holdings, *beni di famiglia.* For these to be viable, extensive State aid in fertilizers, livestock, and machinery was envisaged. This program, largely translated into law, has really changed the face of much of rural Italy and created a new class of peasant proprietors owing their status to the Christian Democratic government. Rural cooperatives and peasant unions have assumed a new importance. The land-reform villages, the layout of which always features a state-built parish church, promise to be a great reservoir of Christian Democratic voting strength, realizing one of the soundest and most consistent programmatic aspirations of the Christian Democratic movement in Italy.

THE ELECTORAL SITUATION OF ITALIAN
CATHOLIC PARTIES, 1919–48

Catholic voting strength varied sharply from region to region at the last two elections held under democratic conditions, 1919 and 1921. As might be expected from the facts of Catholic Action, the Catholic stronghold—Catholic bank and cooperative activity and the circulation of the Catholic press—was in the northern and central areas of the nation, especially Lombardy-Venetia and the Trentino. In 1919 the Popular Party got 25.2% of the popular vote in the North, 12.5% in the South. Of every 100 Popular Party voters, only 19 were Southern. There was no significant change in 1921, when the Popular Party scored heavily in the Veneto (35.9%), the Trentino-Tyrol (32%), and the Marches (29.9%). In the great Lombardy region the Party did well, with 25.6% of the total vote. The Party made an unimpressive showing in Trieste, where nationalist tendencies had made some inroads on Liberalism but left no room for the Catholics, and got less than one-fifth of the total vote in Tuscany and Emilia, areas where the parties of the Left could appeal to discontented rural proletarians and sharecroppers, the rural proletariat above all being organized in the Po valley. In the stagnant electoral area of the South the Popular Party generally made a mediocre or very poor showing, which is not surprising, for the South generally responded to the prevailing winds from Rome. After providing a reservoir of Liberal deputies for the government majorities of Italy from the time of Unity up to 1922, the whole area went Fascist in the coerced elections of 1924. Italy as a whole went 66.3% for the Fascist list, but the South far exceeded that: 77.8% of its voters were recorded as favoring the new masters.

When free elections were resumed in 1946, the picture changed in certain features, though retaining its basic pattern: the Christian Democrats swept the old Popular Party strongholds, the bedrock area of Italian Catholicism in Lombardy-Venetia and the Trentino. However, there was a general rise in the Catholic vote throughout Italy: instead of the prewar 21% of the total vote, the Christian Democrats now got 35.2% in 1946 and 48.5% in 1948. These additional votes came from all over Italy, and the reasons for them are not hard to conjecture: the decadence of Italian Liberalism and the fear of Communist revolution suffice to account for them. However, there is a striking shift toward the Christian Democratic Party in the South, where its percentage of the total vote almost equals that which it obtained in the North in 1946 (35.0% and 35.3%, respectively), and in 1948 the Christian Democrats did a shade *better* in the South than in the North (49.6% and 47.9%, respectively), a reversal of all previous trends. In the 1946 and 1948 elections 31.6% and 33.6%, respectively, of all Christian Democratic voters were Southern. The South had again responded to the new masters.[1]

The Italian Ministry of the Interior, in analyzing the 1946 returns, made some discoveries of sociological importance. The Christian Democrats did best in the countryside and in small towns, and their percentage of the total vote lessened in large towns and cities: their lowest percentage (26.9%) was gathered in cities of over 500,000 inhabitants, and their highest in towns and districts of less than 30,000.[2]

These facts accord well with the common observation that the Italian countryside is far more imbued with Catholic feeling and practice than the city. For example, when Monsignor Dalla Costa assumed the see of Florence in 1932, he made a four-year visitation of his archdiocese, and found that in the country parishes almost everyone fulfilled his principal religious duties, that traditions such as the family recitation of the rosary were still respected, and that the conditions of country life favored the maintenance of Catholic faith and piety. Dalla Costa said that the peasantry was benefited by sharecropping contracts that provided for the peasants' life-needs without making them rich.[3]

Unfortunately, statistics of Catholic Action do not antedate 1946. In that year in all Italy there were 150,866 members in "Catholic Men," 369,015 in "Catholic Women," 367,392 boys in Catholic Youth and 884,992 girls; unfortunately these first statistics are not broken down according to region. At a glance, they suggest that postwar female suffrage has had great effect in increasing the Christian Democratic vote in Italy if these Catholic Action members can be taken as a small sample of the larger Catholic voting public.

In 1954, for which statistics are more detailed, there were 284,455 "Catholic Men," 161,576 of whom were in North Italy. In that same year of 597,394 "Catholic Women," 344,399 were North Italian. Catholic Youth also shot up between 1946 and 1954: like the other major branche of Catholic Action, it too is predominantly North Italian. In 1954 it numbered 556,752 boys and 1,215,977 girls. Lombardy-Venetia is the strong hold of all these mass organizations, far exceeding in members the othe populous regions of North Italy.

The higher educational branches of Catholic Action are much smalle and more evenly distributed throughout the nation: in 1954 there wer only 5,488 members of FUCI, of both sexes, and 12,643 *Laureati Cattolic*. In these elite organizations North Italy does not outweigh the Central an Southern zones. It is worth noting that FUCI is, surprisingly, the mos "anemic" of the Catholic Action branches, though its role in the recen past of Catholic and Christian Democratic Italy has been so significan These figures suggest something well known to contemporary observer that Italian culture is more secular than Italian political life.[4]

NOTES TO CHAPTERS

1. See Achille Plebano, *Storia della finanza italiana* (Turin, 1899), I, 495, 502. Gino Luzzatto, *Storia economica dell'età moderna e contemporanea* (Padua, 1952), II, 390, and Aldo Romano, *Storia del movimento socialista in Italia* (Milan-Rome, 1954), I, 298. Military conscription further embittered the Italian peasantry: see the many references in Emilio Sereni, *Il capitalismo nelle campagne* (Turin, 1947), and important literary sources such as Verga's great novel *I Malavoglia*.

CHAPTER ONE

1. The early history of the Catholic movement is ably presented by Fausto Fonzi, *I cattolici e la società italiana dopo l'unità* (Rome, 1953). A more general view may be found in Pietro Scoppola, *Dal neo-guelfismo alla democrazia cristiana* (Rome, 1957). These authors are both Catholic. The work of the Liberal Giovanni Spadolini, *L'Opposizione Cattolica* (Florence, 1954), is also useful, though perhaps unnecessarily wordy; a Marxist point of view is put forth by Giorgio Candeloro in *Il Movimento cattolico in Italia* (Rome, 1953), a polemical work bristling with useful statistics.

2. Scoppola, *Dal neo-guelfismo*, pp. 48–49, Fonzi, *I cattolici*, pp. 65–66, and Gabriele De Rosa, *Storia politica dell'Azione Cattolica in Italia* (Bari, 1953), I, 143–50, hereafter cited as *L'Azione Cattolica*.

See also Gabriele De Rosa, *Filippo Meda* (Florence, 1959), pp. 123–32, for an interesting profile of a peasant priest of Lombardy, one of the labor-chaplains commissioned in 1900 by the Archbishop of Milan to forestall rural socialism by establishing militant Catholic peasant unions, based on the principles of *Rerum Novarum*. Catholic unions were aggressive in securing more decent conditions of labor from landlords and textile mill owners in Lombardy; often, going further, they set up genuine rural cooperatives. Parish priests taught many of their peasants to read and write, so that they could qualify to vote for Catholic candidates to local and eventually national office. It should be noted that this Christian-Democratic foundation was in greatest part the work of parish clergy, a fact that was to have consequences sometimes harmful to the autonomy of lay parties inspired by Catholic social doctrines and dependent upon Catholic votes.

3. Fonzi, *I cattolici*, p. 56.

4. See Sereni, *Il capitalismo*, pp. 198–205, and Fonzi, *I cattolici*, pp. 34–50.

5. See I. Felici, *G. B. Scalabrini* (Monza, 1954).

6. See the successive volumes of Murri's *Battaglie d'oggi, 1899–1905*, in their *edizione definitiva* (Rome, 1903–5).

7. Aside from the many works of Toniolo himself, see the hostile discussion by Piero Gobetti, *La Rivoluzione Liberale, Saggio sulla lotta politica in Italia* (Turin, 1950), pp. 74–77, and the sympathetic summary by Maurice Vaussard, *L'Intelligence catholique dans l'Italie du XXe siècle* (Paris, 1921), pp. 21–62.

8. De Rosa, *L'Azione Cattolica*, I, 200.

9. This is the opinion of one of his authoritative biographers, Count Edoardo Soderini, in *Il pontificato di Leone XIII* (Milan, 1932–33), III.

10. By 1903 the *Opera dei Congressi* was beginning to coordinate Catholic voting in local administrative elections, the first step toward outright partisan political action on a national scale. The program of the *Opera* was officially defined as "Christian Democratic": this amounted to making the single official Catholic Action organization of Italy into an overtly political mass movement. See De Rosa, *Filippo Meda*, pp. 48–49.

11. See De Rosa, *L'Azione Cattolica*, II, for a lively narrative and discussion of the period 1904–18. On Pius X's early political attitudes, see Nello Vian, "Due lettere del Vescovo di Mantova Giuseppe Sarto intorno al processo Stoppani–Osservatore Cattolico," *Rivista di storia della Chiesa in Italia*, VIII (1954), 383–96.

The future Pius X, when he was still Patriarch of Venice, had in a covert way—*alla chetichella*—done much to put forward municipal alliances between Catholics and Liberals, favoring a common front against "subversives" of the Left. See Giovanni Spadolini, *Giolitti e i cattolici* (Florence, 1959), pp. 228 and 253. Spadolini observes, in his general review of the period 1901–14, that after 1904 and the break between the French Republic and the Holy See, Catholics had good reason to favor an Italian government loyal to the Triple Alliance, which came to appear as the principal bulwark of conservatism in Europe. Thus, Italian Catholics had international as well as domestic grounds for rallying to the Italian Monarchy. *Ibid.*, pp. 238–40.

12. Scoppola, *Dal neo-guelfismo*, pp. 93–94. Suardi later published an account of the 1904 transactions in *La Nuova Antologia*, 1 November 1927 and 1 May 1929.

13. See Luigi Albertini, *Venti anni di vita politica* (Bologna, 1951), II, 253.

14. See Beniamino Palumbo, *Il movimento democratico cristiano in Italia* (Rome, 1950). The journal *L'Azione* of Cesena remains the best source for the history of this movement. It is interesting to note that Donati came from Faenza, the one city in the Romagna of a definitely "Clerical" leaning. For Donati's early writings see *La Voce*, 25 November 1909 and 5 January, 16 March 1911. As a young disciple of Salvemini, Donati was much concerned with the ignorance and illiteracy of the South Italian countryside, which he attributed largely to the way in which that area was slighted by Italian educational laws and appropriations; he indicted Parliament and the Government with a wealth of statistics and legal citations.

15. See the illuminating article by the Marxist Mario Ronchi, "Le origini del movimento contadino cattolico nel soresinese," *Movimento Operaio* (May–August, 1955), pp. 423–38, and De Rosa, *L'Azione Cattolica*, I, 206.

16. See De Rosa, *L'Azione Cattolica*, I, 151 *et seq.*, 246 *et seq.*, and L. Sturzo, *I discorsi politici* (Rome, 1951), pp. 351 *et seq.*

Sturzo differed from the Catholics of the prosperous Po valley in his attitude toward Giolitti's moderate regime. While the North actually benefited from Giolitti's methods, the South did not; indeed, in Sturzo's view the moderate "clienteles" of the South, a necessary parliamentary support of Giolitti's governments, had to be fought without compromise. A Northern Christian Democrat like Meda might see some reason for holding fire on Giolitti, if only momentarily, in order to halt the further de-Christianization of Italian public life and stem the tide of socialism; but Sturzo saw the central government at Rome, in the person of its school administrators, as the very agent of further de-Christianization, and distinguished himself in the Sicilian Catholic opposition. Sturzo held that the Giolitti system in the South was corrupting the parish clergy and reducing it, at certain times and places, to the level of an election agent for local moderate-Liberal cliques; the papal ban on voting received at best a formal and hypocritical compliance in the Southern constituencies. Hence Sturzo's advocacy of a militant, autonomous and lay party of Christian inspiration as the only hope for thoroughgoing reform in Italy. See De Rosa, *Filippo Meda*, pp. 66 and 108, and Spadolini, *Giolitti e i cattolici,* pp. 119–21.

17. See Vaussard, *L'Intelligence catholique,* pp. 63–83.

18. The Holy See in December, 1912, actually reproved the Trust. See Vaussard, *L'Intelligence catholique,* pp. 75–76, 334–38.

19. See Barbier, *Histoire du catholicisme libéral et du catholicisme social en France* (Bordeaux, 1924, V, 225–27). See also *Civiltà Cattolica,* IV (1927), 285–400; II (1928), 13, 55–68; III (1928), 158–60, and De Rosa, *L'Azione Cattolica,* I, 100 *et seq.*

20. See Candeloro, *Il Movimento cattolico,* pp. 334–41, and Tupini's journal *L'Organizzatore* of Rome. Catholic cooperatives were as important as Catholic unions in North Italy.

CHAPTER TWO

1. Albertini, *Venti anni di vita politica,* II, 123.
2. Gabriele D'Annunzio, *Le Canzoni della gesta d'Oltremare* (Milan, 1915), pp. 17 *et seq.* This is the fourth book of the *Laudi.*
3. De Rosa, *L'Azione cattolica,* II, 329–37.
4. Candeloro, *Il Movimento cattolico,* pp. 343–45.
5. *Civiltà Cattolica,* IV (1911), 244, 358–63.
6. *L'Azione* (Cremona), 7 October 1911.
7. *Ibid.,* 16 September 1911.
8. *La Torre,* 6 November 1913.
9. *Ibid.,* 6 January 1914.
10. *Ibid.,* 21 May 1914.
11. *Corriere d'Italia,* 12 August 1912.
12. *Idea Nazionale,* 20 February 1913.
13. *Ibid.,* 30 January 1913.
14. Alfredo Rocco, *Scritti* (Milan, 1938), I, 81.
15. De Rosa, *L'Azione cattolica,* II, 375–78.

CHAPTER THREE

1. The Clerico-Moderate policies of the pontificate of Pius X were well described by an eminent forerunner of Italian Fascism:
"For the Catholics of Italy entrance into politics was singularly hard. . . . But slowly and cleverly the Clerical Party organized the multitudes which revolutionary liberalism had failed to draw: it founded clubs, mutual-aid societies, country banks; it shook the inertia of clergy and aristocracy, overcame the bishops' reluctance, published magazines and newspapers, tested its early strength in municipal elections and got a parliamentary training in its congresses. Nevertheless its political consciousness was still weak, and the masses were too passive; it lacked a name, a standard, a program. Meanwhile the Moderate Party, wearing itself out in action, went on losing votes and dropping its best leaders along the road day by day. Hence, rejected by the great public

seething with Jacobin slogans, it shrank almost to an academy. The highest types were still in its ranks, but instead of being an army it remained only a General Staff.

"An alliance with the advance guard of the Clerical Party was hence unavoidable: the one had the political personnel, the other the votes, and both had almost the same necessity of social defense; the Clericals accepted Rome as Italian, together with the State and the new fundamental freedoms, the Moderates forgot the old [Catholic] denial of the Fatherland in order to protect that Fatherland with a new class of citizens, against all opposition open or hidden, as summed up in the attack against the monarchical and bourgeois government." (Alfredo Oriani, *La Rivolta ideale*, Part II, Chapter 6, written in 1946.)

2. See Gino Luzzatto, *Storia economica dell'età moderna e contemporanea* (Padua, 1952), II, 468–73, and Antonio Fossati, *Lavoro e produzione in Italia* (Turin, 1951), pp. 449 *et seq*.

3. Fossati, *Lavoro e produzione*, p. 494.

4. Albertini, *Venti anni di vita politica*, II, 229, 271. Mussolini, then editor of *Avanti!*, did much to embitter these conflicts in his belief that they were the prelude to a revolution.

5. Fossati, *Lavoro e produzione*, pp. 439–40.

6. For a bitter but enlightening account of Giolitti's withdrawal in 1914 see Albertini, *Venti anni di vita politica*, II, 277–81. Ivanoe Bonomi, *La Politica italiana da Porta Pia a Vittorio Veneto* (Turin, 1944), pp. 306–7, discusses the spring 1914 crisis from a Social-Democratic point of view.

7. Saverio Cilibrizzi, *Storia parlamentare* (Rome, 1951), IV, 322–24. Since Cilibrizzi gives a partial account of Labriola's speech and barely mentions Comandini's, these must be consulted in the *Atti Parlamentari, Discussioni alla Camera dei Deputati, Tornata del 3 aprile 1914*. For Salandra's notion of Catholicism as an instrument of the "ethical State" see De Rosa, *L'Azione Cattolica* II, 317–19. Salandra regarded Catholic instruction as a means of keeping the masses subservient to the State, while the superior citizen, he thought, could find the moral law within himself. These views recall the motives of the Fascist Regime in establishing religious training through the *riforma Gentile*.

8. *Civiltà Cattolica*, 1914, III, 108.

9. *Ibid.*, p. 102.

10. Albertini, *Venti anni di vita politica*, III, 256–59, draws on Austrian and Bavarian diplomatic documents to show the real sympathies of Pius X and Cardinal Merry Del Val for the Austrians, and their fear of Pan-Slavism. But *Civiltà Cattolica*, III (1914), 499 and 637–38, showed indignation at the German violation of Belgian neutrality, presumably a reflection of the Holy See's view.

11. Matthias Erzberger, *Erlebnisse in Weltkrieg* (Stuttgart-Berlin, 1920), 4.

12. Albertini, *Venti anni di vita politica*, II, 260–62, De Rosa, *L'Azione Cattolica*, II, 387–89, illustrate this point of view by quoting from the intransigent *Unità Cattolica* of Florence.

13. See the previously cited works on Mussolini and Corridoni.

14. *Lega Democratica Cristiana Italiana V° Congresso Nazionale* (Cesena, 1915), 2, hereafter cited as *Lega D.C.I.*

15. Donati noted proudly in *L'Azione* (Cesena), 11 October 1914, that "from the integralists of *Unità Cattolica* to the modernizers of the *Corriere d'Italia* ... all the Clericals are for a pro-Austrian neutrality. ... Only we democratic Catholics can say that we were ... right from the beginning, favorable to the national war." Yet there was no confusion with Italian Nationalism, which the

Christian Democrats regarded as "a danger for the Catholics," treating the Church as a servant rather than a mother. See *L'Azione,* 28 June 1914.

16. *Lega D.C.I.,* 53.

17. *L'Azione* (Cesena), 23 May 1915.

18. *Lega D.C.I.,* 106.

19. See Filippo Meda, *I Cattolici italiani nella guerra* (Milan, 1928), pp. 9–43. It is clear from what Meda says that most Catholics could find no distinctively *Catholic* position in 1914–15. On the one hand, they regarded war as a scourge which might be averted by prayer. On the other, Catholics like Meda had the conventional conception of just national interests in the pursuit of which war might become necessary. The two positions were never reconciled.

The same dangerous equivocations of Catholic neutrality were authoritatively expressed in *Segretariato generale dell'Unione Populare fra i Cattolici d'Italia, Guerra e neutralità nel pensiero dei cattolici italiani* (Padua, 1915). See also Antonio Salandra, *La neutralità italiana* (Milan, 1928), pp. 222–24.

20. *Il Cittadino di Brescia,* 17 April and 14 May 1915.

21. *Ibid.,* 7 May 1915.

22. *Ibid.,* 30 April 1915.

CHAPTER FOUR

1. Meda, *I cattolici,* p. 30.

2. De Rosa, *L'Azione Cattolica,* II, 422–63.

3. *Ibid.,* II, 425–30.

4. Agostino Gemelli, *Il nostro soldato* (Milan, 1917).

5. See Arrigo Serpieri, *La guerra e le classi rurali italiane* (Bari, 1930).

6. *Ibid.,* pp. 177, 257–58. Catholic cooperatives underwent a similar evolution.

7. De Rosa, *L'Azione Cattolica,* II, 432–53, and Francesco Luigi Ferrari, *L'Azione Cattolica e il regime* (Florence, 1957), pp. 1–2, 7. On Tupini see *L'Organizzatore* (Rome, 1916), a labor journal.

8. Sturzo's conception of the Catholic movement was sociological, not theological: "Since Socialism, especially German Socialism, has given theoretical expression to the proletarian movement that has resulted from the economic changes brought about by the domination and centralization of powerful economic forces, the Socialist Party has therefore been its natural interpreter and exponent. In like manner, the Christian-Social movement has for the most part represented the economic interests of agriculture, the crafts, and small industry; having developed within State and regional boundaries, in greater contact with home and national life, and being supported by a mingling of middle-class groups and city professional people, who have the interests and mentality of small producers or *rentiers* and a prevalently juridical culture, it has therefore theorized and represented their constituent elements. . . . The basic specific characteristic of this school is its organic tendency to recognize this middle class as the legal, economic, and political base of society; the movement ultimately aims at suppressing the class struggle as a social right, though admitting it as a passing phenomenon, to be eliminated, as far as possible, from the interclass dynamics of state organization." See Don Sturzo, *Riforma statale e indirizzi politici* (Florence, 1923), pp. 10–12. See also his *I discorsi politici,* pp. 1–25. Note the significant omission of any mention of the Roman Question.

9. De Rosa, *Partito Popolare,* pp. 30–31.

10. De Rosa, *ibid.,* pp. 61–65.

CHAPTER FIVE

1. The Popular Party has been dealt with in a voluminous literature, of which no complete account can be given here. Even during its brief life much was written on it, of which Salvemini's brilliant essay *Il partito popolare a la questione romana* and Sturzo's *Popolarismo e Fascismo* are outstanding. Since World War II, which brought in its wake a period of Catholic hegemony in Italian political life, interest in Sturzo's party has been considerable: the *Popolare* veteran Stefano Jacini published a standard *Storia del partito popolare* (Milan, 1951), which is interesting in what it does *not* say, as well as in its precise and detailed narrative. Much light was thrown on the inner history of the Italian Catholic masses during the crisis of 1919–26 by a posthumously published work, F. L. Ferrari, *L'Azione cattolica e il regime* (Florence, 1957). However, the most valuable work, partly because it is the latest and partly because it is based on new archive materials, is De Rosa, *Storia del Partito Popolare*. De Rosa skillfully defends Sturzo's point of view through most of his book, which must be read very critically, but much of what he has to say is derived from both a deep understanding of the whole Catholic movement and a diligent reading of new sources.

The crisis of the Italian State after World War I has also attracted much attention once the Fascist Regime disappeared. Without presuming to exhaust the field, it may be safely said that Angelo Tasca, *Nascita e avvento del Fascismo* (Florence, 1950), an expansion of an earlier work written under the pseudonym A. Rossi, is much the most useful guide to the period 1919–22. Nino Valeri, *Da Giolitti a Mussolini* (Florence, 1957) and Gabriele De Rosa, *Giolitti e il Fascismo in alcune sue lettere inedite* (Rome, 1957) offer new source material of capital importance. In 1946 Pietro Nenni published his *Storia di quattro anni*, which had been suppressed by the Fascists at its first printing twenty years before; it remains an extremely useful guide to the curious degeneration of the Italian Left between 1919 and 1922. The Democratic-Center point of view is well represented by Count Carlo Sforza, *L'Italia dal 1914 al 1944 quale io la vidi* (Rome, 1944); the author was foreign minister in Giolitti's 1920–21 government. Giovanni Giuriati's two published books of memoirs are perhaps the best index to the progress of the Fascist movement, although Mussolini and Farinacci's occasional writings should be read as well.

In this chapter I have generally followed De Rosa's exposition, though dissenting from many of his evaluations; where no other source is indicated, his history of the Popular Party should be consulted.

Edith Pratt Howard, *Il Partito Popolare Italiano* (Florence, 1957) is exhaustive, drawing upon a wide range of published sources. Though more thorough than the work of De Rosa, Howard's work does not have the "inner track" held by De Rosa, who has more insight into the problems of the Catholic world and draws upon unpublished materials difficult for a foreigner to come by.

2. Mussolini had originally founded the *Fasci di combattimento* in Milan on 23 March 1919 as a continuation of the *Fasci di azione rivoluzionaria* of 1915, a distinctly Syndicalist movement of the Far Left combating bourgeois society as well as the official Socialist leadership. The movement had a revolutionary program, antimonarchical, antisenatorial, and anticlerical, and consisted largely of veterans. However, there was no room on the Far Left of Italian politics: that position was pre-empted by the Leninists. When Mussolini and his movement presented themselves to the voters in November 1919 they got little more than 5,000 votes in the whole nation, and it looked as if the *Fasci*

were headed for extinction. What saved Mussolini, his movement and his newspaper, *Il Popolo d'Italia*, was the Fiume expedition. Mussolini managed to ride out the 1919–20 period of discredit and unpopularity by hanging on D'Annunzio's coattails, becoming his most conspicuous spokesman and organizer in Italy; when *Il Popolo d'Italia* took up a collection for the legions of Fiume, it attracted new attention, which Mussolini heightened by a dramatic flight to Fiume itself, across the lines, for a personal interview with the *Vate*. Much of the money collected for the Fiume legions was eventually used to protect and build up the *Fasci* of Mussolini, a constant target of Socialist mob aggression; but the identification with the poet's cause gave the *Fasci* a new popular appeal. As D'Annunzio began thinking of a "march on Rome," Mussolini became one of his counselors, though never of the real inner circle.

As Mussolini pondered the possibilities of a revolutionary coup on behalf of D'Annunzio in October 1920, his attitudes toward Catholicism were already changing. Though he was still in favor of proclaiming a republic, it was clear to him that religion and the Vatican must be given full "respect" as a national force, and Marinetti's *Svaticanamento* had lost its attractions for the onetime anticlerical "specialist." Even before Mussolini became a monarchist, he had already become pro-Vatican, and hoped to be able thus to "work on" the Popular Party.

The turning point in the history of Fascism was November–December 1920. Within two months the Socialists began retreating, having failed to make their revolution, and the Italian middle class took heart. At the same time D'Annunzio was dislodged from his "Regency" by Italian armed forces, and retired in disgust to Lake Garda. Though the poet and his inner circle continued to resent what they felt was betrayal on Mussolini's part—when Fiume was under siege by Giolitti's forces Mussolini had shown no interest in a projected coup that was sure to fail—many legionaries of Fiume went over to the Fascist movement, which had so long been their principal auxiliary within Italy itself. Thus at the beginning of 1921, Mussolini was able to undertake an armed counteroffensive against the Socialists, acting as the heir of D'Annunzio's national tradition.

What happened thereafter in the Fascist movement is perhaps to be summed up in a concise formula: the Syndicalist element in the movement lost priority to the Nationalist element, and in religious policy the ideas of Rocco and Federzoni guided the rising Duce as he made his peace with much of the old Italy, including the Catholic hierarchy. See Pini and Susmel, *Mussolini: l'uomo e l'opera*, II, 68, 81–82, and F. T. Marinetti, *Futurismo e Fascismo* (Foligno, 1924), pp. 201–2.

3. Gaetano Salvemini, *Dal patto di Londra alla pace di Roma* (Turin, 1925), pp. xxix–xxxi.

4. Sturzo, *I discorsi politici*, p. 325.

5. "The *Popolari* represent a necessary phase in the process of development of the Italian proletariat toward socialism. . . . The *Popolari* stand in relation to the Socialists as Kerensky to Lenin; the twenty-fifth Italian Parliament will see the defeat of these hasty political creations based on the peasants' impulsive hunger for power, exactly as in the constitution of the Russian democratic republic." See Antonio Gramsci in *L'ordine nuovo*, 1 November 1919.

6. Nenni, *Storia di quattro anni*, pp. 49–50.

7. *La Vedetta d'Italia* (Fiume), pp. 5, 14, and 25 October 1919, and Howard, *Il Partito Popolare Italiano*, p. 152. But see Paolo Alatri, *Nitti, D'Annunzio e la questione adriatica* (Milan, 1959), p. 438, from which it can be seen that

Sturzo had a middle-of-the-road attitude toward Fiume, favoring the erection of an independent buffer state there. (Alatri's book is an important contribution to the growing Italian literature on the post-1918 crisis; on the base of a wide documentation he maintains that Nitti, rather than the venerable Giolitti, was the last best hope of Italian democracy.)

8. These comments are drawn from Salvemini, *Il partito popolare*, pp. 24–39.

9. De Rosa, *Il Partito Popolare*, pp. 145–53.

10. See Roberto Farinacci, *Storia della rivoluzione fascista*, and Paolo Pantaleo, *Il Fascismo Cremonese* (Cremona, 1931). A day-by-day narrative is given by G. A. Chiurco, *Storia della rivoluzione fascista* (Florence, 1929), III, 64–66, 281, 335, and IV, 366. See also *Civiltà Cattolica*, I (1922), 78–79, 182. Cremona is in many ways a perfect example of Fascist methods and mentality.

11. Salvemini, *Il partito popolare*, p. 47. The Socialists were divided between the parliamentary group of Turati, which was ready for alliance with Sturzo, and the Maximalists of Serrati, who took the intransigent Third International line.

12. The "veto" of the *Popolari* against Giolitti is discussed in Nino Valeri, *La lotta politica in Italia* (Florence, 1945), pp. 533–42, where the opinions of Giolitti, Sforza, Croce, and Sturzo are quoted extensively. Again Valeri examines the "veto" in *Da Giolitti a Mussolini*, pp. 101–3, 117–21, in which he makes the inference, from public and private statements of Cardinal Gasparri, papal Secretary of State, that the question of bearer bonds was at least as serious a cause of the "veto" as the reasons of anti-Fascism put forth by Don Sturzo. In fact, the Popular "veto" was the expression of a genuine incompatibility between the Party and the policies of Giolitti, who was still devoted to prewar ideals in the fields of education and economics; but this incompatibility could have been put aside in the interests of saving the Italian State from a Fascist coup.

13. See Mario Missiroli, *Una battaglia perduta* (Milan, 1924), pp. 277–83.

14. De Rosa, *Il Partito Popolare*, p. 302.

CHAPTER SIX

1. Crispolti, *Pio IX, Leone XIII, Benedetto XV, Pio XI*, p. 219.

2. Salvemini, *Il partito popolare*, p. 45.

3. F. L. Ferrari, *L'Azione cattolica e il regime*, pp. 17 *et seq.* See also Pini and Susmel, *Mussolini: l'uomo e l'opera*, II, 109, 165.

4. Father Rosa had spoken of the Holy See's discontent with the Popular Party in a most secret conversation with Premier Giolitti's private secretary (Valeri, *Da Giolitti a Mussolini*, pp. 116–19), on 25 January 1921. On 29 September 1921 similar statements by Gasparri to the writer Ernest Buonaiuti were published in *Il Messaggero* of Rome. See Buonaiuti, *Pellegrino di Roma* (Rome, 1945).

5. Jacini, *Storia del partito popolare*, p. 80, and Howard, *Il Partito Popolare Italiano*, pp., pp. 259 *et seq.*

6. *L'Eco di Bergamo*, 25 July 1924.

7. De Rosa, *Partito Popolare*, pp. 391, 457–58. Monsignor Pucci extended his pro-Fascist activities to the extent of acting as an informer of the Fascist secret police in later years. See *Gazzetta Officiale, Supplemento ordinario o* No. 145, 2 July 1946.

The whole problem of the undermining of the Popular Party by higher ecclesiastical authority is dealt with exactly and subtly by A. C. Jemolo, *Chiesa e stato in Italia negli ultimi cento anni* (Turin, 1952), pp. 606–8.

8. See Gino Valori, *De Gasperi al parlamento austriaco 1911–1918* (Florence, 1953), pp. 94–102, Giulio Andreotti, *De Gasperi e il suo tempo* (Milan, 1956), pp. 58–65, and Guido Miglioli, *Con Roma e con Mosca* (Milan, 1946), where the neutralist Catholic leader reminisces about early contact with De Gasperi in 1914–15.

9. See Donati's *Il Popolo,* 23 January 1924. *Il Popolo,* the unofficial newspaper of the Popular Party, began publication 5 April 1923, filling a vital need in the Party, since just at this point the Trust journals swung over to Fascism.

10. See Jemolo, *Chiesa e stato in Italia,* pp. 605–8. In January 1923, Santucci arranged a secret talk between Mussolini and Cardinal Gasparri, at which the Bank of Rome was discussed. Ernesto Rossi, *Il Padrone del vapore* (Bari, 1955), p. 123.

11. See the great Trust newspaper, *Il Corriere d'Italia,* 3 April 1924. In these years the Fascists reassured Italian property-owners by repeatedly professing a faith in private initiative.

12. *Il Popolo,* 23 January 1924.

13. *Il Popolo,* 22 January, 22 March, and 3 April 1924. On Gronchi's career, see *ibid.,* 30 March 1924.

14. *Il Popolo,* 29 March 1924.

15. *Ibid.,* 12 April 1924.

16. See *L'Eco di Bergamo,* 4 July 1924, and *Il Cittadino di Brescia,* 10 July 1924.

17. De Rosa, *Partito Popolare,* p. 472.

18. *Il Cittadino di Brescia,* 26 July 1924; Donati, *Scritti politici,* I, 186–87. The Lombard Conservatives who had remained faithful to the Party were against any understanding with the Socialists. See *Il Cittadino di Brescia,* 9 July, 20–22 July 1924.

19. See the remarks of Rodinò carried in *Il Popolo,* 18 November 1924.

20. *Osservatore Romano,* 10 September 1924.

21. *Il Popolo,* 11 September 1924.

22. *Ibid.,* 16 September 1924.

23. *L'Italia,* 11 and 12 September 1924.

24. *Ibid.,* 17 September 1924.

25. *L'Eco di Bergamo,* 13 and 15 September 1924.

26. *Ibid.,* 1 September 1924.

27. Quoted from Giorgio Tupini, *I democratici cristiani* (Milan, 1954), pp. 33–35.

28. For the rift between Catholic Action and the White labor organizations, see Ferrari, *L'Azione Cattolica e il regime,* and De Rosa, *Il Partito Popolare,* pp. 505–21, who shows that the Whites had enemies in the Vatican itself. For Gronchi's role see Giancarlo Vigorelli, *Gronchi* (Florence, 1956), pp. 294–320, and, above all, the numbers of *Cronaca Sociale d'Italia* kept in the Biblioteca Nazionale Centrale at Florence.

29. Igino Giordani, *Rivolta cattolica* (Turin, 1925). See especially pp. 115 and 152.

30. See Augusto Hermet, *La Ventura della riviste* (Florence, 1941, pp. 151, 341–56, 368–78, and Giovanni Papini's *Un Uomo finito* (Florence, 1934). The latter work is a violently written account of Papini's revolt against nineteenth-century "bourgeois" decencies. As a lower middle-class figure with vague aspirations toward grandeur, Papini is highly significant, and offers some clues to the mentality that accepted Fascism.

31. As a man of letters with a propensity for resounding *tours de force* in

religion and politics, Papini is often frantic and brutal, never measured or profound, continually bursting forth with a strange mixture of old and new enthusiasms; as he once put it, *per la Croce e contro il Croce.*

A far deeper literary view of Italian politics may be found in occasional essays of Riccardo Bacchelli, a grass-roots conservative, as aware of the values of the European Christian and Liberal traditions as of the ingrown, regional and factious character of Italian politics. In a remarkably prophetic essay on the fallen Giolitti, published in *La Ronda* of Rome (November-December, 1921), Bacchelli noted that "Italy abhors dictatorship to the same degree that she needs it," although dictatorial exercise of sovereign power had, in his view, to be wisely concealed. In this lay Giolitti's special merit. Bacchelli went on to note that the Italians cannot endure being nagged at over trifles, a feature of Italian character that the Fascists, with their compulsory saluting, forms of address, plumes and uniforms, were to fail to take into account. Bacchelli was especially struck by the curious Italian mass reaction to authority: Italy "protests furiously against the application of a city regulation and then tolerates for months on end with unheard-of patience the most enormous and barefaced abuses." Without any of the affected provincialism of the Tuscan *Frontespizio* group, Bacchelli could appraise seriously the importance of the Italian regions, and the danger they sometimes presented: "we have a lively and influential parliamentary system, but without a certain shade of dictatorship and personal government things do not go forward," for "underneath the abstract divisions by party and the generic divisions by class, there is a concrete division in the Chamber by regional deputation. In managing this sort of parliament lay another of Giolitti's merits.

Anyone who aspired to govern Italy, Bacchelli saw, had to contend with partisan passions and violence on one side, and widespread apathy and skepticism on the other. Giolitti managed to steer the nation between them for many fruitful years, but Mussolini's Regime was ultimately to encourage both of them to an extent previously unknown. However, when Bacchelli wrote this article, the troubles of Fascism were yet to come. Bacchelli himself put much trust in the Savoy monarchy and praised Giolitti as the "Savoy minister." In 1921 it would have seemed fantastic that Fascism would take possession of the State to such a degree that it would finally bring discredit on the Monarchy itself, exposing the royal family to charges of treachery and desertion. In his politics as in his novels Bacchelli aimed to get at human reality, social and historical, seen without the distortions and oversimplifications of "ideology." In this, too, he was unlike Papini, who passed from ideology to ideology in his restless early days. A writer with a strong native vein of Latin Catholicism, Bacchelli provides an instructive contrast to the noisily and obtrusively Catholic chauvinists of *Frontespizio,* offering a far better indication than they of the real temper of a cultivated, traditional Italian mind. See Riccardo Bacchelli, *La Politica di un impolitico* (Milan, 1948), especially pp. 162–83.

For Papini, whose 1920 conversion to Catholicism was widely attributed to the influence of Giuliotti, religion furnished new weapons for the assault upon the modern bourgeois-democratic world which he so hated. After 1931 Papini passed from the "medieval imperialism" of Giuliotti to Clerico-Fascism. His election to the Fascist government's Academy of Italy came in 1937. See Carlo Falconi, *La Chiesa e le organizzazioni cattoliche in Italia (1945–1955)* (Turin, 1956), pp. 163–69.

CHAPTER SEVEN

1. On the 1929 settlement, see Binchy, *Church and State in Fascist Italy,*

Jemolo, *Chiesa e stato in Italia,* pp. 634–59, and Luigi Salvatorelli, *La politica della Santa Sede dopo la guerra* (Milan, 1937), pp. 175–225.

2. On Fascist anticlericalism, see especially Giuseppe Bottai's *Critica Fascista,* June–July, 1931, the Fascist labor union organ *Lavoro Fascista,* April–July 1931, E. Settimelli, *Aclericalismo* (Rome, 1929), and Berto Ricci's lively journal *L'Universale,* published in Florence, 1931–35. Settimelli's diatribe, *Svaticanamento* (the word itself is a coinage of Marinetti's), was suppressed by the Regime after it came out in 1931, and I have not been able to find it. On a more official level, see "Ignotus," *Stato Fascista Chiesa e Scuola* (Rome: Libreria del Littorio, 1929). The Fascist youth publication *Il Cantiere* was scornfully anticlerical like so many of these periodicals put out by fringe elements of the Fascist Party; it only lasted a short time (1934–36). Of the same anticlerical stripe was the "Garibaldian" *Camicia Rossa.* The Regime tolerated this sort of anti-Catholic agitation; it was a harmless outlet for discontent of all kinds, and served as a weapon held in reserve against the Church.

3. The 1931 *dissidio* has been dealt with in most works on Fascism; Binchy and Jemolo have devoted special attention to it. Egilberto Martire, one of the peacemakers, gives a running account of it in his *Rassegna Romana,* March–August, 1931, and recently Achille Tamaro has added some further details in *Venti anni di storia 1922–1943* (Rome, 1954), II, 441–53. Tamaro has drawn on unpublished reminiscences of Giovanni Giuriati, an old D'Annunzio aide at Fiume who in 1931 was Secretary of the Fascist Party and led the campaign against Catholic Action. Incidentally, Giuriati's political fortunes waned after the Church and the Regime came to an agreement.

After the war the *Osservatore Romano* editor, Count Giuseppe Dalla Torre, expressed the Vatican's point of view on the 1931 dispute in a well-documented little work, *Azione cattolica e fascismo* (Rome, 1945).

There is one point about the 1931 dispute which has, to my knowledge, never been properly noted. In 1931 both De Bosis and Malvestiti, though unknown to each other, were promoting anti-Fascist sentiments among Italian Catholics, De Bosis through Vatican intermediaries, and Malvestiti directly among the members of Catholic Action. Is it unreasonable to suppose that the Fascists took alarm at these underground efforts? Certainly *Il Lavoro Fascista,* 8 July 1931, warned about an anti-Fascist plot within the Vatican itself, though carefully specifying that Cardinal Pacelli was not part of it. See Chapters Eight and Twelve. The final agreement of September 1931 provided for the removal of ex-*Popolari* from high positions in Catholic Action, an issue that the Fascists had made much of.

4. The great organ of the Fascist racial campaign was the periodical *Difesa della Razza,* edited by Telesio Interlandi. In its issue of 20 October 1938, it printed an enthusiastic endorsement from Monsignor Giuseppe Beccaria, the King's *capellano maggiore,* but on the whole it got no support or encouragement from Catholic quarters; its readers, mostly young Fascists, were hostile to Catholicism, an embarrassing fact which Interlandi tried to gloss over by frequent references to the fine anti-Jewish traditions of *Civiltà Cattolica.* In the Roman periodical *Quadrivio* the "Catholic" Fascist propagandist Gino Sottochiesa carried on a campaign of provocation, accusing the Catholic press of hostility or lukewarmness toward the doctrines of race that in 1938 had been recognized as part of the Fascist deposit of faith. The attitude of most Catholics is well represented by Mario Bendiscioli and the Austrian Father Wilhelm Schmidt, whose works, published by the *Morcelliana* of Brescia, laid down a sort of antiracist line; Papini's hostile attitude toward German racism is expressed in *La pietra infernale* (Florence, 1934), pp. 231–45. However pleased

some Catholics were over the end of "Masonic" Jewish influences in Italy, there
was little tendency to compromise with German racial doctrines. See Monsignor
Giovanni Cazzani, Bishop of Cremona, *Cristiani o pagani, Lettera pastorale
per la Quaresima 1936* (Cremona, 1936), and Archbishop Schuster of Milan's
homily of 13 November 1938, reproduced in *L'Italia* of 15 November 1938, a
strong condemnation of racism. The yearbook *Il Ragguaglio* of 1939 took a
more conciliatory stand toward Fascist racial laws, justified for reasons of state,
but it avoided endorsing current racial doctrine.

The Fascists themselves were often uneasy about the racial slogans that they
were being asked to swallow suddenly in 1938, and sometimes dared to suggest
that the "Aryan" doctrines of Germany were having an unfortunate effect on
the *italianità* of their Party. See the revealing words of Gioacchino Volpe, *Storia
del movimento fascista* (Milan, 1939), pp. 236–40; the Catholics were far from
isolated in the aversion they felt for racism. The Fascist radicals of *L'Universale*
ridiculed as late as 1937 the "little sergeants" of German racism in Italy. See
Frontespizio, November 1937, p. 860.

5. On the 1938 dispute between Church and Regime, and the estrangement
between Pope and Duce, see Luigi Salvatorelli and Giovanni Mira, *Storia del
Fascismo* (Rome, 1952), pp. 838–39, Giulio Castelli, *La Chiesa e il Fascismo*
(Rome, 1951), pp. 521–22, citing *Osservatore Romano*. On the "wound" inflicted
upon the Concordat, see Jemolo, *Chiesa e stato in Italia*, p. 670. The 1938 fric-
tions between the Fascist Party and Catholic Action were resolved by petty
measures, such as calling the Catholic Action membership card a *pagella* instead of a *tessera*, the latter term being reserved for the Fascist Party card.
Catholic Action ordered its members not to display Catholic Action badges on
Fascist Party uniforms or at political-military functions.

The provincial Catholic journals often faithfully reproduced the observations of *Osservatore Romano*, even when politically embarrassing. For example,
La Difesa del popolo, organ of the Curia of Padua, told its readers on 31 July
1938, in the midst of the racial campaign, that "Communism and Racism are
merely developments of secularism": the next issue, 7 August, was seized by the
police.

On the other hand, there were Catholics here and there who accepted the
Fascist form of racism. See Paolo Bonatelli, *Orientamenti* (Fidenza, 1942).

6. Ciano, *Diario* (Milan, 1946), I, 199–200, 203.

7. See *ibid.*, I, 132, and Jemolo, *Chiesa e stato in Italia*, p. 703. The Fascist
Ministry of Popular Culture was much concerned over the *Osservatore Romano's* anti-Axis reportage. See Francesco Flora, *Stampa dell'era fascista*
(Rome, 1945), pp. 65–66. *Osservatore Romano* continued to belittle racial
doctrines, in the name of a common rational nature of humanity. See the
Fascist reply by Arnaldo Fioretti in *Razza e Civiltà*, April 1940, an official publication of the Italian Ministry of the Interior.

8. See *Il Ragguaglio 1937*, pp. 234–41, and Dino Del Bo, *Il Bene commune*
(Florence, 1942). Of great significance was the condemnation of the works of
Alfredo Oriani, a noted literary forerunner of Fascism, by the Holy Office on
24 April 1940, raising disputes of a sort that had not been heard since Fogazzaro's *Il Santo* was condemned in 1906. Oriani had been dead for thirty years:
why choose the spring of 1940 to strike at his work? See *Il Ragguaglio 1940–41*,
pp. 297–303.

In the regained freedom of August 1943 *L'Italia* of Milan was able to vaunt
some real though recently acquired anti-Fascist merits: "the Catholics have
bent their backs less than anyone else . . . our newspaper, which is, in a way,

the live expression of the Catholics of Lombardy and Piedmont, has, especially in these last and most questionable years of Fascism, borne so many seizures of issues, suspensions and warnings to the editor, that it has stayed on its feet by a miracle. Fascism fell 25 July, and our paper was last seized on 23 July." See *L'Italia*, 25 and 26 August 1943, where like claims are made for the whole Catholic Action press.

CHAPTER EIGHT

1. On Cavazzoni's activities there is only one available source that I know, the *numero unico* edited by Leone Cavazzoni, *Stefano Cavazzoni* (Milan, 1955). See especially pp. 124–25 on the saving of the Catholic banks; p. 101 on his intervention on behalf of the "Guelf" leader Malvestiti; pp. 127–29 on his work as an intermediary between the Catholic University and the Regime; pp. 81–87 on his personal relation with Fascism; and pp. 224–39 on his work in Catholic Action and, again, the saving of the Catholic banks of North Italy.

2. *Ibid.*, pp. 231–32.

3. Galeazzo Ciano, *Diario* (Milan, 1946), I, 40–41.

4. Igino Giordani, *Alcide De Gasperi* (Rome, 1956), pp. 90–91. See also the periodical *Quadrivio* published at Rome in 1937 and 1938, an organ of the racial campaign. In this chapter I have not dealt with small-fry Catholic Fascist publications like *Secolo Fascista* or *Segni dei tempi*, since their influence was not noticeable; they are only important as symptoms of a state of mind.

Among the contributors to *Illustrazione Romana* was the veteran Catholic journalist Giulio Castelli, who also ran an agency of "Vatican and international" news, *La Corrispondenza*. Up to 25 July 1943 Castelli remained faithful to the Regime, and his denunciations of Catholic lukewarmness were quoted by the Fascist press. By 1943 Castelli had fallen out of favor in the Vatican, where finally, according to *L'Italia*, he was not allowed to set foot. See *L'Italia* (Milan), 27 August 1943, which brushed him off as a "horsefly," and also Ernesto Rossi, *Il Manganello*, pp. 9–15, for an account of Castelli's career, in which he has always turned, like a weather vane, to the prevailing winds.

5. Salvatorelli and Mira, *Storia del Fascismo*, pp. 618, 838. On Mussolini's real religious sentiments, see Ciano's reminiscences as quoted in Rossi, *Il Manganello*, pp. 38–42. Don Luigi Sturzo credited Tacchi-Venturi with arranging the agreement between Church and Regime which ended the 1931 dispute. See Rossi, *ibid.*, p. 295.

6. See *Civiltà Cattolica*, IV (1935), 92–105.

7. See Messineo's "L'Annessione territoriale nella tradizione cattolica," *Civiltà Cattolica*, I (1936), 190–202, 291–303, and *idem*, "Necessità economica ed espansione coloniale," *ibid.*, pp. 378–94. Arguing against French Catholic justifications of colonialism, Messineo points out that a people with a declining birthrate can hardly allege economic necessity for expansion. Finally, see *Civiltà Cattolica*, III (1936), 363–73, and 451–60, for Messineo's view of "Necessità di vita e diritto di espansione."

8. *Ibid.*, p. 457.

9. *Ibid.*, pp. 458–60.

10. See Father Antonio Bresciani, S.J., *L'Ebreo di Verona* (Milan, 1855), a novel first published in installments in *Civiltà Cattolica*.

11. See *Civiltà Cattolica*, series XVII, I (24 January 1898), 273–87.

12. See the programmatic article, "Della questione giudaica in Europa," published in several installments in *Civiltà Cattolica*, series XIV, VII (1890), and reprinted by Roberto Mazzetti in his *L'Antiebraismo nella cultura italiano dal*

1700 al 1900 (Modena, 1939), with the permission of *Civiltà Cattolica*, at the time of the Fascist racial campaign. On the blood accusation see *Civiltà Cattolica*, II (1914), 344, and I (1926), 367–68.

13. *Ibid.*, IV (1922), 111–21.

14. *Ibid.*, II (1928), 335–44. The *Protocols* had been published at Florence in 1921 by the *intégriste Fede e Ragione* (see Part I, Chapter One), which might account for *Civiltà Cattolica*'s skepticism concerning them.

15. See the citations in Rossi, *Il Manganello*, pp. 360–69, and *Civiltà Cattolica*, II (1938), 76–82. Father Brucculeri of *Civiltà Cattolica* took a positive view of "moderate" Fascist racism in an article he wrote for *L'Avvenire d'Italia*, 17 July 1938.

16. *Civiltà Cattolica*, IV (1938), 3–16.

17. The episode of the *Alleanza* became generally known after the war, when many of its pamphlets were reprinted together with De Bosis' work. See Lauro De Bosis, *Storia della mia morte e ultimi scritti* (Turin, 1948), with a long historical preface by Salvemini, who knew De Bosis well and followed his movement closely.

18. See the account in Luigi Salvatorelli, "L'Opposizione democratica durante il Fascismo," in the collection of essays, *Il Secondo Risorgimento* (Rome, 1955), pp. 168–69. Salvatorelli himself is a veteran anti-Fascist and a witness of much of what he writes about.

Croce's sympathy for a moderate and constitutional anti-Fascist movement was natural: he had the courage in 1929 to oppose Mussolini on the floor of the Italian Senate by speaking against the Lateran Pacts in the name of the whole Risorgimento tradition of a free Church in a free State. See *Atti parlamentari, Senato del Regno, Legislatura XXVIII, 1ª Sessione 1929*, p. 190. The compilation *Una Lotta nel suo corso* (Venice, 1954), with a preface by the Resistance commander Ferruccio Parri, has a useful biographical index of anti-Fascist militants, many of them *Crociani*.

19. De Bosis, *Storia della mia morte*, pp. 9–10.

CHAPTER NINE

1. See Donati, *Scritti politici*, F. L. Ferrari's periodical *Res Publica*, published at Brussels 1931–33, and his open letter to the President of FUCI, a mimeographed copy of which may be found at Harvard College Library Ital. 839.30.85*. Ferrari had been FUCI president under Pius X, it should be remembered.

2. See Giordani, *Alcide De Gasperi*, and Andreotti, *De Gasperi e il suo tempo*. For his earlier career, Gino Valori, *De Gasperi al parlamento austriaco 1911–1918* (Florence, 1953), and R. A. Webster, "Il primo incontro tra Mussolini e De Gasperi," *Il Mulino* (January, 1958), pp. 51–55.

3. *Lavoro Fascista*, 8 July 1931, and Andreotti, *De Gasperi e il suo tempo*, p. 130. Also *Regime Fascista*, 5 October 1939. De Gasperi always refused to petition Mussolini for clemency, even when the influential Jesuit Father Tacchi Venturi was ready to act as intermediary. See Andreotti, p. 286.

4. It is necessary to go back to De Gasperi's articles as they appeared in *Illustrazione Vaticana*; postwar republications of them are incomplete.

5. *Illustrazione Vaticana*, 1–15 October 1933, pp. 765–66.

6. *Ibid.*, 16–30 September 1933, p. 725.

7. *Ibid.*, 16–31 July 1933, pp. 555–56, and 1–15 January 1934, pp. 28–29.

8. *Ibid.*, March and April, 1934.

9. *Ibid.*, 16–31 May 1934, pp. 447–48; 16–28 February 1935, pp. 179–80.

10. *Ibid.*, 16–31 July 1935, pp. 767–68.

11. *Ibid.*, 16–30 November 1935, pp. 1209–10, in which he speaks of the "golden middle way that is the characteristic and merit of present Catholic politicians."

12. *Ibid.*, 16–31 January 1936, pp. 60–61.

13. *Ibid.*, 1–15 October 1937, p. 834.

14. *Ibid.*, 16–30 November 1937, p. 965.

15. *Ibid.*, 1–15 March 1938, pp. 182–84.

16. *Ibid.*, 1–15 June 1938, p. 448.

17. *Ibid.*, 16–31 March 1938, p. 229. Guido Gonella wrote: "Some judge on the basis of the interest one's own nation has in the establishment of a powerful state unit stretching from Hamburg to Vienna, and some instead judge on the basis of sympathy for political systems or regimes, independently of the consideration of specific national interests. This second criterion of judging the situation tends to prevail over the first."

CHAPTER TEN

1. See especially Sergio Paronetto in *Studium*, VIII–IX (1943), as reprinted in G. B. Scaglia ed., *Il Movimento laureati di Azione Cattolica. Notizie e documenti 1932–1947* (Rome, 1947), pp. 214–22. Paronetto was an associate of De Gasperi during the "preparatory" conferences of 1942–43; see Andreotti, *De Gasperi e il suo tempo*, p. 134. The former Popular Party leaders, G. B. Migliori and Stefano Jacini, regularly wrote for *Studium*, following a political line rather like that of De Gasperi.

2. Baroni, *Igino Righetti*, pp. 92–103.

3. *Ibid.*, pp. 120 *et seq.*, and 205–7.

4. *Ibid.*, pp. 138, 142.

5. *Ibid.*, pp. 156–57, 168 *et seq.*

6. *Ibid.*, pp. 234–38.

7. *Ibid.*, pp. 251–53.

8. *Azione Fucina*, 14 February 1932.

9. See also Guido Gonella, *Il Pontificato di Pio XI* (Rome, 1939), which was cautiously anti-Axis in its implications.

10. *Gazzetta Ufficiale della Repubblica Italiana, Supplemento ordinario* N. 145 of 2 July 1946; see the entry *Bronzini* among the names of the police informers listed there.

11. See *L'Italia*, 28 September 1938. It is not surprising that the Vatican organ *Fides, rivista mensile della pontificia opera per la preservazione della fede in Roma*, took time away from its usual polemics against Protestant preachers and Jehovah's Witnesses to express deep sympathy with the Poles. See *Fides*, November 1939, p. 486; in those years *Fides* was edited by the anti-Fascist veteran Igino Giordani, another Vatican exile.

12. See Guido Gonella, *Presupposti di un ordine internazionale. Note ai messaggi di S. S. Pio XII* (Vatican City, 1942), a reprint of Gonella's *Osservatore Romano* articles of January–May, 1942. Gonella's *Acta Diurna* were avidly read by anti-Fascists such as Piero Calamandrei of Florence, the noted jurist. See Jemolo, *Chiesa e stato in Italia*, p. 703.

CHAPTER ELEVEN

1. See F. Flora, *Stampa dell'era fascista* (Rome, 1945), p. 86, and H. Hermet,

La ventura delle rivista (Florence, 1941), pp. 341–74. Flora, using the Ministry of Popular Culture's press directives, shows that the Regime was always concerned over Catholic opinion and ordered newspapers to feature "Academician Papini."

2. *Principî*, April 1939, pp. 75–80; May 1939, pp. 101–8; June-July 1939, pp. 126–35; also January-February 1940, pp. 31–32.

3. *Ibid.*, August-September 1939, pp. 157–65, 180.

4. *Ibid.*, November-December 1939, pp. 209–10, 213–21. La Pira states (p. 216) that the propagation of the "new order" is not a *casus belli.*

5. *Ibid.*, June-July 1939, p. 125, and January-February 1940, pp. 27–29.

6. *Il Bargello*, 12 May 1940.

7. The source of this police information is *sentenza 73* of *La Commissione Istruttoria presso il Tribunale Speciale per la Difesa dello Stato*, Rome, 4 December 1933 (typescript). General information about the Guelf movement may be found in Malvestiti, *Parte guelfa in Europa* (Milan, 1945), and Democrazia Cristiana Comitato Regionale Lombardo, *Impegno, II° Congresso Nazionale, Parte Prima*, Lina Morino, *Contributo della Democrazia Cristiana lombarda alla preparazione dottrinale e politica del Partito e alla riconquista della libertà*, pp. 11–25.

8. *Il Popolo d'Italia*, 31 January 1934, p. 7.

9. See Monsignor Giuseppe Pecora, *Don Davide Albertario* (Turin, 1934), and the rejoinder by Monsignor Luigi Cornaggia-Medici, *Antesignani della Conciliazione* (Fidenza, 1936).

10. Cavazzoni (ed.), *Stefano Cavazzoni*, p. 101.

CHAPTER TWELVE

1. *Rivista del clero italiano*, October 1934, p. 664.

2. *Ibid.* See also the fulsome praise of the Fascist military program by Alberto Amante in *Vita e Pensiero*, November 1934, pp. 638 *et seq.*

3. Binchy, *Church and State in Fascist Italy*, pp. 422–28.

4. See *Vita e Pensiero*, August 1934, pp. 470–71.

5. *Ibid.*, pp. 489–96. After the war Giacchi became a Christian Democratic deputy.

6. *Rivista internazionale di scienze sociali*, April-May, 1928, p. 368; February-March, 1929, pp. 99–129; April 1929, pp. 163–65; and *Rivista del clero italiano*, February 1934, pp. 124–29. The latter periodical was part of the *Vita e Pensiero* chain of publications. See also Volpe, *Storia del movimento fascista*, p. 175.

7. *Annuario missionario italiano 1936*, pp. 30–58, and *Annuario missionario italiano 1937*, pp. 209, 216. See also *Popolo d'Italia*, 10 April 1937, p. 1, reporting the expulsion of foreign Protestant missionaries from Ethiopia.

8. See Pio Bondioli, *L'Università cattolica in Italia dalle origini al 1929* (Milan, 1929), a *Vita e Pensiero* publication.

9. *Rivista internazionale*, March 1939, pp. 141–46.

10. Andreotti, *De Gasperi e il suo tempo*, p. 392.

11. *Rivista internazionale*, March 1933, p. 173.

12. *Ibid.*, July 1933, pp. 410–11.

13. *Ibid.*, November 1933, pp. 732–34.

14. A. Fanfani, *Il significato del corporativismo* (Como, 1937), p. 150.

15. See Mario Rivoire, *Vita e morte del Fascismo* (Milan, 1947) pp. 128, 148–49. Rivoire, an old member of Bottai's *Critica Fascista* group, recalls many of

the false hopes and expectations that Fascist corporativism had raised, especially among idealistic young Italians. Among the latter were to be found many Catholics. In the same vein, see Camillo Pellizzi, *Una rivoluzione mancata* (Milan, 1948). Though authoritative Catholic spokesmen like Count Giuseppe Dalla Torre, editor of *Osservatore Romano*, urged the similarity between Catholic and Fascist corporative doctrine in the special May 1934 issue of *Vita e Pensiero*, devoted entirely to corporativism, these resemblances were not so apparent to many Fascists. See *Rivista internazionale*, November 1934, pp. 831 and 854, commenting on various articles in Italian journals.

16. See the Istituto Coloniale fascista publication, *Colonialismo europeo ed impero fascista* (Milan, 1936), pp. 11–31.

17. *Rivista internazionale*, May 1936, pp. 229–31.

18. *Vita e Pensiero*, June 1936, p. 250.

19. *Rivista internazionale*, May 1939, p. 256.

20. *Ibid.*, September 1939, p. 835.

21. *Rivista internationale*, March 1941, pp. 255–57.

22. *Vita e Pensiero*, July 1938, pp. 322–30, and Luigi Gedda, "A proposito di razza," *Vita e Pensiero*, September 1938, pp. 408–16. Dr. Gedda is a person of some importance in the Catholic world; for many years after the war he was head of Catholic Action in Italy.

23. *Regime Fascista*, 14 January 1939, and *Il Popolo d'Italia*, 10 January 1939. For other political statements by Father Gemelli see R. W., "Pezze d'appoggio per un cappello cardinalizio," *Il Ponte*, February 1956, pp. 316–18.

24. P. E. Taviani, *Prospettive sociali* (Milan, 1945), an interesting contrast with his *Decadenza del capitalismo* (Savona, 1935). A similar transition was undergone by Dino Del Bo, as stated in our first chapter. See *Il Ragguaglio* 1937, pp. 235–41, and the various articles by Del Bo and the polemics between Catholic and Fascist youth in the Florentine monthly *Rivoluzione* between January 1940 and May 1943.

25. Francesco Vito, *Comunismo e cattolicesimo* (2d ed.; Milan, 1944).

CHAPTER THIRTEEN

1. The sequence of events in the Italian Resistance is not simple, and it might be well to put it before the reader in a short form:

By 1942 it was clear that the "Fascist War" was lost, and the anti-Fascist parties began reorganizing clandestinely. In the spring of 1943 war-weariness and discontent produced strikes in Turin, a clear sign that the Regime was failing. The Allies landed in Sicily.

In Rome, the heads of the anti-Fascist parties began to confer together and to make contact with the Royal House: Orlando and Bonomi took the lead.

On 24 July 1943 an extraordinary session of the Grand Council of Fascism passed a resolution presented by Grandi and Bottai and supported by Ciano which clearly indicated a lack of confidence in Mussolini. When Mussolini went to the King on the next day, he was abruptly dismissed and put in custody.

The new chief of the Government, Marshal Badoglio, abolished the Fascist Party and dismissed the leading Fascist hierarchs. The anti-Fascist parties enjoyed a semi-legal status in which they were able to carry on organization and propaganda. Yet the Badoglio government announced that the war would go on.

On 8 September Marshal Badoglio concluded an armistice with the Allies, but Italy was overrun by the Germans before any further plans could be made.

The army was left without orders, while the King, the Crown Prince, and the Government left Rome in a precipitate flight to Brindisi, under Allied protection. The Germans descended the peninsula as far as Naples, liberated Mussolini, and set up a "Social Republic" under his leadership in North Italy. The army dissolved and the administration of the State went to pieces, while the anti-Fascist parties conducted a resistance to the invaders side by side with dispersed army units that refused to surrender. The ranks of the resisting forces were soon increased by refugees from the Social Republic's conscription and German labor enrollment.

In the South, where the Monarchy carried on its legal existence, the Allies tried to foster a new Italian government capable of aiding them in the campaign against the Germans. At first there was a deadlock, for the anti-Fascist parties refused to have anything to do with the discredited King and his Marshal. But in March 1944 the Soviet Union recognized the new Government and sent Togliatti, secretary of the Italian Communist Party, back to Italy. The Communists broke the deadlock by agreeing to a coalition government, in which the Christian Democrats promptly joined them. After the liberation of Rome in June 1944 a new cabinet, under Ivanoe Bonomi, was formed, with Crown Prince Humbert acting as Lieutenant-General in place of his father. The Communists and Christian Democrats, together with the Liberals, formed the government, for the Socialists and the Party of Action still maintained a veto against collaborating with the Monarchy.

However, in the North all five parties worked together under a rule of unanimity on the Committees of National Liberation which coordinated and directed the Resistance, and in the spring of 1945 an arrangement was finally concluded between the Government, the Allies, and the Committee of National Liberation of North Italy, by which the provisional authority of the latter was recognized. By the end of the war Italy was being governed by a coalition of all anti-Fascist parties (except the Republicans); in the South and Center the old governmental apparatus was soon put back together, while in the North the Committees maintained an insurrectionary people's regime until 1946, though checked by Allied military occupation.

2. The literature on the Resistance may be followed closely in the historical journal *Il Movimento di liberazione in Italia,* published at Milan since 1950.

3. See Franco Catalano, *Storia del C.L.N.A.I.* (Bari, 1956), which draws on the Committee's archives.

4. See Catalano, *Storia del C.L.N.A.I.,* pp. 316–19, and Cardinal Schuster, *Gli ultimi tempi di un regime* (Milan, 1946), a collection of documents and notes on which our account of his activities is based.

5. See G. Rovero, "Il clero piemontese nella Resistenza," in Istituto storico della Resistenza in Piemonte, *Aspetti della Resistenza in Piemonte* (Turin, 1950). On the use made of the Lateran Palace by the Committee of National Liberation, see the many references in Ivanoe Bonomi, *Diario di un anno* (Milan, 1947).

6. The German Ambassador, Rahn, found Schuster "of clearly anti-Fascist tendencies" during this period. See a memorandum of the Social Republic's Foreign Office in Istituto Nazionale per la storia del Movimento di Liberazione in Italia (Milan), *Archivio CVL,* DN IV (6).

7. The last talk between the Duce and the Cardinal throws unaccustomed light on the characters of both men. When the Duce came to the Archiepiscopal Palace at 3 o'clock on the afternoon of 25 April the delegates of the Resistance forces had not yet arrived. Schuster and Mussolini chatted for a while.

Schuster, noting that the Duce seemed stunned by his disasters, received him kindly and assured him that he was making a great sacrifice by surrendering and beginning a new life of prison or exile. When Schuster mentioned the fall of Bonaparte, Mussolini, evidently brightening a little, observed that for himself, too, the hundred-day Empire was about to end.

Schuster characteristically told Mussolini that the Church in Italy would never forget the Lateran Concordat; if all its hoped-for fruits had not been gathered, this was due in large part to the unfortunate way in which the Duce had been served by many of his party chiefs. Mussolini in turn insisted that he was outside of and hostile to Farinacci's schismatic *Crociata Italica* movement. Schuster did not pursue this subject, for he had always held Mussolini responsible. Mussolini then told of his renewed interest in religion and his reading of Ricciotti's *Life of Christ* while he was imprisoned in the summer of 1943. He and the Cardinal then began to talk about the superior influence and character of the Ambrosian clergy. Mussolini asked Schuster whether the Ambrosian rite, at least in its essential "dogmas," was in harmony with that of the Roman Church! "At this new question," remarked the Cardinal rather artlessly, "I had a sense of surprise, ascertaining the scanty religious culture of a man who had had in his hands the fate of Catholic Italy." The Cardinal might well have been shocked, for less than eight years before he had hailed this man as a new Constantine.

The conversation was broken off by the arrival of the Resistance delegates. It is clear from Schuster's account that Mussolini's queries about the Church were inspired more by admiration of its influence and efficiency than by any inward spiritual concerns. Schuster emerges from this and other testimonials as an essentially monkish and almost naïve churchman, far out of his depth in the difficult political situation of Fascist Italy; only when some religious matter was at stake did he behave with firmness and courage, as during the racial campaign of 1938 or in his relations with Farinacci. During this last interview between him and Mussolini he did something most revealing: he gave the Duce a bulky life of St. Benedict which he had just written. The mixture of monastic piety and probable joy of authorship seems characteristic not only of Schuster but of many prelates like him. See Schuster, *Gli ultimi tempi di un regime,* pp. 160–66.

8. See the Bishop of Mantua's injunctions against partisan violence, *Italia Cattolica,* 5 December 1943, and Cardinal Elio Dalla Costa, *Le Vie della pace* (Florence, 1944) and *I Cristiani veri oggi e domani* (Florence, 1944). See also *Conferenza episcopale della Regione Triveneta, Notificazione* (Venice, 1944), to which there was a Fascist reply in an anonymous pamphlet without name or date, *Contro Notificazione.* The Fascist National Republican Guard reported from Imperia in December 1944 that "the clergy continues in its anti-national propaganda." See *Archivio CVL,* DN (B), document 3.

Indeed, the higher clergy was capable of taking an active role whenever conditions allowed it. The special situation of the Trentino, where the Germans had named a Liberal prefect and banned the Social Republic, was ideal for a revival of Catholic-inspired movements. The Fascist foreign ministry was informed 20 October 1944 that "the ecclesiastical authorities [of Trent] in all this confusion have a wide field of action and seek with every means to orient the population toward an extreme clericalism of Socialist shading"; see *Archivio CVL,* DN IV (B). The Fascists were well informed, for in the first postwar elections Trent was the most strongly Christian Democratic area of Italy, the Christian Democratic vote there rising to 57.4 per cent of the local total.

9. See *Archivio CVL,* LO VIII–IX and LO VII (G).

10. See *Relazione del consultore nazionale Enrico Mattei al Congresso Nazionale del partito della D.C., tenutosi a Roma il 24 aprile 1946* (mimeographed), and the testimony of Achille Marazza in *Mercurio,* December 1945, pp. 252–54. Marazza, Christian Democratic representative in the great Committee of National Liberation of North Italy (CLNAI), emphasizes the military-political liaison network set up by his party, which maintained contacts between the partisan forces, especially the *Fiamme Verdi* and *Di Dio* units, and the prelates of North Italy. Many prisoner exchanges and eventual surrenders were negotiated with the Germans by means of the North Italian bishops, the only authority left in many areas. However, Catholic militia itself in Lombardy, including the *Fiamme Verdi,* ran to only 14.2 per cent of the 1945 total. See *ibid.,* pp. 323–26.

In Florence itself the Christian Democrats played an important part. During the final battle to free the city in the summer of 1944 the city was divided into sectors, each entrusted to one of the parties of the local Committee of National Liberation; 55 Christian Democrats were killed in action there. See the wartime reports of Avvocato Francesco Berti, a Christian Democratic member of the Committee, in his own collection.

11. *Archivio CVL,* GE XVII.

12. See the undated booklet *La Divisione Fiamme Verdi "Tito Speri"* (Brescia), prepared by the historical office of the division at Cividate Camuno, and *Mercurio,* December 1945, pp. 224–26 and 230, where the *Fiamme Verdi* clandestine press is described. The *Fiamme Verdi* leader Olivelli held that "social propaganda in depth among the masses is not called for at this moment," a point that many Catholic and conservative elements in the Resistance would find acceptable. But Olivelli was well aware of a widespread restlessness in the North. In his view, Catholic Action had a "pre-political" task of "formation" among the people, to hold off Communism and prepare the way for social reconstruction along Catholic lines. See Caracciolo, *Teresio Olivelli,* p. 169.

13. *Archivio CVL,* LO X. Communists often tried to dominate local partisan movements. The Party of Action GL (*Giustizia e Libertà*) partisan formations operating in this area, the Valtellina, complained that the Communists were trying to absorb them by threats. See *ibid.,* LO VII (G. 13 and 23).

14. Francesco Cargnelutti, *Preti patrioti* (Udine, 1947).

15. Paola Zancan, *Luigi Pierobon* (Padua, 1946).

16. In 1945 the Catholic Communist movement took the form of a political party, the Christian Left, as it called itself. The leaders of the Party had conceived of the Christian Left as part of a great federated party representing the entire Italian working class; within such a "front" the Christian Left would carry on the traditions of Don Albertario and Murri, putting forward the demands of the revolutionary Catholic peasantry. But the facts belied their aspirations as soon as the war ended. After fruitless months of trying to set on foot a Christian party of the far Left, Franco Rodano, the leading thinker of the group, admitted at the last Christian Left Party Congress, 10 December 1945, that "we have not been *objectively* able to separate Christian laborers from the ruling capitalistic groups of the Catholic world . . . in time." For, as Rodano saw it, by December 1945 the "national, democratic, anti-Fascist movement" was in the descending phase of its wartime parabola. As the prospects for a united workers' party faded, it had become clear that by itself the Christian Left Party was merely a lightning rod drawing down bolts of condemnation from the Vatican, a source of disunity and confusion for Catholics

and workers alike. The solution adopted by Rodano and the Congress was to break up the Party and join the Communists. Rodano, hailing Togliatti's expressed desire to build the Communist Party as a great party of a new type, called the Italian Communist Party "the most decisive instrument of defense of the democratic positions conquered in our country." For Catholics desiring to enter the Communist Party there were no real barriers on the side of the Party itself, for "work in the Communist Party, according to the regular terms of its statute, does not commit one to acceptance of the atheist ideology, but only of the program and political line of the Party." Thus the Catholic Communist movement ended in failure. In several respects—its distinction between "Church" and "Vatican," its interest in Christian Left movements in Eastern European popular democracies, its concern with the working class as the key to the political future—it was interesting and symptomatic of a state of mind widespread among open and alert Catholics of the Italian Left, even the Christian Democratic Left. See *Voce Operaia*, 3 December and 13 December 1945.

17. See Roberto Angeli, *Poi l'Italia è risorta* (Pinerolo, 1953), and *Rivista di Livorno, Il Decennale della Resistenza*, pp. 23–45.

18. See the clandestine newspapers of Padua, *La Libertà* (1944) and *Voce Democratica, Foglio del Partito Democratico Cristiano* (1945), as well as *La Campana, L'Ora del Popolo, organo del partito democratico cristiano* (Verona, 1944). These organs of the Resistance naturally upheld the "sacred union" of anti-Fascist parties in the Committees of National Liberation, a fact which sometimes scandalized Catholics. Interestingly, these Christian Democrats often expressed regret for the years gone by, in which Catholics had lauded the Fascist Regime because of the 1929 Concordat.

19. Clandestine pamphlet *Ai Giovani intellettuali d'Italia (a proposito di un manifesto comunista), Edizioni della Democrazia Sociale Cristiana, Toscana, Giugno 1944*. The Florentine Christian Democrats had added "Social" to their title and had as their ideal a mixed economy of State, cooperative and private management, to be brought into existence by gradual reforms on a regional level to avoid the entanglements of centralized bureaucratic control. Like many Christian Democratic resistance groups, the Tuscan "social" Christian Democrats were strongly opposed to the Monarchy. See the clandestine pamphlet *Problemi e orientamenti No. 2, La missione sociale e politica della Democrazia Cristiana, Roma, 1944*, which was actually printed at Florence. In this work, as in their other statements of ideals and programs, the La Pira group showed little sense of the values of the Liberal tradition, identifying it with "egoistic individualism" and economic exploitation. Catholics in Tuscany clashed not only with Communists, but also with the much less adroit propagandists of the Party of Action, who stressed secular education and the elimination of the Concordat as desirable goals. See the clandestine periodical *Azione Sociale, Rivista dei Giovani Italiani,* June 1944 (Florence), p. 31, and also July-August 1944, pp. 22–24, attacking the Party of Action's "laic religion of liberty" as a French-Masonic coinage imported into Italy.

20. For the background of the Party of Action see Aldo Garosci, *La Vita di Carlo Rosselli* (Rome-Florence-Milan, 1945), and Guido Calogero, *Difesa del Liberalsocialismo con alcuni documenti inediti* (Rome, 1945). C. L. Ragghianti in *Disegno della liberazione italiana* (Pisa, 1954), describes the formation of the Party of Action in 1942 by such anti-Fascist veterans as Mario Vinciguerra, who had since the death of De Bosis evidently given up hope of working "legally" through the Monarchy.

21. See the clandestine booklet by a Party of Action ideologue, "Carlo In-

verni," *I Partiti e la nuova realtà italiana* (Turin, 1944), pp. 30–33, for a hostile but penetrating view of the wartime Demo-Christians, as of 20 March 1944.

"Today it seems that the Vatican prefers a plurality of Catholic parties, in order to safeguard all future possibilities. . . . It does not seem improbable that a Clerico-Moderate party will break off from the Christian Democracy itself, which would increase notably Christian Democracy's freedom of action, cut it loose from De Gasperi's policy, and allow a closer approach to the progressive Catholic masses of certain Italian regions such as Venetia and Liguria.

"We do not believe that the Vatican will long maintain its reserve with regard to the various parties. It is probable that after the liberation of the country, or at least of Rome, when the Curia gains freedom of movement, there will be a return to a single party, most likely the Christian Democracy, with the entrance of the Christian-Socials as a splinter of the Left. . . .

"The activity of the Christian Democratic Party is uneven in various regions, both in work and in political orientation. This unevenness is caused by the fact that the Christian Democracy, which will unquestionably be a mass party, today (except in some regions) does not work among the masses. It wants to compromise nothing, and hence wants not to commit itself too much in essential questions. From this arises a tendency to wait for the Germans to leave and for the situation to clear up, with an aversion toward the rising of the masses, an attitude that is, in substance, conservative, quite aside from the more or less radical statements of its political program. On a diplomatic plane, that is, within the Committee [of National Liberation], the Christian Democracy, more than anything else, puts in an appearance, and seems to be concerned not to assume too definite a commitment in joint responsibility."

The Party of Action writer here had caught the essentials of Christian Democratic policy. In the postwar period the Christian Democratic Party was to appeal to millions of Italians who had little use for the Resistance.

22. See Catalano, *Storia del C.L.N.A.I.*, pp. 308–13.

23. See *Il Popolo* (Milan), clandestine edition of 28 February 1945 carrying *La Parola di Alcide De Gasperi agli italiani delle regioni settentrionali*, a plea from Rome for moderation and renunciation of extreme political demands.

24. See Catalano, *ibid*.

25. See Valiani, *L'Avvento di De Gasperi*, and Panfilo Gentile's account in *Il Secondo Risorgimento*, p. 387, as well as Tupini, *I democratici cristiani*, pp. 124–25.

26. See Valiani, *loc. cit.*, and Andreotti, *De Gasperi e il suo tempo*, pp. 165–69, where two quite different impressions of the same event are given.

EPILOGUE

1. One of the eminent "front" figures of the Christian Democratic Right turned out to be Don Luigi Sturzo, who came back to Italy after the war and was made a life Senator under the Republic. This conservative role, quite new for the Sicilian priest, came most into evidence in April 1952, in a curious and revealing episode. The Communists, in a bid to capture the municipality of Rome, managed to launch a "Left" ticket headed by the ailing Francesco Saverio Nitti and composed of independent secular candidates. The forces of Catholic Action were alarmed at the prospect of the capital of Italy and of Catholicism falling into the hands of the Reds, and the idea of a "civic" ticket to oppose the Communists soon went the rounds. This "civic" ticket was to include the parties of the extreme Right; and Catholic Action candidates, it was said, were

refusing the Christian Democratic label in order to run under this coalition. The power behind the ticket came largely from Father Lombardi and other organizers and agitators of the Catholic Action organization, but a respectable façade was provided by the venerable founder of the Popular Party himself. Only when the Christian Democratic Center protested against this scheme, which would have put the Party completely at the mercy of resurrected Clerico-Moderates or Clerico-Fascists, did Don Sturzo suddenly withdraw his backing and return to his natural party position. In the municipal elections the Christian Democrats received Catholic Action support after all, and won; Gedda, leader of Catholic Action, hastened to smooth over this momentary but significant public rift with the Party. See the embarrassed accounts of the affair by Christian Democratic observers in Andreotti, *De Gasperi*, p. 325, and Tupini, *I democratici cristiani*, pp. 278–81.

The involution of Don Sturzo in his old age should not be used to reflect on his political past, either in Italy or in the anti-Fascist migration when he carried on a lonely battle in London and New York. Nevertheless, the history of the Popular Party itself gives evidence of certain fundamental limitations in Sturzo's political outlook: his insistence on isolating the Party from both Giolitti and the Socialists until it was far too late to stop Mussolini, his failure to free the Popular Party from clerical pressures, and his error in believing that a largely rural party could exercise political leadership in a country where the industrial proletariat had just become aware of its real power—all these mark the weaknesses and shortsightedness of a man who was, with all his failings, one of the few great democratic leaders in the history of Italian Catholic movements.

2. See especially *Il Popolo* of 25 April, 1955, a Resistance commemorative issue of the Party organ.

3. Carlo Falconi, *La Chiesa e le organizzazioni cattoliche in Italia (1945–1955)* (Turin, 1956), pp. 358 *et seq.*, notes acutely that the Italian Catholic Action lay member has never fully recovered the autonomy he lost as a consequence of the 1931 and 1938 agreements between the Church and the Fascist Regime. On the other hand, Catholic Action itself has gone far beyond the limits once set for it by Fascism, and has reached the point of affirming a political vocation over and above the various parties, including the Christian Democratic Party; witness the success of Dr. Gedda's Civic Committees in mobilizing votes during the crucial elections of April 1948, and the consequent rise of Gedda, from 1934 to 1946 head of Catholic Youth, to the supreme lay presidency of Italian Catholic Action. Incidentally, the Civic Committees, not officially a part of Catholic Action, can by this fiction carry on political activities forbidden to Catholic Action itself by Article 43 of the Concordat.

The ascendancy of Gedda, whose policies had the publicly expressed approval of Pius XII, is in itself an interesting indication of the temper of the postwar Italian Catholic movement. Not only had Gedda shown in 1938 a tendency to accommodate himself to the racial directives of the Fascist Regime (see Chapter Thirteen), but he had been among the authors of "Operation Sturzo" (see the preceding note), which would have allied Neo-Fascists and Catholics; indeed, there was much talk of surreptitious meetings between Gedda and the MSI leader Ezio Maria Gray. However, an equally important clue to the state of postwar Italian Catholicism is furnished by the dogged opposition that Gedda kept encountering from young Catholic Action leaders, who had to be brought into line by severe measures from above.

Falconi, himself a disillusioned former adherent of autonomously minded

Catholic Left groups, sees little hope of Catholic lay autonomy in Italian politics. Rather, Italy will become the Papal State of the twentieth century, if the Vatican's aspirations are ever fully realized. The autonomy allowed French Catholics is hence unthinkable in Italy, which is destined to be an exemplary "confessional" state. The drift in that direction has been more marked since the stubborn and highly principled De Gasperi departed. See *ibid.*, pp. 415–38, and Jemolo, *Chiesa e stato in Italia*, pp. 731–39.

The great question suggested by Italy of the 1950's and 1960's is essentially this: Can there be, in Italian or European political life, any valid distinction between being a Catholic and being a Clerical? Within the Catholic world itself the distance between a De Gasperi and a Gedda is great, though to non-Catholics it may seem a mere shade of difference. However, this distinction has great *practical* consequences for non-Catholics living in or dealing with a prevalently Catholic nation.

APPENDIX ONE

1. See the program texts in Tupini, *I democratici cristiani*, pp. 326–43.

APPENDIX TWO

1. SVIMEZ, *Associazione per lo sviluppo dell'industria nel Mezzogiorno, Statistiche sul Mezzogiorno d'Italia 1861–1953* (Rome, 1954), pp. 952 *et seq.*, and Ministero dell'economia nazionale, Direzione generale della statistica, *Statistica delle elezione generali politiche per la XXVI legislatura (15 Maggio 1921)* (Rome, 1954), p. xliii.

2. See *Istituto centrale di statistica e Ministero dell'Interno. Elezioni per l'assemblea costituente e referendum istituzionale (2 giugno 1946)* (Rome, 1948), pp. liii and 26–27.

3. See Elio Dalla Costa, *Al Clero e al Popolo dell'Arcidiocesi, Lettera pastorale* (Florence, 1936).

4. See Falconi, *La Chiesa e le organizzazioni cattoliche*, pp. 399 *et seq.*, based on official Catholic Action yearbook figures.

BIBLIOGRAPHY OF WORKS CONSULTED

The most up-to-date bibliographical essay on the Italian Catholic movement is by Guido Verrucci, "Recenti studi sul movimento cattolico in Italia," *Rivista Storica Italiana*, III and IV (1955), 425–48 and 529–54. Of great critical value is the short study by Fausto Fonzi, "I cattolici e l'Italia moderna," *Itinerari* (December 1956), 603–24. Fonzi shows that postwar concern with the history of the Italian Catholic movement is not a mere reflection of Christian Democratic political successes, but also part of a general awakening of interest in the deep social aspects of history so often neglected in traditional historiography. Since the Italian State Archives have made available their materials up to 1900, studies in depth of the late nineteenth-century "Clerical" movements are now possible; if the Church should show a similar latitude, serious researches could be conducted on the inner life of Catholic prelates, their relation to the Holy See, and their connection with Catholic tendencies abroad. Fonzi points out the fundamental weakness of many non-Catholic studies of the Catholic movement, their inability to grasp religious problems and their tendency to reduce religious movements to political-economic terms exclusively. In Fonzi's view the historiography of the Italian Catholic movement must be European in its scope, must take into account local source materials, so varied in Italy, and must be shot through with an awareness of specifically religious problems.

All archive materials referred to come from the Archivio Corpo Volontari della Libertà (Partisan Military Archives), Istituto per la storia del movimento di liberazione in Italia, Piazza Duomo 14, Milan.

I. GENERAL WORKS, ARTICLES, AND PAMPHLETS

Alatri, Paolo. Nitti, D'Annunzio a la questione adriatica. Milan, 1959.

Albertini, Luigi. Venti anni di vita politica. 5 vols. Bologna: Zanichelli, 1950.

Andreotti, Giulio. De Gasperi e il suo tempo. Milan: Mondadori, 1956. (A slick piece by a Christian Democratic minister who worked with De Gasperi in the early 1940's, when the Party press was reconstructed.)

Angeli, Roberto. Pòi l'Italia è risorta. Pinerolo, 1953. (A priest and former leader of the Christian-Social movement of Leghorn, Don Angeli has since become a Christian Democrat.)

Anichini, Guido. Cinquant'anni di vita della F.U.C.I. Rome: Studium, 1947.

216 *Bibliography*

Astori, Guido. "S. Pio X ed il vescovo Geremia Bonomelli," *Rivista di Storia della Chiesa in Italia* (May-August, 1955), pp. 212–66. (A selection of unpublished documents throwing light on Pius X's politics; his quiet insistence on the Temporal Power, his refusal to permit a lay Catholic party, and his recurrent fears of Modernist heresy.)

Bacchelli, Riccardo. La politica di un impolitico. Milan, 1948.

Il Banco di Roma nell'economia coloniale. Estratto dagli atti del Terzo Congresso di Studi Colonali. Florence, 1937.

Barbier, Emmanuel. Histoire du catholicisme libéral et du catholicisme social en France. . . . 5 vols. Bordeaux: Cadoret, 1924. (An *intégriste* work, illustrating the point of view prevalent under Pius X. The book goes from 1870 to 1914.)

Baroni, Augusto. Igino Righetti. Rome, 1948.

Battaglia, A., *et al*. Dieci anni dopo 1945–1955. Bari: Laterza, 1955.

Bendiscioli, Mario. Germania religiosa nel III Reich. Brescia: Morcelliana, 1938. (An Anti-Nazi work by a democratic Catholic.)

Berti, Francesco. Relazione al P.W.B. (Typescript.) (Avvocato Berti was Christian Democratic partisan commander at Florence in 1944, and has kept a collection of his wartime reports.)

Binchy, D. A. Church and State in Fascist Italy. London: Oxford University Press, 1940. (A standard and indispensable work by an independent Catholic of Dublin.)

Bok, Pacifico V. Lux in tenebris. Rome: Partigiani ferrovieri, Ufficio Cultura e Propaganda, 1946. (Words of a Communistically inclined priest.)

Bonatelli, Paolo. Orientamenti. Fidenza: Segni dei tempi, 1942.

Bondioli, Pio. L'Università cattolica in Italia dalle origini al 1929. Milan: Vita e Pensiero, 1929.

Bonomi, Ivanoe. Diario di un anno. Milan: Garzanti, 1947. (The first anti-Fascist premier tells of how the united front of anti-Fascist parties was formed in 1943–44.)

———. La Politica italiana da Porta Pia a Vittorio Veneto. Turin: Einaudi, 1944.

Bottai, Giuseppe. Vent'anni e un giorno. Milan: Garzanti, 1947. (The memoirs of one of Mussolini's most independently minded ministers, up to the fatal Grand Council session of 24 July 1943.)

Bresciani, Fr. Antonio. L'Ebreo di Verona. Milan: Tipografia Arcivescovie, 1855. (A classic of Jesuit anti-Jewish propaganda.)

Buonaiuti, Ernesto. Pellegrino di Roma. Rome: Darsena, 1945. (Memoirs of a Modernist heresiarch, which reveal many interesting particulars about Monsignor Benigni and Cardinal Gasparri.)

———. Pio XII. Rome: Universale, 1946. (Chapters IV, V, and VI recount, tendentiously but amply, the positions taken by *Osservatore Romano* 1939–43. In spite of himself, the author shows that *Osservatore Romano* gave continual, public concern to the Fascists by its reports and comments. The Party went so far as to organize bonfires of the offending Vatican journal.)

Calogero, Guido. Difesa del liberalsocialismo con alcuni documenti inediti. Rome: Edizione U., 1945. (Calogero was one of the professors who founded the Party of Action.)

Candeloro, Giorgio. Il Movimento cattolico in Italia. Rome: Edizioni Rinascita, 1953. (A Marxist interpretation. The best chapters are those concerned with the pontificates of Leo XIII and Pius X.)

Caracciolo, Alberto. Teresio Olivelli. Brescia, 1947. (The biography of an important young Catholic Resistance leader who had been raised as a Clerico-Fascist.)

Cargnelutti, Francesco. Preti patrioti. Udine, 1947. (On "autonomous" Catholic partisan forces in the Friuli area.)

Castelli, Giulio. La Chiesa e il Fascismo. Rome: Arnia, 1951. (A well-documented work by a veteran Catholic journalist on the cordial relations that generally existed between the Regime and the Holy See. In 1946, according to Ernesto Rossi, Castelli had written *Il Vaticano nei tentacoli del Fascismo* to show exactly the reverse!)

Catalano, Franco. Storia del C.L.N.A.I. Bari: Laterza, 1956.

Cavazzoni, Leono. Stefano Cavazzoni. Milan, 1955. (A privately printed book giving testimonials by Gemelli, Colombo, and other Clerico-Fascist leaders on Cavazzoni's mediation between Mussolini and Italian Catholicism.)

Cazzani, Giovanni. Cristiani o pagani (Lettera pastorale per la Quaresima 1936). Cremona, 1936. (As bishop of Farinacci's diocese, Monsignor Cazzani, though no anti-Fascist, often had to protest against Blackshirt extremes.)

Chiurco, G. A. Storia della rivoluzione fascista. 5 vols. Florence: Vallecchi, 1929. (The detailed story of how the Blackshirts raided and occupied North Italy, told by a veterinarian.)

Ciano, Galeazzo. Diario. 2 vols. Milan: Rizzoli, 1946.

Cilibrizzi, Saverio. Storia parlamentare. 8 vols. Rome: Tosi, 1951.

La Commissione istruttoria presso il tribunale speciale per la difesa della stato. Rome (4 December 1933). (Typescript.)

Conferenza episcopale della regione Triveneta, notificazione. Venice, 1944. (A circular of protest against Axis outrages and deportations, signed by all the bishops of Istria, Friuli, Veneto, and Trent.)

[Anon.] Contro notificazione. (A Fascist answer to the protests of the Veneto bishops in 1944.)

Crispolti, Filippo. Pio IX, Leone XIII, Benedetto XV, Pio XI, Ricordi personali. Milan, 1939.

Croce, Benedetto. Speech against ratifying the Lateran Pact. Atti parlamentari, Senato del Regno, Legislatura XXXVIII, 1ª Sessione 1929, p. 190.

Dalla Costa, Elio. Al Clero e al popolo dell'arcidiocesi (Lettera pastorale). Florence, 1936.

———. I Cristiani veri oggi e domani. Florence, 1944. (A pastoral message warning Catholics against committing acts of violence during the Axis occupation.)

———. Le vie della pace. Florence, 1944.

Dalla Torre, Giuseppe. Azione cattolica e fascismo. Rome, 1946.

De Ambris, Alceste. Filippo Corridoni. Rome, 1922.

De Bosis, Lauro. Storia della mia morte e ultimi scritti. Turin, 1948.

De Gasperi, Alcide ("Demofilo"). La parola dei democratici cristiani. Rome: SELI, 1944. (A clandestine pamphlet reprinted. A traditional middle-of-the-road Catholic social program, but emphasizing "methods of freedom.")

Del Bo, Dino. Il bene commune. Florence, 1942.

De Rosa, Gabriele. Giolitti e il Fascismo in alcune sue lettere inedite. Rome: Edizione Letteratura e Storia, 1957.

De Rosa, Gabriele. Storia del Partito Popolare. Bari: Laterza, 1958. (De Rosa, a former Catholic Communist, is now apparently an autonomous, "Sturzian" Christian Democrat.)

——. Storia politica dell'Azione Cattolica in Italia. 2 vols. Bari: Laterza, 1953–54.

——. Filippo Meda e l'età liberale. Florence: Le Monnier, 1959.

La Divisione Fiamme Verdi "Tito Speri." Brescia, n.d.

Donati, Giuseppe. Scritti politici. 2 vols. Rome: Cinque Lune, 1956.

Erzberger, Matthias. Erlebnisse im Weltkriege. Stuttgart-Berlin, 1920.

Falconi, Carlo. La Chiesa e le organizzazioni Cattoliche in Italia (1945–1955). Turin: Einaudi, 1956.

Fanfani, Amintore. Il significato del corporativismo. Como, 1937. (A standard textbook explaining the Fascist corporate state, which went through several editions.)

Farinacci, Roberto. Storia della rivoluzione fascista. 3 vols. Cremona, 1931.

Felici, I. G. B. Scalabrini. Monza, 1954.

Ferrari, Francesco Luigi. L'Azione cattolica e il regime. Florence: Parenti, 1957. (A posthumously published essay by the Left *Popolare* leader, showing how Pius XI isolated the Popular Party and the "White" labor unions, 1922–26.)

Fiocchi, Ambrogio M., S.J. Padre Enrico Rosa S. I. scrittore della "Civiltà Cattolica (1870–1938). Rome: Edizioni "La Civiltà Cattolica." 1957.

Flora, Francesco. Stampa dell'era fascista. Rome, 1945. (Contains long extracts from the press directives of the Fascist "Minculpop.")

Fogarty, Michael P. Christian Democracy in Western Europe, 1820–1953. Notre Dame: University of Notre Dame Press, 1957.

Fonzi, Fausto. I cattolici e la società italiana dopo l'unità. Rome: Studium, 1953. (A short but excellent essay based on first-hand material.)

——. "Giuseppe Tovini e i cattolici bresciani del suo tempo," *Rivista di Storia della Chiesa in Italia* (May-August, 1955), pp. 233–48. (Describes the formation of a Clerico-Moderate, later Right-Center *Popolare* stronghold at Brescia under the Montini dynasty. Fonzi shows how Catholic banks and journals, originally "papal" and anti-Liberal, became the pillars of bourgeois-nationalist conservatism during World War I.)

Fossati, Antonio. Lavoro e produzione in Italia. Turin, 1951.

Francovich, Carlo. "La Stampa clandestina a Firenze," *Il Ponte* (September, 1954), pp. 1459–79.

Garosci, Aldo. La vita di Carlo Rosselli. Rome-Florence-Milan: Edizione U., 1945. (The life of a martyred forerunner of the Party of Action.)

——, et al. Il Secondo Risorgimento. Rome: Istituto Poligrafico, 1955. (See especially the essay by Mario Bendiscioli, "La Resistenza: aspetti politici," which brings out De Gasperi's moderating role among the Rome party leaders 1943–44, and Salvatorelli, "L'Opposizione democratica durante il Fascismo.")

Gazzetta Ufficiale della Repubblica Italiana, supplemento ordinario, n. 145, 2 July 1946. (A list of Fascist police informers, now very hard to find.)

Gedda, Luigi. "A proposito di razza," *Vita e Pensiero*, September 1938, pp. 408–16.

Gemelli, Agostino. Il nostro soldato. Milan: Treves, 1917.

Giordani, Igino. Alcide De Gasperi. Rome, 1956. (A work of pulpit eloquence, interesting only because the author knew De Gasperi for many years.)

——. Rivolta cattolica. Turin: Gobetti, 1925.

Gobetti, Piero. La Rivoluzione Liberale, Saggio sulla lotta politica in Italia. Turin: Einaudi, 1950. (Audacious political observations originally published at Turin in 1924.)

Gonella, Guido. Il pontificato di Pio XI. Rome, 1939.

———. Presupposti di un ordine internazionale. Note ai messaggi di S.S. Pio XII. Vatican City, 1942.

Gramsci, Antonio. L'Ordine Nuovo 1919–1920. Turin: Einaudi, 1954. (A reprint of the Italian Leninist chief's articles: see pp. 284–86 on the Popular Party.)

Hermet, August. La ventura della riviste. Florence: Vallecchi, 1941. (A lively bibliographical essay on Italian literary-political reviews, written from a Catholic-Fascist point of view.)

Howard, Edith Pratt. Il Partito Popolare Italiano. Florence, 1957.

"Ignotus" [pseud.] Stato fascisto, chiesa e scuola. Rome: Libreria del Littorio, 1929. (A set of Fascist complaints against Catholic attempts to dominate Italian education and undermine Fascism. Righetti is singled out on p. 96.)

Istituto centrale di Statistica e Ministero dell' Interno. Elezioni per l'assemblea constituente e referendum istutizionale (2 giugno 1946). Rome, 1948.

Jacini, Stefano. Storia del partito popolare. Milan: Garzanti, 1951.

Jemolo, A. C. Chiesa e stato in Italia negli ultimi cento anni. Turin: Einaudi, 1952. (The classical work on Church-State relations in modern Italy.)

La Pira, Giorgio. "Crisi della morale," *Il Ragguaglio,* 1940–41, pp. 269 *et seq.*

Lega Democratica Cristiana Italiana. Vº Congresso Nazionale. Cesena, 1915.

Luzzatto, Gino. Storia economica dell'età moderna e contemporanea. 2 vols. Padua: Cedam, 1952.

Malvestiti, Piero. Parte guelfa in Europa. Milan, 1945.

Marinetti, F. T. Futurismo e Fascismo. Foligno, 1924.

Masotti, Tullio. Corridoni. Milan: Carnaro, 1932.

Mazzetti, Roberto. L'Antiebraismo nella cultura italiana dal 1700 al 1900. Modena: Soc. Tip. Modense, 1939.

Meda, Filippo. I cattolici italiani nella guerra. Milan: Mondadori, 1928.

Medici, Luigi Cornaggia. Antesignani della conciliazione. Fidenza: Tipografia Commerciale, 1936.

Merlini, Luciano. "Il C.L.N. di Livorno," *Rivista di Livorno, Il Decennale della Resistenza,* pp. 23–45. (Merlini was one of the leaders of the Christian Social movement.)

Messineo, Fr. Antonio. "L'Annessione territoriale nella tradizione cattolica," *Civiltà Cattolica,* I (1936), 190–202.

———. "Necessita economica ed espansione coloniale," *Civiltà Cattolica,* I (1936), 378–94.

———. "Necessità di vita e diritto di espansione," *Civiltà Cattolica,* III (1936), 363–73, 451–60.

Miglioli, Guido. Con Roma e con Mosca. Milan: Garzanti, 1946. (An autobiography by the "White Bolshevik.")

Missiroli, Mario. Date a Cesare. Rome: Libreria del Littorio, 1929. (A Fascist answer to the extreme 1929 claims and interpretations of Pius XI, by one of Italy's most adroit journalistic pens. See a hostile Fascist comment on Father Enrico Rosa on p. 129.)

———. Una battaglia perduta. Milan: Corbaccio, 1924.

Momigliano, Eucardio. Storia tragica e grottesca del razzismo fascista. Milan, 1946.

Monelli, Paolo. Roma 1943. Rome: Migliaresi, 1945.

Morino, Lina. "Contributo della democrazia cristiana Lombarda alla preparazione dottrinale e politica del partito e alla riconquista della libertà," *Democrazia cristiana comitato regionale Lombardo*, Impegno, 1° Congresso Nazionale, Parte Prima. (Contains an account of Malvestiti's movement.)

Murri, Romolo. Battaglie d'oggi, 1899–1906. Rome: Cultura Sociale, 1905.

Nenni, Pietro. Storia di quattro anni. Turin: Einaudi, 1946.

Oriani, Alfredo. La Rivolta ideale. Bologna, 1906.

Palumbo, Beniamino. Il movimento democratico cristiano in Italia. Rome, 1950.

Pantaleo, Paolo. Il Fascismo Cremonese. Cremona, 1931.

Papini, Giovanni. La pietra infernale. Florence: Vallecchi, 1934.

Pecora, Giuseppe. Don Davide Albertario. Turin, 1934. (This biography, exalting the rebellious priest, enraged Clerico-Fascists.)

Pellizzi, Camillo. Una rivoluzione mancata. Milan: Longanesi, 1948.

Pini, Giorgio, and Susmel, Duilio. Mussolini: l'uomo e l'opera. 4 vols. Florence: La Fenice, 1953. (A Neo-Fascist compilation, well documented.)

Plebano, Achille. Storia della finanza italiana. 2 vols. Turin, 1899.

Pucci, Enrico. La Pace del Laterano. Florence: Libreria Editrice Fiorentina, n.d. (Contains some guarded personal reminiscences by a Monsignor who acted as an intermediary between the Regime and the Vatican in the 1920's.)

Ragghianti, C. L. Disegno della liberazione italiana. Pisa: Nistri-Lischi, 1954. (Largely concerned with the Party of Action, this book nevertheless sheds light on the general conditions of Italian Anti-Fascism 1941–44.)

Relazione del consultore nazionale Enrico Mattei al Congresso Nazionale del partito della D.C., tenutosi a Roma il 24 Aprile 1946. (Mimeographed.)

Rivoire, Mario. Vita e morte del Fascismo. Milan: Edizioni Europee, 1947.

Rocco, Alfredo. Scritti. 3 vols. Milan, 1938. (With a preface by Mussolini.)

Romano, Aldo. Storia del movimento socialista in Italia. Vol. I. Milan-Rome: Bocca, 1954.

Ronchi, Mario. "Le origini del movimento contadino cattolico nel soresinese," *Movimento Operaio* (May-August, 1955), pp. 423–38. (Shows why Miglioli was successful at Soresina, among "backward" peasants who were still paid in produce, not cash.)

Rosa, Fr. Enrico. "La questione giudaica e la Civiltà Cattolica," *Civiltà Cattolica*, IV (October, 1938), 3–16.

Rossi, Ernesto. Il Manganello e l'aspersorio. Florence: Parenti, 1958. (A polemical anticlerical work without much finesse, but bristling with useful quotations and facts, conscientiously documented. Rossi stresses the Church's acts of complicity with Fascism.)

Rossini, Giuseppe. "Un contributo alla biografia di Giuseppe Donati," *Civitas* (September-October, 1956), pp. 65–85.

Rovero, G. "Il clero piemontese nella resistenza," *Istituto storico della resistenza in Piemonte, Aspetti della resistenza in Piemonte*. Turin, 1950.

Salandra, Antonio. La neutralità italiana. Milan: Mondadori, 1928.

Salvatorelli, Luigi. La politica della Santa Sède dopo la guerra. Milan: ISPI, 1937.

——, and Mira, Giovanni. Storia del Fascismo. Rome: Novissima, 1952.

Salvemini, Gaetano. Dal patto di Londra alla pace di Roma. Turin: Gobetti, 1925.

——. Il partito popolare a la questione romana. Florence, 1922.

Scaglia, G. B. (ed.). Il Movimento laureati di Azione Cattolica, Notizie e documenti 1932–1947. Rome: Studium, 1947.

Bibliography

Schuster, Ildefonso. Gli ultimi tempi di un regime. Milan, 1946.

Scoppola, Pietro. Dal neo-guelfismo alla democrazia cristiana. Rome: Studium, 1957. (A Left-Wing, autonomously minded Catholic interpretation of the Catholic movement in Italy.)

Segretariato generale dell'Unione Popolare fra i Cattolici d'Italia. Guerra e neutralita nel pensiero dei cattolici italiani. Padua, 1915.

Sereni, Emilio. Il capitalismo nelle campagne. Turin: Einaudi, 1947. (A Marxist essay on Italy from 1860 to 1900. There are many references in it to the Catholic peasant and landowner.)

Serpieri, Arrigo. La guerra e le classi rurali italiane. Bari: Laterza, 1930.

Settimelli, E. Aclericalismo. Rome, 1929. (An abusive anticlerical pamphlet, by an old Futurist.)

Sforza, Carlo. L'Italia dal 1914 al 1944 quale io la vidi. Rome: Mondadori, 1944.

Soderini, Edoardo. Il pontificato di Leone XIII. 3 vols. Milan: Mondadori, 1932–33.

Spadolini, Giovanni. Giolitti e i cattolici. Florence: Le Monnier. 1959.

———. L'Opposizione Cattolica. Florence: Vallecchi, 1954. (A verbosely written but clever book by a young associate of Mario Missiroli.)

Sturzo, Luigi. I discorsi politici. Rome: Istituto Sturzo, 1951.

———. La Mia battaglia da New York. Milan: Garzanti, 1949. (Sturzo became bitter during the war, and in 1946 urged De Gasperi not to sign the Paris Treaty. Sturzo's lonely battles were fought in 1940–46, all of them failures.)

———. Popolarismo e Fascismo. Turin: Gobetti, 1925.

———. Riforma statale e indirizzi politici. Florence: Vallecchi, 1923.

[Note: Don Sturzo's Opera omnia are in process of publication at Bologna by Zanichelli (1954–).]

Suardi, Gianforte. "Quando e come i cattolici poterono partecipare alle elezioni politiche," Nuova Antologia, November 1, 1927, pp. 118–23. (A narrative of the alliance between Catholics and Liberal-Conservatives at Bergamo, and the relaxation of the non expedit in 1904, as a result of discreet government pressures.)

Svaticanamento. (Anonymous pamphlet banned by the Fascists in 1931.)

SVIMEZ. Associazione per lo sviluppo dell'industria nel Mèzzogiorno, Statistiche sul Mèzzogiorno d'Italia 1861–1953. Rome, 1954.

Tamaro, Achille. Due anni di storia, 1943–1945. 3 vols. Rome: Tosi, 1948. (A Neo-Fascist work.)

———. Venti anni di storia 1922–1943. 2 vols. Rome: Tosi, 1954. (Tamaro was a Fascist diplomat, with an Irredentist political past.)

Tasca, Angelo [pseud. A. Rossi]. Nascita e avvento del Fascismo. Florence: La Nuova Italia, 1950. (A standard work.)

Taviani, P. E. Decadenza del capitalismo. Savona, 1935.

———. Prospettive sociali. Milan, 1945.

Tupini, Giorgio. I democratici cristiani. Milan: Garzanti, 1954. (Young Tupini is a rising political figure in the Party he writes about.)

Una lotta nel suo corso. Preface by Ferruccio Parri. Venice: Neri-Pozza, 1954.

Valeri, Nino. Da Giolitti a Mussolini. Florence: La Nuova Italia, 1957.

———. La lotta politica in Italia. Florence: La Nuova Italia, 1945.

Valiani, Leo. L'Avvento di De Gasperi. Turin: Silva, 1949.

Valori, Gino. De Gasperi al parlamento austriaco 1911–1918. Florence: Parenti, 1953. (Helps to deflate the legend that De Gasperi was an Irredentist or a friend of Cesare Battisti.)

Vaussard, Maurice. L'Intelligence catholique dans l'Italie du XX⁰ siècle. Paris, 1921.

Vian, Nello. "Due lettere del vescovo di Mantova, Giuseppe Sarto . . . ," *Rivista di Storia della Chiesa in Italia*, September–December, 1954, pp. 383–98.

Vigorelli, Giancarlo. Gronchi. Florence: Vallecchi, 1956. (A "Gronchian" biography of President Gronchi, wordy but valuable, which makes much of his ties with Murri and, later, Donati.)

Vito, Francesco. Comunismo e cattolicesimo. 2d ed. Milan: Vita e Pensiero, 1944. (The only publication of the Catholic University group of Gemelli during the Resistance period.)

Volpe, Gioacchino. Storia del movimento fascista. Milan: Garzanti, 1939.

Webster, Richard A. "Il primo incontro tra Mussolini e De Gasperi," *Il Mulino*, January 1958, pp. 51–55. (De Gasperi's first meeting with the agitator Mussolini in 1909 at Maia Bassa, then Untermais; an episode ignored by his Christian Democratic biographers, Giordani and Andreotti, but amply attested by the Catholic and Socialist publications of Trent.)

——. "Pezze d'appoggio per un cappello cardinalizio," *Il Ponte*, February 1956, pp. 316–18. (An anthology of Father Gemelli's pro-Axis and anti-American speeches and written remarks, 1937–41, with reference to their sources.)

Zancan, Pablo. Luigi Pierobon. Padua, 1946. (A Resistance biography.)

II. Periodicals, Clandestine and Official

Ai giovani intellettuali d'Italia (a proposito di un manifesto comunista), Edizioni della Democrazia Sociale Cristiana, Toscana, giugno 1944. (A clandestine pamphlet, evidently of the La Pira group.)

Annuario missionario italiano 1936, 1937.

L'Avvenire d'Italia. Bologna. (One of the most important Catholic newspapers of Italy which survived the Fascist period.)

L'Azione (Cesena). (Organ of the Romagnole Christian Democrats, 1914–15.)

L'Azione (Cremona). (The journal of Miglioli's Catholic peasant movement.)

Azione, Fucina. (The newsletter of F.U.C.I. after 1932.)

Azione Sociale, Rivista dei giovani italiani, June–July–August, 1944 (Florence). (This little periodical was published illegally by a group of Catholic anti-Fascists based at the Dominican church of Santa Maria Novella.)

Camicia Rossa. (Published at Rome by Ezio Garibaldi under the Fascist Regime, this periodical represented itself as the continuation of the Garibaldian patriotic and anticlerical tradition.)

La Campana, L'Ora del popolo, organo del partito democratico cristiano (Verona). (A clandestine newspaper, 1944–45.)

Il Cantiere. (A radical Fascist youth publication, 1934–35.)

Il Carroccio. (A small Irredentist-Nationalist journal, 1908–10.)

Il Cittadino di Brescia. (The standard Catholic newspaper of Brescia, controlled by the Montini family, 1899–1925, of Clerico-Moderate but Anti-Fascist coloring.)

Civiltà Cattolica. (Published at Rome by the Jesuits since 1850.)

Civitas. (Published by Filippo Meda at Milan when he was a Popular Party leader.)

Comunismo e i cattolici, edizioni di "Voce Operaia," Movimento Comunista Cattolica. (Clandestinely printed at Rome in 1944.)

Bibliography

223

Corriere d'Italia. (The Roman organ of the *Trust*, it did not survive the general contraction of Italian newspapers in the early years of the Fascist Regime.)

Critica Fascista. (Published at Rome all during the Fascist period by Giuseppe Bottai: organ of Fascist "nonconformists.")

Crociata Italica (Cremona). (An effort by priests to rally Catholics to the Axis cause 1943–45. Edited by Don Tullio Calcagno, it was violently anti-Semitic. The Pope was regarded as a prisoner of the Allies.)

Cronaca Sociale d'Italia. (Published by Gronchi and other Catholic "White" labor leaders for a few months in 1926.)

Difesa Della Razza. (The semiofficial organ of the Fascist racial campaign of 1938, edited by the pro-Nazi and covertly anticlerical Telesio Interlandi.)

La Difesa del Popolo. (Organ of the Curia of Padua.)

L'Eco di Bergamo. (The Catholic newspaper of Bergamo, neither *Popolare* nor Clerico-Fascist.)

Emilia, Rivista mensile di cultura. (Special issue dedicated to the Resistance, April 1955.)

Fede e Ragione. (An *intégriste* publication, full of antidemocratic and anti-Semitic diatribes, that came out in Florence, 1919–23.)

Fides, Rivista mensile della Pontificia opera per la preservazione della fede in Roma. (Edited in the late 1930's by the anti-Fascist Igino Giordani, who had found refuge as an employee of the Vatican Library.)

Geopolitica. (Rome, 1939–41. Launched with the honorary editorship of Bottai, with personal blessings of the Duce, to spread "living-space" theories in Italy. Fanfani was a consulting editor.)

Idea Nazionale. (The leading organ of the Italian Nationalist Party, 1910–14.)

Illustrazione Vaticana. (1933–38.)

Italia. (Successor to Albertario's Osservatore Cattolico, this newspaper was never completely "Fascistized," and has always been the authentic voice of the Milanese curia and of Lombard Catholic Action.)

Italia Cattolica. (Venice, 1943–45: it favored the Social Republic.)

Italy Today. (Monthly Bulletin issued by Friends of Italian Freedom, May 15, 1930.)

Lavoro Fascista (Rome). (The Fascist labor-union newspaper, which was a spearhead of the Fascist campaign against Catholic Action in 1931.)

La Libertà (Padua). (A clandestine Christian-Democratic sheet.)

La Liguria del Popolo. (The *intégriste* weekly of Genoa.)

Il Movimento di liberazione in Italia (Milan). (A historical journal of the Resistance.)

L'Organizzatore (Rome). (A Catholic white-collar workers' paper, 1914–16, illustrating the early career of Umberto Tupini, later a prominent figure associated with Sturzo and De Gasperi.)

Il Popolo. (Newspaper of the Popular Party, 1923–25, under Donati. The masthead was revived by De Gasperi, Gonella and Andreotti in 1943, when the Christian Democratic Party was organized at Rome.)

Il Popolo (Florence). (Published clandestinely by the Christian Democrats, 1943–44.)

Il Popolo (Milan). (Published clandestinely, 1944–45.)

Popolo d'Italia. (Mussolini's newspaper, 1915–43.)

Principî. (A supplement to the Florentine archdiocesan review *Vita Cristiana*, edited by La Pira, suppressed in 1940.)

Problemi e orientamenti, No. 2. La missione sociale e politica della democrazia cristiana. Rome, 1944. (A clandestine pamphlet actually printed at Florence.)

Quaderni di cultura e Storia Sociale. (A postwar independent Catholic publication of Leghorn.)

Quadrivio. (A racist sheet published at Rome, 1937–39. Sottochiesa wrote articles aimed at Catholic readers.)

Il Ragguaglio. (Catholic cultural yearbook published 1935–41.)

Rassegna Romana. (A Clerico-Fascist monthly edited by the Honorable Egilberto Martire, which did its best to smooth over the 1931 dispute.)

Razza e Civiltà (Rome).

Regime Fascista (Cremona). (Edited by Farinacci.)

Il Regno (Florence). (First journal of the Italian Nationalist movement 1903–8, under Corradini.)

Res Publica (1931–33). (Published by Ferrari at Brussels to warn Catholics against Fascism.)

Rivista del clero italiano (Milan).

Rivista internazionale di scienze sociali (Milan). (Part of Gemelli's press.) (Founded by Toniolo, now controlled by Gemelli.)

San Marco. (Florence, August-September, 1943, a successor to *Principî* of 1940, put out by the La Pira group.)

Secolo Fascista. (A radical Fascist journal, edited by Giuseppe Fanelli, which professed to be Catholic.)

Segni dei tempi. (A Clerico-Fascist publication of Fidenza.)

Unità Cattolica (Florence). (An intransigent clerical newspaper that finally died in 1927, typical of the first generation after Pius IX.)

L'Universale (Florence, 1931–35). (A cultural journal of young Fascist nonconformists, which often verged on anticlericalism, obscenity, and talent.)

La Vedetta d'Italia (Fiume).

La Voce (Florence, 1908–13). (One of the most serious and influential political-literary reviews of Giolittian Italy.)

Voce Operaia. (Clandestine, later legal, organ of the Catholic Communists of Rome.)

Voce Democratica, Foglio del Partito, Partito Democratico Cristiano (Padua). (A clandestine publication, 1944–45, in a center of militant Catholicism.)

INDEX

Africa, Italian East, 155, 159
Albertario, Don Davide (journalist-priest), 5, 7, 152, 152n, 220
Albertini, Luigi (senator), 15, 26, 27, 38
Alleanza Nazionale, 126–28, 204
Allies (Anglo-American, of World War II), 163–64, 167, 174, 176, 177, 178, 207–8
Amendola, Giovanni, 77
Andreotti, Giulio, 87, 137, 141, 169, 183, 223
Angeli, Roberto, 215
Amoroso, Luigi, 157
Aquilanti, Francesco, 35
Arias, Gino, 157
Autonomy, political, 105, 139, 141, 149, 172, 180–81, 185, 214
Avanti! of Italian Socialist Party, 39, 42, 194
Azione Fucina, 137
L'Azione (Cesena), 17
L'Azione (Cremona); on Libyan War, 30–31; on Mussolini, 47

Bacchelli, Riccardo, 200
Badoglio, Marshal Pietro, 169, 170, 207–8
Balbo, Italo, 90
Bank of Rome, 29–31, 109, 119, 199; relations with Fascist Regime, 119–20
Bargellini, Piero, 106, 127n, 145, 145n
Bassani, Ettore, 150
Battelli, Guido, 32–34
Battista, Cesare, 83
Bendiscioli, Mario, 201, 216
Benedict XV (Pope 1914–22) (Giacomo Della Chiesa), 21, 44, 78
Benigni, Monsignor Umberto, 21
Bernareggi, Monsignor, Bishop of Bergamo, and *Movimento Laureati*, 140–41
Berti, Francesco, 216
Bicchierai, Don, and war crisis of 1943, 163, 164

Bilenchi, Romano, 144n
Binchy, Daniel, 153, 216
Bissolati, Leonide, 45, 59–60
Blackshirts, 57, 77, 80, 81, 82, 93, 112, 116n
Bok, Pacifico V., 168n, 216
Boldrini, Marcello, 159
Bonomelli, Monsignor, Bishop of Cremona, 6, 30, 31
Bonomi, Ivanoe, 14, 70, 71, 74, 173, 174–75, 207–8, 216
Borgoncini-Duca, Monsignor, papal Nuncio, 122
Bottai, Giuseppe, 93, 113n, 116n, 144, 207, 216, 223
Brucculeri, Father Angelo, 122n, 204
Bruni, Gerardo, 169
Bülow, V. K. A. von, 87

Cacciaguerra, E., 16, 47
Calcagno, Don Tullio, editor of *Crociata Italica*, 163, 223
Calogero, Guido, 216
Casonini, Fausta, 160
Castelli, Giulio, 203
Catholic Action, 50–51, 52–53, 54, 57, 79, 80, 81, 103–5, 110–12, 115, 118n, 120, 127, 138–42, 144–45, 148, 151, 167–68, 182, 184–85, 189–90, 201–3, 207, 212–13, 223
Catholic Communist movement, 168–69
Catholic Congresses, 4, 5, 6, 9, 11
Catholic movement in Italy: and Christian Democracy, 9–12; intransigent origins of, 3–9; Left, Right, and Center elements of, 16–23; and Libyan War, 31; and Nationalism, 23–25; and Pius X, 12–16; and relations with Vatican, 30–31; social programs of, 9, 10–12, 15, 20, 21–23
Catholic University of Milan, 57, 119–20, 142, 155, 157–58; and Fascists, 109, 120
Cavazzoni, Stefano, 54, 73, 76, 104, 119–20, 152, 162, 203

Cavour, Count Camillo, xi, 24
Christian Democracy: as anti-Fascist movement, 116–18; beginnings of movement, 9–12; and Catholic voting, 9; and Crispolti, 9–10; and De Gasperi, 131, 135, 141, 174–77; and Fanfani, 161; and Guelfs, 144, 148–52; and La Pira group, 144–48; and Leo XIII, 12; and Libyan War, 31; and Meda, 9–10, 10n; and Murri, 9; and Pius XI, 79; and Popular Party, 54, 62; programs of, 187–88; and reconstruction of Italian State, 178–85; and Red Week, 42; revival under Fascism, 111, 129, 131, 137, 169–77, 209, 210, 211, 212; and Taviani, 161; and Toniolo, 10–11; and World War I, 45–46
Christian Socialists, 169
Ciano, Galeazzo, 113n, 114–15, 116n, 121, 207
Civiltà Cattolica, vii, 122–27
Clerico-Moderates, 19, 20, 41, 48–49, 50, 52, 54, 55, 63, 64; and Fascism, 89, 119–22
Colombo, Luigi, 79, 120
Committees of National Liberation, 162–76, 178, 208, 210, 211
Communist Party, Italian, 59, 69, 144, 163–77, 178–80, 184, 208, 210–12
Concordat, Lateran (1929), 209, 211; and Church-State relations, 110–13, 115; and education, 156
Coppola, Francesco, 34
Cornaggia-Medici, Monsignor Luigi, 151, 162, 206, 218
Corporative systems (Fascist), 11, 156, 157–58, 161
Corporativism, 10–12, 22, 23, 112, 122n, 131, 132, 157, 207
Corradini, Camillo, 68
Corradini, Enrico, 23n, 27, 37, 224; and *L'Idea Nazionale*, 34
Corridoni, Filippo, 40n, 45
Corriere della Sera, 15, 26; and D'Annunzio's war poetry, 27–29
Crispi, Francesco, xii, 55
Crispolti, Marquis Filippo, 9, 11, 15n, 19, 20, 89
Croce, Benedetto, 36, 59, 72, 127, 204, 217

Dalla Costa, Monsignor Elio, 164, 190
Dalla Torre, Count Giuseppe, 142, 201

D'Annunzio, Gabriele, 24, 27–29, 46, 59, 65, 66, 197
Davanzati, Roberto Forges, 34
De Bosis, Lauro, 126–28, 201, 204
De Gasperi, Alcide, 55n, 69, 73, 82–88, 91, 95–97, 100–102, 128, 129–36, 137, 141, 142–43, 144, 152, 157, 169, 171, 174, 175, 176, 177, 178–83, 204, 218, 221, 223; and Mussolini, 222
Del Bo, Dino, 116–17, 118, 183, 207
Demochristians, 16; nature of movement, 17; absorbed into Popular Party, 17
De Rosa, Gabriele, 196, 218
De Rossi, Don Giulio, 96
De Stefani, Alberto, 157
Di Dio partisans, 166, 210
Di Rudinì, Antonio, xii
Donati, Giuseppe, 16, 17, 46, 55n, 94, 96, 129, 192, 194–95, 223
Dossetti, Giuseppe, 182

Educational legislation, 4, 41, 110, 156
Electoral systems, xii–xiii, 38, 54, 55, 57, 88
Erzberger, Matthias, 44
Ethiopian war, 123–24

Facta, Luigi, 73, 75–77
Falconi, Carlo, 213–14
Fanfani, Amintore, 157–61, 183–84, 223
Farinacci, Roberto, 71, 93, 116n, 125–26, 130, 142, 160, 163, 165, 198, 209, 224
Fascist Regime, 77, 81, 82, 99–100, 109, 120–21, 162, 164, 172, 180, 207, 211, 213; and banks, 119–20; and Catholic journals, 90–91; and Catholic University, 120, 153–61; and the Crown, 94; and De Gasperi, 133; and Don Sturzo, 82–83, 89, 90; and labor, 79, 102–5; and Nazism, 113; and racial doctrines, 113n; relations with Church, 91, 92, 96–98, 104, 109–13, 119–28, 130; religious policy of, 37
Fascists (Fascism), vi, 57–59, 67n, 68–69, 70–71, 73, 75, 76, 77, 78, 81, 93, 96, 100, 196–97, 220; and Catholic social organizations, 79; and economic and labor organizations, 59, 67, 68, 70, 102–5; and *Osservatore Romano*, 216; and Popular Party, 79

Federzoni, Luigi, 34, 36, 38, 120
Ferrari, Francesco Luigi, 82, 90–91, 129, 204, 218, 224
Fiamme Verdi, 166, 167, 210
Fiume, seizure of, 59, 65, 197, 198
Fogazzaro, Antonio, 6
Frontespizio (1931–42), 34n, 106, 145, 200; and racism, 114
FUCI (Catholic University Student Federation), 36n, 82, 117, 129, 137–43, 144, 169, 204
Futurists, 39

Gasparri, Cardinal (papal Secretary of State), 53n, 78, 80, 83, 199, 216
Gedda, Dr. Luigi, 160, 182, 207, 213
Gemelli, Father Agostino, 51, 54, 118, 120, 155–57, 160–61, 162
Gentile, Giovanni, 165n
Gentiloni, Count, head of Catholic Electoral Union, 14, 15n, 43
"Gentiloni Pact" of 1913, 14, 15n, 33, 38, 46
German National Socialism, vi; and Catholic University, 156–57, 161; relations of Fascism with, 113; and De Gasperi, 132
German Third Reich, 113, 115, 117
Giacchi, Orio, 154, 206
Gini, Corrado, 155
Giolitti, Giovanni, xii–xiii, 12, 17, 26, 30, 40, 43, 55, 58, 66–72, 74, 76, 77, 81, 94 194, 198, 200; and "Gentiloni Pact," 14
Giordani, Igino, 105, 223
Giuliotti, Domenico, 32–34, 106, 127n
Gnocchi, Don Carlo, 153
Gobetti, Piero, 100, 106
Gonella, Guido, 137, 141–43, 169, 183, 205, 223
Granata, Giorgio, 144n
Grandi, Dino, 17, 17n, 104, 116n, 152, 171, 207
Gronchi, Giovanni, 17, 52, 55n, 91–92, 103, 104, 105, 152, 169, 182–83, 222
Grosoli, Count Giovanni, 19, 20, 54, 89, 119
Guelf movement, 144, 148, 164, 219
GUF (Fascist University Youth), 138, 139

Humbert, Prince, 173, 174, 208
Hurley, Monsignor J. P., 120

L'Idea Nazionale, 34
Illustrazione Romana, 120–21
Illustrazione Vaticana, 130, 141, 142, 204–5
Imperialism, 23–24, 30–31, 47
Intégristes, 20–21, 30
Intransigency, 5, 6, 7, 8, 11, 12, 20

Jacini, Stefano, 152
Jesuits, *see Civiltà Cattolica*

Labor unions, 9, 15, 20–23, 39, 50, 52, 59, 65, 66, 67, 79, 102–5
Labriola, Arturo, 41
La Liguria del Popolo, 20, 148–49, 153
La Pira, Giorgio, 140, 142, 144, 145–48, 165, 170, 172, 183
Lateran Pacts (1929), 37, 53n, 105, 109–12, 121, 217; and Constitution, 171, 179
La Torre (Siena), 32–34, 106
Leo XIII (Pope 1878–1903), 4, 7, 8, 11, 12, 20, 216; and Christian Democracy, 12
Liberal Party, 170, 174–76, 178, 184, 211
Libyan War (1911–12), 26–37, 39; and Bank of Rome, 29; and D'Annunzio's poetry, 27–29; and the Vatican, 30–31, 35
Literary movements, 32–34, 105–6
Lombardi, Father, 182, 213
Longinotti, Giovanni, 89
Ludwig, Emil, 113n

Macchio, Baron, 87
Malvestiti, Piero, 98, 144, 150–52, 172, 201, 219, 220
Manacorda, Guido, 145, 145n, 106, 160
Manzoni, Count Alessandro (senator), 6
Maraviglia, Maurizio, 34
Marazza, Achille, 152, 164, 174, 210
March on Rome, 71, 76
Marriage legislation, 40, 41, 110, 115, 155, 159
Martire, Egilberto, 36, 88, 121, 201, 224; and Clerico-Fascists, 89–90; and Popular Party, 90
Massi, Ernesto, 159
Mattei, Enrico, 118, 166, 183
Matteotti murder, 93, 95, 101
Maurras, Charles, 20, 23
Mazzini, Giuseppe, xi

Mazzolari, Don Primo, 140, 165
Meda, Filippo, 9, 11, 19, 20, 34–36, 38, 41, 65–68, 72, 75, 77, 87, 89, 91, 95, 102; political views, 10n, and World War I, 47–48, 50–51, 52, 195
Meda, Luigi, 151, 152
Medici, *see* Cornaggia-Medici
Merry Del Val, Cardinal, 194
Messineo, Father, 123–24
Miglioli, Guido, 71, 87, 129, 219; and Catholic peasants, 220, 222; and Libyan War, 30, 31; political views, 17–18, 20; and World War I, 46, 47, 51
Minzoni, Don, 90
Molteni, Giuseppe, 98
Monarchy, xii, 57, 58, 81, 179, 200
Montini, Monsignor G. B., 89, 91, 137–38, 140, 142
Moro, Aldo, 137, 141, 169, 183
Movimento Laureati, 116, 138, 139, 140–41, 144, 169
Murri, Don Romulo, 10, 11, 13, 15n, 16, 23; political views, 9
Mussolini, Arnaldo, 164
Mussolini, Benito, 34n, 45, 47, 58–60, 67, 70, 75–77, 81, 82, 93, 99, 110, 115, 116n, 122, 126, 154, 156, 159, 162, 164, 196–97, 199, 207–9; and *Avanti!*, 39, 194; and De Gasperi, 84–86, and Italian Socialist Party, 39, 470; and racism, 113n, 114–15; and Red Week, 42; relationship with Pius XI, 79; religious sentiments, 122, 203

Nationalists, 23–25, 31, 34–37, 38, 39, 60, 111
Nenni, Pietro, 42n, 130, 175, 180, 196; on Popular Party, 61–62
Nitti, Francesco Saverio, 64–66, 78, 197, 198, 212

Olgiati, Father Francesco, 54, 155
Olivelli, Teresio, 117, 118n, 210, 217
Orano, Paolo, 31–32
Oriani, Alfredo, 23, 202
Orlando, Vittorio Emanuele, 74, 207
Osoppo partisans, 166–67
Osservatore Romano, vii, 103, 142, 143, 160, 202, 216

Pacelli, Ernesto, 29
Pacelli, Francesco, 109

Paganuzzi, Giambattista, 11
Papini, Giovanni, 23n, 106, 127n, 145, 165, 199–200, 201
Parish clergy, 6, 62, 145–47, 162, 163, 165, 191, 193
Parri, Ferruccio, 17, 17n, 173–76
Party of Action, 170, 172–75, 177, 178, 180, 210, 211–12, 216, 220
Pascoli, Giovanni, 27
Pelloux, Luigi, xii
Piccioni, Attilio, 92, 183
Pius IX (Pope 1846–78), xi, 3, 4
Pius X (Pope 1903–14) (Giuseppe Sarto), 8, 15, 21, 38, 45, 192, 216; Austrian sympathies, 194; on Catholic voting, 14; and Clerico-Moderates, 193–94; political attitudes, 12–14
Pius XI (Pope 1922–39) (Achille Ratti), 78, 110, 138, 139, 140, 218, 219; and Catholic political autonomy, 80, 95, 96–99, 103–4; and Facists, 79; and Mussolini, 79; and Popular Party, 78, 82–83; and racial doctrines, 114–15
Pius XII (Pope 1939–58) (Eugenio Pacelli), 29, 141, 201, 213; and German Reich, 115
Popular Party: and Cardinal Gasparri, 53n, 78, 80, 83; and De Gasperi, 82–83; and Don Sturzo, 52–55, 82–83; programs of, 187–88; relations with other political groups, 58 ff.; and Vatican, 52, 58, 71, 78–80, 82, 92, 95–99
Prezzolini, Giuseppe, 16, 23n
Principî, 145–47
Protestantism, 154, 155
Pucci, Monsignor Enrico, 109, 198, 220

Racism, 34, 113–15, 117, 121, 122, 145, 156, 159–61, 201–2, 204, 216; Jesuit attitudes toward, 124–26
Red Week (June 1914), 41–44
Rerum Novarum, of Leo XIII (1891), 7, 8, 9, 21, 191
Resistance movements, 117, 117–18n, 144, 161, 162–73, 207–8
Righetti, Igino, 137–41
Risorgimento, xi, 24
Rivista internazionale di scienze sociali, 156, 157, 159, 160
Rocco, Alfredo, 36–37, 109; and Lateran Pacts, 37

Rodano, Franco, 210–11
"Roman Question," 3, 4, 7, 9, 57, 78, 110. *See also* Lateran Pacts
Rosa, Father Enrico, 80, 125–27, 219
Rossi, Don Giulio, 99
Rossoni, Edmondo, 105

Salandra, Antonio, 40–41, 87, 99, 194; and World War I, 195
Salvatorelli, Luigi, 204, 218
Salvemini, Gaetano, 16, 45, 71, 78–79, 204; on Nationalists, 59–60; on Popular Party, 62–64
Santucci, Carlo, 89, 199
Scalabrini, Monsignor G. B., Bishop of Piacenza, 6, 7
Scelba, Mario, 169, 183
Schmidt, Father Wilhelm, 114, 201
Schuster, Cardinal Ildefonso (Archbishop of Milan), 114, 142, 146n, 151, 163–65; and Mussolini, 208–9; and racism, 202
Segni, Antonio, 91, 183
Sforza, Count Carlo, 66, 196
Siri, Monsignor Giuseppe, 140
Socialism, xii, 4, 24, 35
Socialist Party, Italian, xii, 13–14, 39, 57–59, 61, 62, 64–65, 67–70, 71, 73–74, 76, 80, 84, 95, 99, 170–71, 173, 178, 180, 184, 196–97, 198
Social Republic, Italian, 162, 163, 164, 165
Sonnino, Sidney, 40, 87
Sottochiesa, Gino, 121–22, 201
Soviet Union, 163
Spataro, Giuseppe, 169, 183
Studium, 137, 139, 140, 147n
Sturzo, Don Luigi, 11, 16, 20, 23, 30, 61, 67, 72, 72n, 73, 78, 79, 80, 82, 129, 203, 212–13, 221; political views, 18–19; and Popular Party, 52–55, 83;

sociological views, 195; and World War I, 51, 53
Suardi, Gianforte, 14, 221
Suffrage, xii–xiii, 7, 8, 9, 14, 38, 54
Syndicalists, 26, 39, 40n

Tacchi-Venturi, Father, and Mussolini, 115, 122, 203, 204
Taviani, Paolo Emilio, 159, 160, 161, 183
Tittoni, Tommaso, 14
Togliatti, Palmiro, 171, 174n, 175, 177, 179, 180, 208
Toniolo, Giuseppe (professor), 21, 22, 51, 156; political views, 10–11
Tovini, Livio, 47, 88, 119, 121
Tozzi, Federigo, 32
Trentino, Il, 83–85, 86–87, 88
"Trust" (*Società Editrice Romana*), 19, 20, 30, 31, 63, 91, 119, 199
Tupini, Umberto, 22, 52, 221, 223
Turati, Filippo, 95, 99

Valiani, Leo, 174n
Vercesi, Don Ernesto, 152
Victor Emmanuel III, King, 65, 72, 75, 77, 93–94, 99, 115, 207–8
Vinciguerra, Mario, 126, 128, 211
Vita e Pensiero, 154, 155, 156, 159, 160, 161
Vito, Francesco, 161
Voting, 15, 38; abstention by Catholics, 8, 9, 10n, 14; procedures, 44; prohibition by Pope, 8, 9. *See also* Gentiloni Pact

White Labor Confederation, 102–5
World War I, 43–49, 50–52
World War II, 115–16, 162, 166, 207–8

Zoli, Adone, 170n